INVESTING

in

REAL ESTATE

Fourth Edition

ANDREW McLEAN & GARY W. ELDRED

WILEY

John Wiley & Sons, Inc.

For general information on our other products and services, or technical support, please contact our Customer Care Department within the United States at 800-762-2974, outside the United States at 317-572-3993 or fax 317-572-4002.

Wiley also publishes its books in a variety of electronic formats. Some content that appears in print may not be available in electronic books. For more information about Wiley products, visit our web site at www.wiley.com.

Library of Congress Cataloging-in-Publication Data

McLean, Andrew James.
    Investing in real estate / Andrew McLean, Gary W. Eldred.— 4th ed.
        p. cm.
    Includes bibliographical references and index.
    ISBN 0-471-32339-X (pbk.)
    1. Real estate investment—United States. I. Eldred, Gary W. II. Title.

HD255 .M374 2003
332.63'24—dc21   2002190904

Author's Note

I would like to thank Andrew McLean for his work in preparing the first edition of this best-selling book. Subsequently, though, Andy felt the need to withdraw from the project. Accordingly, I would like to inform readers that, as with the second and third editions, this fourth edition remains my sole responsibility. To contact me with questions or comments, please e-mail garye@stoprentingnow.com or phone (800) 942-9304, extension 20691. (Please include a telephone number with your e-mail.) May your real estate investing bring you years of satisfaction and good fortune.

GARY W. ELDRED

Contents

9 MORE TECHNIQUES FOR HIGH YIELDS AND FAST PROFITS 187

1

WHY INCOME PROPERTIES REMAIN YOUR BEST ROUTE TO A PROSPEROUS FUTURE

My telephone rings. I pick it up, and it's Dr. Cynthia Stephens from Los Angeles (where during the past three years property prices have jumped nearly 30 percent).

"I'm so worried," she says. "I think I've chosen the absolute worst time to buy a home."

I calmly assure her, "No you haven't."

"What do you mean?" she replies.

"Well, I'll tell you an even worse time to buy—five years from now, ten years from now, or any other time in the foreseeable future."

◆ ◆ ◆

Coincidentally, around the same time that I heard from Dr. Stephens, I was interviewed by *Business Week* (Susan Scherreik), *Fortune* (Brian O'Keefe), National Public Radio (Chris Farrell, Katherine Scott), *Smart Money* (Gerri Willis), *Mutual Fund* (Mark Klimek), the *Wall Street Jounral* (Terri Cullen), and the *New York Times* (James Schembari). In one way or another, each of these journalists asked similar questions and expressed concerns similar to those of Cynthia and many other homebuyers, investors, and journalists who frequently call me.

"Are we in a real estate bubble? Are properties still a good investment? Is it better to start switching money back to stocks? Can we expect property prices to stop appreciating? Won't stock returns outperform all other types of investments over the long run? Doesn't owning property create too many headaches? Shouldn't property buyers lay low until prices come back down?"

In two words, I answer all of these doubting Thomas questions with a resounding "Absolutely not!" Although no one can predict the short-term future, convincing evidence confirms that during the coming 20 years, people who own single-family homes, duplexes, quads, and small apartment buildings will continue to build wealth that they can count on. As a savvy real estate investor, your properties will outperform stocks because your profits will build in six ways:

1. A dependable and growing flow of income
2. Value increases (appreciation)
3. Mortgage payoff (amortization)
4. Value creation (property improvement)
5. Instant gain (bargain purchase price)
6. Government benefits (tax credits, tax deductions, rent vouchers, advantageous loans, etc.)

In the chapters that follow, you will discover how to make each of these sources of return work best for you. You will discover how income properties can provide you a near certain path to financial security and prosperity. But before you begin that journey, first carefully examine the economic and demographic evidence that firmly supports strong gains for investors who choose real estate.

REVIEW THE PAST *AND* FORECAST THE FUTURE

All too frequently, authors try to guide their readers with lessons learned from history and experience. You know the line: "This worked for me, so it will succeed for you." While that approach offers some credibility, it's certainly not the end of the story. Markets change. Opportunities ebb. What worked yesterday may not work tomorrow.

So I'm not merely going to persuade you with tales about the riches earned by property owners of the past (myself or others). More importantly, before you invest time, energy, intellect, and money, you're invited to envision the future. You must ask, "Do emerging demographic trends still point to profits? Do reasonably expected returns justify the price you're required to pay? Does a downturn in the housing market signal a great time to buy, or a quick trip to the exit? Will more (or less) inflation spell boom or gloom for your investment? Given what we know about the unfolding future, what investment offers the best returns along with the most controllable risks?"

Today, investing profitably stands critical to your health, wealth, and peace of mind. With pension plans, the stock market, social security, and lifetime jobs all engulfed in a fog of uncertainty, you must take investing more seriously than any previous generation in U.S. history.

With this seriousness in mind, then, we will explore the answers you need to the foregoing questions. You are not advised to choose income properties because they have yielded superior profits in the past. You are encouraged to own property because provable economic and demographic facts confirm a profit-generating future.

A DEPENDABLE AND GROWING FLOW OF INCOME

During the bull run of the late 1990s, dot-com investors forgot a central truth: The justifiable price of an investment never exceeds the present worth of the income that investment can reasonably be expected to generate. Of course, these dot-com investors (speculators) don't stand alone in history. The same story with the same results has been told a hundred times before: Amsterdam tulip bulbs in the 1700s, the Florida land boom in the 1920s, the stock market craze for conglomerates in the early 1970s, Houston apartments in the early 1980s, Boston condominiums in the late 1980s, and maybe Silicon Valley houses since 2000. Fate offers no safe escape for the foolish or greedy.

Before you choose an *investment*, you must weigh the amounts of *income* (rents, dividends, or interest) that investment is likely to yield relative to other potential investments. Is the flow of income dependable? Will it grow over time? Will it guard you against inflation?

Always recognize this truth: An investment that falls behind other types of investments in terms of income must (sooner or later) suffer in value. In contrast, investments that yield superior flows of income will show higher rates of long-term appreciation. *Investors* never buy assets, per se. They buy flows of future income.[1] With that said, let's see how income properties stack up against stocks, bonds, and annuities.

Property versus Stocks

Compare two investors, Sarah and Roy, who have each accumulated investments worth $1,000,000. Sarah owns rental houses; Roy owns

---

1. For the definitive exposition of this critical (yet too little understood) point, see John Burr Williams, *The Theory of Investment Value* (Cambridge: Harvard University Press, 1938).

stocks. Who is likely to achieve the most annual income? The average dividend yield on stocks has been bouncing around 1.4 percent—a near record low.[2] In contrast, the dividend yield (i.e., net operating income) on rental houses and small apartment buildings (owned free and clear) typically falls within the 6 percent to 12 percent range. Let's say Sarah's properties yield around 8 percent.

Based on these respective yields, the corporate management of the companies in which Roy owns stocks would mail him checks totaling $14,000 a year. As a reward for owning income properties, Sarah's property manager would mail her checks totaling $80,000 a year.

Even if we assume that Sarah's current returns from property actually fall in the low range (say, 6 percent) and that Roy achieves a dividend yield from stocks that's double the S&P average (say, 2.8 percent instead of 1.4 percent), Roy's stocks will pay him only $28,000 per year versus the $60,000 a year that Sarah's real estate will pay her. Note, too, that we've ignored income taxes. In real life Roy's dividends will be fully taxed as ordinary income, whereas Sarah's rental income will (in part) escape taxation due to tax breaks for the noncash deductions of depreciation.

Also, to keep matters simple, we didn't count leverage (discussed in Chapter 2). Through long-term mortgage financing, Sarah could greatly boost the amount of property cash flow that her $1,000,000 yields. By using mortgage money to help her buy more properties, Sarah could actually pull in $100,000 to perhaps as much as $140,000 a year.

Unfortunately, Roy can't use borrowed money to enhance his yearly income from dividends. He would have to pay interest on his margin account at the rate of 8 percent to 12 percent a year. Yet he earns an annual cash return of 3 percent or less. Even the mathematically challenged will realize that Roy could soon go broke following that losing strategy.

The Nest Egg Dilemma.   Financial planners are gradually beginning to acknowledge the problem that low dividend yields create for stock market investors. Absent a much larger cash-on-cash return, relatively few Americans can ever hope to accumulate a stock market nest egg large enough to provide them a livable income in their later years. In recognizing this fact, financial Web sites now display "retirement calculators" that presumably help you figure out safe rates of portfolio liquidation. The "stocks for retirement" crowd now admits that to live comfortably, future retirees must plan to eat much of their seed corn. Yet anytime you consume capital, you face the risk that you will run out of money before you run out of life.

---

2. Each issue of *BusinessWeek* reports the latest dividend yield in its "Figures of the Week" section, which is regularly found in the magazine's back pages.

On the other hand, if you just nibble your seed corn conservatively, you will probably have to give up your golf club membership, your frequent dinners at Café à Riche, and those cross-country trips to visit the kids.

Because stocks don't produce much income, retired stock investors are pinched between that proverbial rock and a hard place: (1) Draw down cash too quickly, and you end up living on food stamps and Section 8 housing vouchers; or (2) spend cautiously, clip coupons, search out every senior discount you can find, and you miss the enjoyable lifestyle that accumulated wealth should make possible.

Volatility of Returns.   More bad news for those who want to count heavily on stocks for the long run. We return to March 2000. The S&P is flying high, and the NASDAQ has sailed into the stratosphere. Your plans to retire comfortably at age 55 in the year 2006 are moving along quite nicely. In fact, you're already shopping for a vacation-retirement home. Then, wham! You're hit with previously unimaginable losses. During the next two and one-half years, the value of your portfolio sinks 40 percent. By July 2002, it's fallen back to where it was in 1996—six years earlier. What do you do?

Up until March 2000, most investors erroneously believed that the stock market just plugs along dependably, handing out appreciation gains of 10, 12, or 16 percent year after year. Market blips? No worry, the S&P will surely bounce right up again. Only recently have these investors begun to learn that depressed markets don't always roar to new highs. Bear markets can sometimes slumber for decades (e.g., 1907–1924; 1929–1954; 1964–1982).

And that unhappy fact presents another type of stock market nest egg dilemma: If, over the next 20 years, you want to build a nest egg of $1,000,000 (today's dollars), how much do you sock away each year? No one knows the answer.

You can assume stock market appreciation of 6, 8, 10, or even 12 percent a year. But persistent (and sometimes lengthy) ups and downs of the market render financial planning tougher than predicting sunny days in Seattle. Not only do stocks fail to yield a high level of income, but you can't even reliably estimate the amount of income (or wealth) you will receive. Stock price volatility along with low dividend yields can shatter the best-laid nest eggs.

What about Bonds?

Quality bonds typically pay more annual income than stocks, but they still lag returns from income properties. However, let's say that to boost his income, Roy moves his portfolio from stocks that earn a dividend yield of 2.8 percent to 30-year bonds yielding 7 percent. Sounds good until you think longer term. Unfortunately, that $70,000 a year that Roy now receives in interest will remain at $70,000 year after year for the next 30 years. This annual income will never go up, and its purchasing power will continue to fall. If the consumer price index (CPI) advances at an average annual rate of 3 percent during the next 20 years, that $70,000 of bond interest would yield a purchasing power in today's dollars of just $38,757; after 30 years, $28,839.

Now compare this bond interest with Sarah's (low) current rental income of $60,000. The bond interest looks better for now (income taxes aside). Over time, though, Sarah's rental income will continue to increase by 3 to 5 percent a year. If Sarah's properties average a 4 percent rent increase each year, here's how her $60,000 of net income could grow:[3]

5 Years	10 Years	20 Years	30 Years
$72,900	$88,700	$131,300	$194,325

Investors must recognize that income properties are called *income* properties not only because they yield competitively favorable incomes today but also because that income will multiply itself over time. For future income that you can live well on for as long as you live, no investment comes close to matching the amount and certainty of income provided by properties that produce ever-growing rental revenues.

Don't Fall for the Annuity Sales Pitches

With stock market jitters and low CD rates rattling the retired and near retired, peddlers of annuities have tried to grab an increasing share of the investment and savings dollar. One such company regularly runs an ad in the *Wall Street Journal* with the following headline:

Lock in 6.00 Percent Interest Rate
Fixed annuities are today's ideal investment. Compared to dividend yields of less than 1.5 percent and CD rates of 2.5 to 5.0 percent, 6.00 percent interest might seem attractive.

But as with bonds, fixed annuities expose you to substantial inflation risk. Even worse, as with stocks, to pay a decent income, annuities must con-

---

3. Actually, a 4 percent increase in rents would typically produce more than a 4 percent gain in cash income. But for now, we'll keep this example perfectly simple.

sume your capital. Just as bad, many annuities include heavy front-end expense loads and fees in addition to early redemption fees. Don't be misled (as my retired parents almost were). Most people cannot wisely use annuities to satisfy their need for a sufficient, dependable, and growing source of income. And if you get in and want out, you will pay dearly for that privilege.

Are Rent Collections Dependable?

"Okay," you may be saying, "You've convinced me that dollar-for-dollar rental properties throw off more income than stocks, bonds, CDs, or annuities. But what about vacancies and deadbeat tenants? Who needs that kind of headache?"

Good point. That's why Chapters 11 and 12 show you how to manage your rentals with minimal time, effort, and risk. When you follow the policies and practices discussed later in this book, you will see how to achieve low turnover, high tenant retention, and an eager waiting list of good people who will prefer your properties to inferior rentals offered by other owners.

Review Your Market.   As a check on what I say, review your local rental market. Can you find any well-located, well-kept houses or (competently managed) small apartment buildings that remain available for rent for any lingering period of time? Probably not, especially if they're priced and promoted effectively. Except in isolated cases, smaller residential rentals typically suffer vacancy and collection losses of less than 5 percent per year.

Beware of Superficial "Market" Vacancy Rates.   As I write, news stories are reporting increasing apartment vacancies, falling rents, and increasing use of rental concessions. Nationally, average apartment vacancy rates have climbed above 6 percent.

Beware of putting too much meaning into these types of "market" averages. Typically these averages do not pertain to the types of properties that you will own. Instead, so-called market vacancy rates and rent concessions primarily apply to two types of properties: (1) apartment megacomplexes whose hundreds of units persistently suffer revolving-door occupancy, and (2) ill-maintained properties that attract the dregs of the human populace.[4]

---

4. For example, I recently received a Department of Housing and Urban Development (HUD) foreclosure offering for a 22-unit rental property that not even rats and cockroaches would want to call home. Of the 22 units, only 9 were occupied.

Don't misunderstand. By citing the misleading nature of market averages, I don't imply that a glut of new construction (houses, condos, or apartments) or a severe uptick in unemployment will never pressure small investors to reduce their rents. Even owners of well-managed small properties must adapt to the law of supply and demand. Over time, though, nearly all competent property owners will enjoy increasing amounts of rent receipts. (Severe underbuilding always follows excessive overbuilding.)

Why Rents Will Continue to Increase

Although short-run economic downturns may jack up vacancies and depress rents, rent levels will go up over time because future demand will increase faster than future supply. Here are four reasons why:

1. *Population growth.* During the next 20 years, moderate projections show that the U.S. population will grow from a current population of 280 million to a nation of 330 million—an increase of 50 million people. In just two decades, the United States will add more people than currently live in the states of Florida and California.
2. *Household growth.* To adequately house this population increase will require a net gain of 20 to 25 million housing units. Americans now average about 2.3 persons per household. But given the relative decline of families with children, more singles living alone, and a bulging contingent of empty nesters (as boomers move into late middle age and retirement), the per-person-household figure could fall to around 2.0.
3. *Incomes.* To rent or buy homes and apartments, people need money. Correspondingly, people earn more money when the U.S. economy becomes more productive. Fortunately, the outlook for productivity remains bright. Technological innovation, higher levels of education, heightened competition among businesses, and continued corporate cost cutting will bring strong gains in productivity and incomes. The ever-growing number of two- (or more) earner households also adds measurably to household buying power.
4. *Second homes.* At present, around 7 million households now own second homes. Nearly all forecasters expect this number to mushroom during the next two decades. By 2025, 15 to 20 million households will own two or more homes.

From Baby Bust to Echo Boom

From 2000 to early 2003, some rental markets did soften. Partly, that weakening reflected low (nominal) interest rates that caused many renters to realize that they could own for less than they were paying to rent. Just as important, this softening reflected "baby bust" demographics.

For the past several years, the largest renter demographic segment (ages 25 to 34) has significantly fallen from its previous high levels, and that fall was especially steep between the ages of 25 and 30. For contrast, consider that during the late 1980s and early 1990s, approximately 26 million baby boomers occupied the 25 to 30 age group, whereas by 2002, the population of 25- to 30-year-olds had hit a low point of approximately 20 million. (From the early 1970s through 1978, the number of U.S. births averaged just 3.2 million a year—a post–World War II low—whereas previously, during the early to mid 1960s, parents produced around 4.2 million babies a year.)

In looking to the future, an emerging wave of echo boomers spells profits for income property investors. In 1978 the nation began to experience a wave of increasing births (often called the echo boom). During the 18 years thereafter, births steadily climbed from around 3.5 million to approximately 4.1 million per year. (Do you recall the boom in housing markets of the 1970s? Prepare for a repeat performance.) To the benefit of investors, this steadily emerging number of echo boomers will compete mightily for their first apartments and starter homes.

You can now easily see that the approaching decades will produce near record levels of new renters and homebuyers. Property owners will continue to enjoy strong upward pressures on both rents and home prices. "But wait," you say. "Aren't you forgetting about supply? Won't builders again go into fits of construction frenzy and glut the market?" No. Here's why.

New Construction Can't Keep Pace

In the academic world of economic theory, supply increases to meet demand. Extensive competition thus tightens the leash on runaway price increases. For Big Macs, long-distance telephone rates, and airfares, this theory works pretty well. But housing prices can't be tamed as easily. Absent some completely unforeseeable events, builders won't be able to construct all of the homes and apartments that people will want. In housing markets, builders and developers are tightly leashed by five factors:

1. *High costs.* Most people can't afford to buy or rent new construction. The median price of a new home now approaches $175,000. To build new apartment complexes, developers typically spend upward of $90,000 per unit. And unlike AT&T, Ford, and Compaq, home builders can't easily slash costs through economies of scale or massive layoffs.
2. *Lack of land.* Although in total the United States enjoys an abundance of land, most of it isn't located where people want to live. And when it does sit in a choice location, you can bet that it's premium priced.
3. *Cumbersome regulatory approvals.* Large-scale land development requires dozens of costly and lengthy government permits. Major developments require an investment of many years and millions of dollars before the first house or apartment unit is ever built.
4. *NIMBY power.* Even if builders are able to weave their way through the webs of bureaucracy, they must increasingly face off against a battalion of upset neighbors, environmentalists, and a variety of so-called public interest groups (PIRGs) who want to influence (restrict) development.
5. *Inadequate infrastructure.* New developments require additional (or expanded) roads, schools, parks, waste disposal and water systems, and recreational areas. In cases where developments lack adequate infrastructure, governments frequently block new construction or alternatively assess builders thousands of dollars per unit in impact fees.

Taken together, these five restrictions mean that the housing market can't quickly and economically respond to bursts of demand. No doubt, some local markets will from time to time produce an excess of "for rent" and "for sale" signs. But in most times and places, builders will play a perpetual game of catch-up. Over the next 20 years, rental property owners are sure to profit from the constrained supply of new construction.

MORE GOOD NEWS FOR PROPERTY APPRECIATION

You now know that market fundamentals (i.e., renters and homebuyers with money and limited housing choices) will push rents and property prices to successive new highs. But that's not the whole story behind strong appreciation. We can also expect to see more investors bidding up the prices of houses and apartment buildings.

But First, the Reckoning

Today relatively few of America's 60-plus million stock market investors seem ready to shift their portfolios from equities to income properties. Most of these investors remain deterred by two false beliefs:

1. *The perils of landlording.* According to this myth, owning properties means spending Saturdays with a pipe wrench under a tenant's sink and taking calls at midnight to deal with a stopped-up toilet. As someone who has owner-managed as many as 32 houses and apartment units at one time, I can assure you that I have never once repaired a sink, roof, or stopped-up toilet. Nor did any tenant ever call me outside the hours of 8:00 A.M. to 8:00 P.M. (and even those calls were rare).

2. *Stocks for the long run.* The second false belief that deters investors from rental properties is the mantra "Over the long run, stocks will outperform all other investments." During several recent weeks of stock market turmoil, I've read a dozen or more personal finance articles telling investors to hang tight. All will turn out well for those who keep the faith.

Naturally, the Wall Street public relations machine otherwise known as the financial press must perpetuate these two myths to keep their advertisers happy and their circulation numbers high. Think about it. Look through *Kiplinger's Personal Finance, Money, Bloomberg, Smart Money, Forbes,* and *Barron's.* Who buys the ads in these publications? Mutual funds, insurance companies, and stock brokerage firms. How many of these advertisers would stick with a publication that told the truth:

SUBSCRIBER ALERT!
The stock market cannot and will not provide 50 million Americans the income they will need for a prosperous and secure future.

How would readers of these publications respond if they discovered that picking stocks (or mutual funds) can't yield the riches they've all been promised? Mass cancellation of subscriptions, plunging sales at newsstands, that's how. The financial press must try to keep the dream alive. Otherwise they too will hit hard times.

Yet I'm confident the truth will eventually prevail.[5] Even without boldface, full-page announcements in the financial press, many thoughtful investors will come to realize that stock market math does not add up. It's not possible to spread the relatively small and finite amount of available corporate dividends among 50 million (or more) retired Americans and expect these retirees to feast for the rest of their lives. A day of reckoning becomes inevitable.

The Relevance to Property Appreciation

Thoughtful investors pay attention to the relative *expected* returns among asset classes. So congratulations to you. You're to be counted within that wise group. By virtue of the fact you're reading a book on investing in real estate, you already suspect that stocks offer too little expected return for too much risk. But potentially, millions of other investors are standing behind you. They, too, will eventually awake to the predominantly inferior risk-reward relationship for stocks vis-à-vis income properties.

When that reckoning hits (indeed, the trend to property investment has already turned upward), cash-on-cash yields will be pulled down as property prices are pushed up.

Here's How the Numbers Work. Property investors typically value income properties according to a simple formula:

$$\text{Value} = \frac{\text{NOI (\textit{net} operating income)}}{\text{R (\textit{capitalization} rate)}}$$

NOI equals gross rent collections less all operating expenses such as repairs, maintenance, property taxes, and insurance. R equals the unleveraged (i.e., no financing involved) prevailing rate of return for a given locale and property type (house, condo, quad, 16-unit). (You'll find a full explanation of this value formula in Chapter 3. For now, though, we'll focus on the basics.)

Throughout much of the United States, cap rates (Rs) range between 8 and 12 percent. Say you're looking at a six-unit property with a net operating income (NOI) of $24,000 and a local market-based R of 10 percent.[6]

5. For a detailed risk/return comparison of stocks and income properties, see my book *Value Investing in Real Estate* (New York: Wiley, 2002).

6 .Earlier we assumed that Sarah bought single-family houses. Quite often, houses carry a lower cap rate (R) than apartment buildings.

With numbers like these, the present owner could sell the property for around $240,000.

$$\text{Value (selling price)} = \frac{24{,}000 \text{ (NOI)}}{.10 \text{ (R)}}$$

$$V = \$240{,}000$$

Now think back to that 1.4 percent market dividend yield for stocks discussed earlier. At that level of yield, a $240,000 investment in stocks will pay only $3,360 (.014 x $240,000) in annual income. When property owners earn a 10 percent (more or less) income yield from real estate, why would sensible investors buy stocks? Because they hope stock prices will appreciate strongly.

Now comes the tough question: Why would anyone expect an asset that yields around 1.4 percent to appreciate strongly and thus drive down its cash-on-cash yield even further? Does the term "irrational exuberance" come to mind? As investors get closer to the age when they need or want income (or as they lose "irrational patience"), more and more of them will bid for the more bountiful cash flows provided by rents. Next you'll see too many new investors chasing too few good properties. Sellers will then force buyers to accept lower yields. Cap rates (R) will fall. Property values will jump even higher. How far will yields drop? No one can say for sure. But in coastal California and other low-yield real estate markets, you frequently find cap rates (R) of 6 percent or less. Here's a glimpse of the potential price-lifting effects of lower cash-on-cash yields (i.e., cap rates):

$$\frac{\$24{,}000 \text{ (NOI)}}{.09 \text{ (R)}} = \$266{,}666 \text{ (V)}$$

$$\frac{\$24{,}000 \text{ (NOI)}}{.08 \text{ (R)}} = \$300{,}000 \text{ (V)}$$

$$\frac{\$24{,}000 \text{ (NOI)}}{.07 \text{ (R)}} = \$342{,}857 \text{ (V)}$$

$$\frac{\$24{,}000 \text{ (NOI)}}{.06 \text{ (R)}} = \$400{,}000 \text{ (V)}$$

$$\frac{\$24{,}000 \text{ (NOI)}}{.05 \text{ (R)}} = \$480{,}000 \text{ (V)}$$

Cash Yields plus Higher Rents.   Where precisely yields come to rest depends on a variety of factors. But one face stands firm: The yield spread between stocks and properties is much too wide to persist. Any investor who buys before R reaches bottom will receive a nice appreciation bonus. But if you act now, here's an even better offer. Your property appreciation won't merely reflect the price-lifting effects of lower yields. You will also gain as the growing numbers of echo boomers (and millions of recent immigrant children) bid up rents as they compete to acquire a place of their own.

Say you buy a six-unit today for $240,000. Five years pass. Rents have gone up. Yearly NOI for the property has climbed from $24,000 to $30,000. Yield (R) has dropped from 10 percent to 8 percent. Your $240,000 property now sports a value of $375,000:

$$\frac{\$30,000 \ (NOI)}{.08 \ (R)} = \$375,000 \ (V)$$

The Interest Rate Kicker

As the cost of 30-year mortgage money hovered in the 6.0 to 6.5 percent range during the summer of 2002, journalists persistently oohed and aahed over the "historically low" interest rates. They told us that rates couldn't stay at this rock-bottom level. By the end of the year, interest rates would surely move higher and thus puncture the housing bubble that these low rates had pumped up. But it didn't happen. Rates stayed lower and lower.

"Historically Low" Rates? Not Even Close.   At some point, however, *short-term* mortgage costs may rise. And even with the approaching growth of the echo boomers, steady double-digit home price gains won't continue without respite. Exhausted buyers in some frenzied markets must choose to take a breather—regardless of where interest rates go. So my analysis hereafter doesn't challenge the possibility of short-term rate boosts and localized dips in home prices.

However, to forecast *longer-term* property appreciation, investors must not accept the erroneous notion that 6.0 to 6.5 percent mortgage rates sit anywhere near their historical lows—and therefore over time must trend upward. Indeed, in real (inflation-adjusted) terms, mortgage rates during 2002 floated near their historical highs. Once you understand that fact, you will see why during the coming years, 15- to 30-year mortgage rates could drop to 5 percent or lower. If that drop does occur, property investors will receive an astonishing appreciation kicker.

Table 1.1   Historical Nominal and Real (Inflation-Adjusted)

Year	Nominal Rate	CPI Increase	Real Rate
1945	4.0	2.3%	1.7
1950	4.5	1.3	3.2
1955	5.0	−0.4	5.6
1960	5.0	1.7	3.3
1965	5.89	1.6	4.29
1970	8.56	5.7	2.86
1975	9.14	9.1	.04
1980	13.95	13.5	.45
1990	10.08	5.4	4.68
1995	7.86	2.8	5.06
2002	6.5 (est.)	1.5 (est.)	5.0 (est.)

Nominal Interest Rates. Recent mortgage costs have seemed historically low only because most people don't know that from the 1940s through 1965, U.S. mortgage rates steadily ranged between 4.0 and 6.0 percent. In fact, during some periods of U.S. history, mortgage interest rates have dropped as low as 2.5 percent.

The mortgage rates of 8 to 14 percent that prevailed throughout most of the 1970s, 1980s, and 1990s do not represent a reasonable norm against which we should judge today's rates. High nominal interest rates prevailed throughout most of the past 30 years because we also experienced (and then came to expect) historically high rates of inflation.

CPI-Adjusted (Real) Rates. In other words, to truly understand whether recent interest rates sit high or low, you must adjust the nominal (quoted) rates for the annual rate of increase in the CPI.[7] The cost of money is cheap when *real* rates are low, and expensive when *real* rates are high.

As you can see from Table 1.1, mortgage borrowers today are paying historically *high* real rates of interest. Viewed correctly, history suggests that—as long as Federal Reserve Board chairman Alan Greenspan (or his successor) keeps inflation low—nominal *and* real interest rates are likely to continue their downward trend during the next 5 to 10 years. With the Federal Reserve's dedicated resolve, the mortgage rate levels of the 1940s, 1950s, and early 1960s could return.

---

7. The nominal mortgage interest rate less the annual percentage increase in the CPI equals what economists call the *real* rate of interest.

Should that fortunate turn of events come to pass, property prices would spike upward again. Lower interest means lower monthly payments; lower payments mean investors and homebuyers alike could (and would) pay more for their properties.

More Good News: Even Higher Interest Rates Can Spur Greater Property Appreciation. Assume that for some unforeseen reason, inflation does again rear its ugly head. The Federal Reserve Board fails to tame this unruly monster, and mortgage interest rates reverse course and run up past 10 percent. What would happen to the prices of investment properties? In the short run, property prices could fall. But not necessarily. When interest rates steadily rose higher and higher between 1965 and 1980, housing appreciation rates generally remained strong. Here's why.

More Inflation, Higher Building Costs. Inflation not only drives up interest rates but also drives up the costs of construction. Builders suffer. Their potential buyers retreat in the face of much higher mortgage payments and more difficult qualifying. Owing to a much-changed profit outlook (fewer buyers, higher costs), builders shut down job sites. They wait for the storm to pass. Fewer new houses and apartments get built. Existing properties appreciate until their prices climb high enough to again make wide-scale building profitable.

More Inflation, Investors Flee to Hard Assets. Have you noticed how the financial news folks track Mr. Greenspan's moves as closely as hounds track a fox? Whenever the Fed signals that inflation could reappear, stock and bond prices take a hit. Investors flee Wall Street securities in favor of hard assets like real estate. Investors know that a skyward-bound CPI wipes out the values of financial assets (e.g., 1965–1982). If you anchor on a rising tide, your boat gets swamped. In response, property prices gain as investors rush to rebalance their portfolios with inflation-protected rental revenues.

More Inflation, Higher Rents, Greater Profits. In other words, as an owner of income properties, you'll gain during a period of inflation because tenants will pay you higher rents. Even better, if you've financed your properties with a fixed-rate mortgage, your largest expense (mortgage interest) will stay low. If you've financed your properties with an adjustable-rate mortgage (ARM), unexpectedly high inflation may still lift your net cash flows.

Your ARM's interest rate adjustments will be capped. The interest rate you pay may still lag the market rate. Or your lender may have tied your ARM increases to a slow-moving index. Without bringing the ARM cap into play, your interest rate may still rest firmly below market. And because loan terms often permit new buyers to assume an adjustable-rate mortgage, your below-market interest rate would tempt investors to pay you a premium price for your property.

REASON, NOT FAITH

When it comes to investing, facts eventually expose illusions. Eventually reason trumps faith. Today more than 80 million Americans need to invest successfully. Most of us can no longer count on a lifetime job, a large pension, or social security to guarantee our financial prosperity—or survival. Yet most investing Americans still believe they can find salvation in stocks. They keep plugging money into their 401(k)s, 403(b)s, IRAs, Keoghs, and 529s. They keep chanting, "Stocks for the long run."

Stocks Can't Deliver

Unfortunately, the stock market can't deliver the bounty that these tens of millions of people are expecting. Mathematically, corporations don't (and can't) pay high-enough dividends to satisfy the income needs of hopeful investors. And no investment can show sustained appreciation without yielding a competitively strong flow of income.

Sure, some people will win the stock market game. They will buy and sell the next Microsoft or eBay at precisely the right times. But for the great majority, disappointment must prevail. The number of players in this poker game has multiplied ten times faster than the size of the pot.

You Can Still Win with Income Properties (for Now)

The discussions throughout this chapter have provided the facts and reasoning to support my advocacy of income properties. All reasonable views of the future show more and more people chasing after a limited supply of homes and apartments.

In addition, the gaping cash-on-cash yield spread between stocks and property clearly indicates that sooner or later (probably sooner), investors with retirement in their sights will rebalance their portfolios toward property, thus putting more pressure on property prices. In terms of both expected income and appreciation, income property currently remains your best route to wealth and financial security.

Use Your Reasoning to Beat the Market.   Although the market forces of supply and demand look favorable for property, you can do even better.

In the chapters that follow, you will learn how to enhance your profits through intelligent use of leverage (mortgage financing), bargain hunting, sharp negotiating, creative improvements, strategic management, and tax avoidance (not evasion). As you develop knowledge and talent with each of these skills, you will be able to earn good profits—even when markets temporarily turn down. (In fact, as an investor, I much prefer down markets. Down markets offer choice buying opportunities. Bargain prices, creative financing, and foreclosures become abundant. Don't fear a down market. Take advantage of it.)

The General Problem: Opportunities Will Get Tougher to Find.   When, as a college student, I began buying investment houses and apartments, I encountered few competing investors. I could find bargains any day of the week. Cap rates of 12 to 16 percent were common. I frequently earned (with financing and tax shelter) annual after-tax, cash-on-cash yields of 30 to 50 percent. Owner financing was typically available for the asking.

Indeed, to show how much prices and cash yields have worsened for today's new investors, I urge you to read the late William Nickerson's *How I Turned $1,000 into $1,000,000 in My Spare Time*, or David Schumacher's *The Buy and Hold Real Estate Strategy*.

Please, though, don't take away the wrong message. I don't bring up the easier past to discourage you with an "it's too late, you've missed your chance" attitude. Instead, you must see the trend. All types of investing present more difficulties today. And no doubt, investing will become even more difficult in the future. Too many people with money are chasing after too few good investment opportunities.

In the past, most Americans worked hard without any thought of living 15 to 30 years after the age of 65. Retiring at age 55 was unheard of—unless your last name was Rockefeller, Ford, or DuPont. Now, tens of millions of us expect and desire both longevity and prosperity. How will we all succeed? We can't. Stocks, bonds, real estate? Even if you total the income from all of these investments, you still can't come up with anywhere near enough money to fund the hopes and dreams of everyone.

The Solution: Start Now.   Times are tougher. Prices are higher. So, should you wait? Absolutely not. In the early 1990s, the press overwhelmingly told Americans not to buy real estate. They said, "Housing is no longer a good investment." Two Harvard economists published a widely quoted article that predicted housing prices were about to collapse. These economists forecast that by 2002 housing prices would sit 40 percent lower than in 1989.

I took the opposite view. In my 1993 book *Stop Renting Now!* I told Americans to get off the sidelines. Get into the game now! Housing prices would soon climb to startling new heights.[8] For the reasons stated in this chapter, I make the same forecast today. By the year 2013, you will see prices and rents shoot up as much as (or more than) they did between 1993 and 2003. I also predict that cash-on-cash yields for rental properties will continue to fall. The baby boomers will be scrambling for their retirement incomes.

So, as I first wrote 10 years ago, I similarly advise you now. Get into the game. Develop your knowledge and talents. Select your strategy (from those discussed later). Put your strategy and goals in writing. Then execute, execute, execute. Played skillfully, the game of real estate will reward you with not only a prosperous life but also the thrill of the chase.

---

8. In the first edition of my book *The 106 Common Mistakes Homebuyers Make—and How to Avoid Them* (1994; 3d ed., 2002), I listed two mistakes as fatal: number 105, "We aren't buying. We're afraid of making a mistake," and number 106, "We thought it over. We think we're better off renting."

2

FINANCING: BORROW SMART, BUILD WEALTH

Nearly all real estate investors use borrowed money to help them build wealth. But to succeed, you must distinguish between "smart borrowing" and "dumb borrowing." Smart borrowing leads to magnified returns. Dumb borrowing leads to sleepless nights and shattered finances. Unfortunately, too many beginning investors do get in over their heads. To understand why, let's look back to the late 1970s and early to mid 1980s.

In the glory days of the get-rich-quick real estate gurus, property prices were escalating 10 to 20 percent a year. Just as with stocks in the late 1990s, back then nearly every would-be investor wanted to get a piece of the property action. Yet the great majority of these investors lacked cash, credit, or both. They had the will, but they lacked the means.

THE BIRTH OF "NOTHING DOWN"

Enter Robert Allen, Carlton Sheets, Tyler Hicks, Al Lowry, Ed Beckly, Mark Haroldson, A. J. Kessler, and other shameless promoters of "nothing down." To sell their books, tapes, and seminars, these pundits promised the masses a solution to their dilemma. "No cash, no credit, no problem." Just learn the tricks and techniques of creative finance and you too can become a real estate millionaire.[1]

---

1. The term *creative finance* does not lend itself (no pun intended) to precise definition. In general, it refers to the use of multiple sources of credit (e.g., sellers, real estate agents, contractors, partners) and out-of-the-norm financing techniques such as mortgage assumptions, subject-to purchases, land contracts, lease options, second or third mortgages, credit card cash advances, master leases, and so forth. In some circumstances, investors can use creative financing to buy real estate even though they lack cash or good credit. Each of these topics is discussed in this chapter.

In his book *Multiple Streams of Income: How to Generate a Lifetime of Unlimited Wealth* (Wiley, 2000), Robert Allen recounts his famous boast to the skeptical *Los Angeles Times:* "Send me to any city," Allen told the newspaper. "Take away my wallet. Give me $100 for living expenses. And in 72 hours, I'll buy an excellent piece of property using none of my own money" (p. 140).

In response, the *L.A. Times* hooked Allen up with a reporter, and off they went. "With this reporter by my side," Allen writes, "I bought seven properties worth $722,715. And I still had $20 left over." The *Times* ate crow and headlined a follow-up article "Buying Homes without Cash: Boastful Investor Accepts Challenge—and Wins." "Yes, these techniques do work," Allen writes.

No question, Robert Allen and others who have preached a similar gospel are right. You *can* buy with nothing down, but that begs the real question. The real question is whether you *should* buy with little or no cash or credit.

SHOULD YOU BUY WITH LITTLE OR NOTHING DOWN?

If buying real estate with little or no cash or credit were a sure route to wealth, this country would be awash in real estate millionaires. Overall, more than 10 million people have bought various nothing-down books, tapes, videos, courses, and seminars. With all this knowledge of creative finance floating about, you might think that the secrets of building real estate wealth were available to almost everyone.

So where's the catch? Why have so many stepped forward, yet so few have made the grade?

What's Wrong with "Nothing Down"?

To begin with, let me emphatically stress that various forms of creative financing can and should be used to finance some types of property acquisitions. I don't mean to bash creative finance. However, I've seen so many of these deals crash and burn that I must advise caution. Without a doubt, the promoters of creative financing have oversold its advantages and undersold its potential perils. Before you imbibe such an intoxicating elixir, think through the following issues:

Do You Live below Your Means?   In their runaway best-seller *The Millionaire Next Door* (Longstreet, 1997), Thomas Stanley and William Danko repeatedly discuss how self-made millionaires typically live *below* their means. As a rule, self-made millionaires do not drive new Jaguars or

BMWs, dress for success in Brooks Brothers suits, spend lavishly with their platinum American Express cards, or wear $200 (let alone $2,000) wristwatches. Serious wealth builders display no foolish affectations of conspicuous consumption.

In fatal contrast, far too many of the hopeful dreamers attracted to the schemes of the real estate gurus have never learned to spend and invest wisely. They primarily see real estate as a means to circumvent their money and credit problems—a quick and painless way to live the envied lifestyles of the rich and famous.

In fact, the promoters of nothing down encourage this lavish image. They nearly always place themselves in fabulous settings. Mark Haroldson's photo on the cover of his book (*How to Wake Up the Financial Genius Inside of You*) shows him lounging on the hood of a Rolls Royce. Irene and Mike Milin (*How to Buy and Manage Rental Properties*) instead chose a Mercedes 600 for their photo backdrop. And, of course, nearly everyone has seen the TV infomercial where Carlton Sheets sits by the pool enjoying his beautiful Florida bay-front estate.

Take a hard look at yourself. Is your goal to sensibly pursue the inner security and confidence of a millionaire next door? Do you presently live *well below* your means? Do you save a large percentage of your earnings? Or do you frequently fail to exercise financial discipline and fiscal responsibility? Do you long to show the world you've "made it"? Do you believe creative finance can substitute for your need to shape up your financial fitness?

If a borrow-and-spend personal profile describes you, please reexamine your motives and priorities. The creative-finance gurus have enticed too many people into believing that, as one such promoter puts it, "nothing down can make you rich." Wrong! Nothing down can help get you started in real estate, but only fiscal discipline can pave the way for long-term wealth and financial security. Before you look to creative finance, critically review and adjust (revolutionize, if necessary) your own habits of spending, borrowing, and saving.

Price versus Terms.   Many creative-finance gurus urge their students to lure sellers into creative-finance schemes with an enticing gambit: "You can set the price, if you let me set the terms." In this way the seller will (ostensibly) receive a price that exceeds his property's market value (along with great bragging rights). In exchange, the creative-finance buyer asks for terms that may include seller financing, little or nothing down, a below-market interest rate, and other seller concessions.

Regrettably, in their eagerness to do these kinds of deals, novice buyers frequently fail to adequately inspect the property for problems. In addition, they end up owing more than their properties are worth. When problems develop that a buyer can't afford to pay for—or otherwise remedy—he or she also faces the problem of owning a property that can't be sold for a price high enough to pay off the mortgage balance.

The lesson: Anytime you agree to pay more than a property is worth, you invite financial trouble. The terms of your creative financing can seldom overcome the tenuous position that an overfinanced property presents. (You'll see a specific financial example of "you name the price, I'll set the terms" later in this chapter.)

Credibility versus Creativity.   Many would-be buyers of property try to use creative financing not just to buy with little or nothing down but also to work around credit problems (no credit record, slow pay, write-offs, bankruptcy, foreclosure, self-employment, etc.). However, never forget that regardless of your credit history, before you can secure any type of sensible financing, you must establish your credibility.

Yet credibility and creativity often clash. In contrast to the gurus' glory years, today's deal makers have wised up. If you suggest a deal that seems strange, risky, or simply off-the-wall, other would-be participants in the transaction (broker, seller, mortgage lender) may doubt that you really know what you're doing. Or they may come to believe that you lack financial resources, experience, or both.

Before you try to negotiate some type of creative-finance scheme, sound out the views and possible responses of the other players in the deal. If you go too far out on a limb, others may simply walk away and dismiss you as a flake (big hat, no cattle). For your failure to establish credibility, you'll lose good properties.

Perseverance versus Productivity.   Nearly all nothing-down gurus admit (at least in their fine print) that the vast majority of sellers, brokers, and mortgage lenders will reject most of their financing techniques. "How often does a transaction like this happen?" Robert Allen (*Multiple Streams of Income*, p. 142) asks rhetorically after explaining one of his zero-down techniques. "Very rarely. One in a hundred. It takes luck, chutzpa, and quick feet."

Now, answer this question: Is your search for creative financing likely to result in success? For many in the past, that answer has been no. When these previously ambitious investors have met repeated rejection and disappointment, they gave up. They came to see real estate "investing" as a waste of time.

In doing so, they missed the success they could have enjoyed had they prepared themselves financially and pursued more realistic types of financing and property acquisitions. In other words, if you chase after deals that stand little chance of profitable completion, steel yourself against slammed doors and fatigue. To achieve so-called creative possibilities, you must persevere. Realize, too, that many investors who do build long-term wealth and financial security choose to follow more proven and productive paths.

Leverage: Pros and Cons

For naive investors, "little or nothing down" sounds appealing. It lulls them into believing that they can join the ranks of real estate millionaires without first disciplining their ruinous habits of overspending and undersaving.

On the other hand, many perfectly responsible real estate investors do use little- or nothing-down techniques to reap the wealth-building effects of *leverage*. Through leverage you can magnify your financial returns and build wealth much faster than if you paid 100 percent cash for your properties. But leverage does entail risk. Highly leveraged purchases expose you to greater potential loss. Here's what I mean.

Leverage Magnifies Returns. Essentially, the term *leverage* means that you use a relatively small amount of cash to acquire and control a property. To illustrate through a simple example, suppose you plan to buy a $100,000 rental home that produces a net operating income (NOI) of $10,000 a year.[2] If you finance this unit with $10,000 down and borrow $90,000 (a *loan-to-value ratio* of 90 percent), you have highly leveraged your purchase. You own and control a property. Yet only 10 percent of the purchase price actually came out of your pocket, whereas if you had paid $100,000 cash for the property, you would not have used any leverage (other people's money).

Now, here's how different degrees of leverage can magnify your cash-on-cash returns as compared to buying without financing. The following four examples calculate rates of return based on alternative down payments of $100,000 (an all-cash purchase), $50,000, $25,000, and $10,000.

---

2. Obviously, in high-priced areas of the country, $100,000 won't even buy a run-down shack. But for purposes of illustration, it's the easiest figure to work with.

Example 1: $100,000 all-cash purchase

$$\text{ROI (return on investment)} = \frac{\text{Income (NOI)}}{\text{Cash investment}}$$

$$= \frac{\$10,000}{\$100,000}$$

$$= 10\%$$

In this example, you receive the full $10,000 of net operating income (rental income less expenses such as insurance, repairs, maintenance, and property taxes). However, if you finance part of your purchase price, you will have to pay a mortgage payment on the amount you've financed. If we assume you find financing at 8 percent for 30 years, you will have to pay your lender $7.34 a month for each $1,000 you borrow. Now, using various percentages of leverage, the subsequent examples show how to magnify your rates of return.

Example 2: $50,000 down payment; $50,000 financed. Yearly mortgage payment equals $4,404 (50 x $7.34 x 12). Net income after mortgage payments (which is called cash throw-off) equals $5,596 ($10,000 NOI less $4,404).

$$\text{ROI} = \frac{\$5,596}{\$50,000} = 11.1\%$$

Example 3: $25,000 down payment; $75,000 financed. Yearly mortgage payments equal $6,607 (75 x $7.34 x 12). Net income after mortgage payments (cash throw-off) equals $3,394 ($10,000 NOI less $6,606).

$$\text{ROI} = \frac{\$3,394}{\$25,000} = 13.6\%$$

Example 4: $10,000 down payment; $90,000 financed. Yearly mortgage payments equal $7,927 (90 x $7.34 x 12). Net income after mortgage payments (cash throw-off) equal $2,073 ($10,000 NOI less $7,927).

$$\text{ROI} = \frac{\$2,073}{\$10,000} = 20.7\%$$

With the figures in these examples, the highly leveraged (90 percent loan-to-value ratio) purchase yields a cash-on-cash rate of return double that of a cash purchase. In principle, the more you borrow and the less cash you invest in a property, the more you magnify your cash returns. Of course, the *realized* rate of return you'll earn on your properties depends on the actual rents, expenses, interest rates, and purchase prices that apply to those properties. You will need to work through those numbers at the time you buy to see how much you can gain (or lose) from leverage.

Now, here's even better news. Look at an even more important way leverage can magnify your returns and help you build wealth faster.

In addition to annual income, your rental properties should appreciate in value. If that $100,000 property we've just discussed appreciates at an annual rate of 3 percent, you'll earn another $3,000 a year. If it appreciates at an annual rate of 5 percent, you'll gain another $5,000 a year. And at a 7 percent annual rate of appreciation, your gains will hit $7,000 a year.

Adding together annual rental income *and* annual price appreciation, here are the total returns from each of the previous examples:

$$\text{Total ROI} = \frac{\text{Income} + \text{Appreciation}}{\text{Cash investment}}$$

Example 1: $100,000 all-cash purchase and (a) 3 percent, (b) 5 percent, and (c) 7 percent rates of appreciation:

$$\text{(a)} \quad \text{Total ROI} = \frac{\$10,000 + \$3,000}{\$100,000} = 13\%$$

$$\text{(b)} \quad \text{Total ROI} = \frac{\$10,000 + \$5,000}{\$100,000} = 15\%$$

$$\text{(c)} \quad \text{Total ROI} = \frac{\$10,000 + \$7,500}{\$100,000} = 17\%$$

Example 2: $50,000 down payment and (a) 3 percent, (b) 5 percent, and (c) 7 percent rates of appreciation:

(a)   Total ROI = $\dfrac{\$5,596 + \$3,000}{\$50,000}$ = 17.2%

(b)   Total ROI = $\dfrac{\$5,596 + \$5,000}{\$50,000}$ = 21.2%

(c)   Total ROI = $\dfrac{\$5,596 + \$7,000}{\$50,000}$ = 25.2%

Example 3: $25,000 down payment and (a) 3 percent, (b) 5 percent, and (c) 7 percent rates of appreciation:

(a)   Total ROI = $\dfrac{\$3,394 + \$3,000}{\$25,000}$ = 25.6%

(b)   Total ROI = $\dfrac{\$3,394 + \$5,000}{\$25,000}$ = 33.6%

(c)   Total ROI = $\dfrac{\$3,394 + \$7,000}{\$25,000}$ = 41.6%

Example 4: $10,000 down payment and (a) 3 percent, (b) 5 percent, and (c) 7 percent rates of appreciation.

(a)   Total ROI = $\dfrac{\$2,073 + \$3,000}{\$10,000}$ = 50.1%

(b)   Total ROI = $\dfrac{\$2,073 + \$3,000}{\$10,000}$ = 70.1%

(c)   Total ROI = $\dfrac{\$2,073 + \$7,000}{\$10,000}$ = 90.1%

When you combine returns from annual net rental income and price appreciation, you can see that highly leveraged properties *may* produce phenomenal annual rates of return—*even without high rates of inflation.* That's why, over the years, average investors in rental homes have been able to build net worths that run into the millions of dollars. When you own rental properties, steady rent increases and price appreciation can turn acorns (relatively low down payments) into oak trees (a free and clear property worth hundreds of thousands of dollars). As the years pass and you pay down your mortgage balances, your portfolio of just 5 to 10 rental units can build enough wealth to guarantee a secure and prosperous future. (Note, too, how these income property rates of return outshine the widely heralded (yet overstated) 10 to 12 percent average annual long-term gains that the stock market has supposedly produced since 1926.)

Manage Your Risks. All too often, the low-down, nothing-down advocates of get-rich-quick real estate schemes fail to warn their students that highly leveraged real estate magnifies risks as well as returns. As a result, many naive real estate investors have lost their shirts. These buyers optimistically expected the market values of their properties to appreciate at rates of 12 to 20 percent a year. They lost touch with reality. In fact, many investors barely cared what prices they paid or how they financed their properties. They just "knew" that they would be able to sell their properties in a few years for twice the amount they had paid.

One such investor, for example, bought a $300,000 fourplex with a down payment of $30,000. After paying property expenses and his mortgage payments, the investor faced an alligator (negative cash flow) that chewed up $1,000 a month. But the investor figured that $1,000 a month was peanuts because he believed the sales price of the property would continue to appreciate at 15 percent a year. Based on this rate of appreciation, here's how this investor calculated the annual returns that he (unrealistically) expected to receive:

$$ROI = \frac{\text{Income} + \text{Appreciation}}{\text{Cash investment}}$$

$$= \frac{-\$12,000 \ (12 \times -\$1,000) + \$45,000 \ (.15 \times \$300,000)}{\$30,000}$$

$$= \frac{\$33,000}{\$30,000}$$

$$= \ 110\%$$

As it turned out, this investor, like so many others, was unable to keep feeding the alligator (covering his $1,000 monthly negative cash flow). He fell behind in his mortgage payments, and as the market slowed, he was unable to sell the property. The lender foreclosed, and the investor lost the property, his down payment of $30,000, and the $18,000 of negative monthly outlays he had made before his default.

What lessons can you take away from this investor's bad experience? Here are four:

1. *Never expect the value of real estate, stocks, gold, antique automobiles, old masters, or any other type of investment to increase by 10, 15, or 20 percent year after year.* When you need high rates of appreciation to make your investment look attractive, you are setting yourself up for a big loss. (Avoid dot-com mania.)

2. *Beware of negative cash flows.* If your investment won't pay for itself through the annual income it produces, you are not investing—you are speculating. That's okay if that's what you want to do. Just recognize that speculating creates high risk.

3. *Don't overextend yourself.* High leverage (a high loan-to-value ratio) usually requires large mortgage payments relative to the amount of net income that a property brings in. Even if you don't immediately incur negative cash flows, unexpected vacancies, higher-than-expected expenses, or generous rent concessions to attract good tenants can sometimes push you temporarily into the swamps where alligators feed.

   Over the long term, owning real estate will make you rich. But to get to the long term, you may have to pass through several downturns. Without financial reserves to defend against alligator attacks, you may get eaten alive before you find the safety and comfort of high ground.

4. *Even when the financing looks "good," never substantially overpay for a property.* Too many investors are lured into buying overpriced properties with little or no down payment deals. In the preceding example, the investor agreed to pay $300,000 for his fourplex not because $300,000 was a reasonable price based on the rents the property was producing. Rather, he paid $300,000 because he was excited about his 10 percent down financing. And that $300,000 purchase price looked cheap compared with the $600,000 sales price he expected to reap after just four or five years of ownership.

By pointing out the potential risks of high-leverage financing, I most certainly do not want to discourage you from making low down payments. But always anticipate possible setbacks. To successfully manage the risks of high-leverage finance, follow the following six investment safeguards:

1. *Buy bargain-priced properties.* You build a financial cushion into your deals when you pay less than market value (you can discover how in Chapters 4 through 7).

2. *Buy properties that you can profitably improve.* The best way to build wealth fast and reduce the risk of leverage is to add value to your properties through creativity, sweat equity, remodeling, and renovation (see Chapter 8).

3. *Buy properties with below-market rents that you can raise to market levels within a relatively short period (six to twelve months).* As you increase your rental income, you will reduce the strain of high mortgage payments.

4. *Buy properties with low-interest financing such as mortgage assumptions, adjustable-rate mortgages, buy downs, or seller financing.* Low interest rates boost your ability to safely handle high debt.

5. *Buy properties in up-and-coming neighborhoods that are soon to be revitalized.* Revitalization efforts can easily lift property values by 20 to 50 percent over a three- to five-year period (see Chapter 8).

6. *When all else fails to reduce the risk of high leverage to a comfortable level, increase your down payment to achieve a lower loan-to-value ratio and lower monthly mortgage payments.* If you don't have the cash, bring in a money partner. Don't act penny-wise and pound-foolish. Share gains with someone else rather than risk drowning in the swamps where the alligators prey.

What Are Your Risk-Return Objectives?

Little- or nothing-down finance creates great opportunities for you to magnify your returns. Through smart borrowing, you can quickly pyramid your real estate wealth. But the more you borrow (all other things being equal), the larger your risk. When you're highly leveraged, a slight fall in rents may push you into negative cash flows. A relatively small decline in a property's value may cause you to owe more than your property is worth. So steer clear of pie-in-the-sky optimism. Carefully work through the numbers for the deals that come your way. Carefully decide what profits are worth pursuing and what risks to avoid.

But remember, failing to own real estate also creates risk. Without investment real estate, you may have to accept a downward slide in your standard of living as you get older and move into your retirement years. Surely you don't want to bet your future financial well-being on an employer pension plan, the stock market, or social security. Even if you're now accumulating significant savings in stocks, exercise caution. Who knows how long the current bear market will continue? Who knows when the next bear market will hit? Or how long it will last? Who knows whether, 5 or 10 years from now, we'll again see yearly inflation rates of 6, 8, 10 percent or greater? And as we saw during the 1970s, inflation destroys the values of stocks and bonds.

For these reasons, smart investors should include at least several rental properties in their investment portfolio. Regardless of what happens to your pension, social security, stock portfolio, or inflation, steadily increasing rental income can provide you security and prosperity.

MAXIMIZE YOUR LEVERAGE WITH OWNER-OCCUPANCY FINANCING

Now that you've seen the pros and cons of creative finance and high leverage (little or nothing down), it's time to consider one popular way that you can maximize your leverage (up to your own self-imposed limits): owner-occupied financing.

By far the easiest, safest, surest, and lowest-cost way to borrow all (or nearly all) of the money you need to buy a property involves owner-occupied mortgage financing. Numerous high-LTV (loan-to-value) owner-occupied loan programs are readily available on single-family homes, condominiums, townhouses, and two- to four-unit apartment buildings that offer 95, 97, or even 100 percent financing. With sterling credit, some lenders will even lend you 125 percent of an owner-occupied property's purchase price. In contrast, if you do not qualify for owner-occupied financing (i.e., your property purchase fits into the investor category), most lenders (banks, mortgage bankers, savings institutions) typically limit their mortgage loans to a 70 percent to 80 percent) loan-to-value ratio.[3]

In addition to lower down payments, lenders also qualify owner-occupants with less exacting standards. Plus, interest rates for owner-occupants may sit one (possibly two) percentage points below the rate charged for investor loans. If lenders are charging 6.0 to 7.0 percent for owner-occupied loans, the rate for investor properties will probably sit in the 7.0 to 8.0 percent range. When you are a beginning real estate investor, you should definitely explore owner-occupied mortgage loans.

Owner-Occupied Buying Strategies

If you don't currently own a home, you can begin building your wealth in income properties very easily. Simply select a high-LTV loan program that appeals to you.[4] Buy a one- to four-family property, live in it for one year,

---

3. From the late 1990s to the present, some lenders have been willing to make investor loans with LTVs as high as 90 percent. If (when?) the property market softens, these relatively liberal lenders will undoubtedly raise the amount of their required down payments.

4. Many of these programs are listed and described later in this chapter.

then rent it out and repeat the process again. Once you obtain owner-occupied financing, that loan can remain on the property even after you move out. Because the second, third, and even fourth homes you buy and move into will still qualify for high-LTV financing (low or nothing down), you can quickly accumulate several rental houses in addition to your own residence—all without large cash investments.

Although you will be able to go through this process two, three, or maybe four times, you can't pursue it indefinitely. At some point, lenders will shut you off from owner-occupied financing because they will catch on to your game. Nevertheless, serial owner-occupancy acquisitions make a great way to accumulate your first several income properties.

Homeowners, Too, Can Use This Method

Even if you already own a home, you too should definitely weigh the advantages of using owner-occupied financing to acquire your next several properties. Here's how: Locate a property (condo, house, two- to four-unit apartment building) that you can buy and move into. Find a good tenant for your current home. Complete the financing on your new property and move into it. If you really like your current home, at the end of one year, rent out your most recently acquired property and move back into your former residence. Otherwise find another "home" to buy and again finance this property with a new owner-occupied, high-leverage, low-rate mortgage.

Why One Year?

To qualify for owner-occupied financing, you must tell the lender that you intend to live in the home for at least one year. *Intend*, however, does not mean *guarantee*. You can (for good reason, or no reason) change your mind. The lender will find it difficult to prove that you falsely stated your intent at the time you applied for the loan.

Nevertheless, to succeed in real estate over the short and long term, you must establish, maintain, and nurture your credibility with lenders—and everyone else with whom you want to make deals or build a relationship of trust. Slipping through loopholes, making false promises, sidestepping agreements, or any similar slights will tarnish your reputation for integrity. Unless you really do encounter an unexpected turn of events, honor a lender's occupancy requirement.

Where Can You Find High-LTV Owner-Occupied Mortgages?

Everywhere! Look through the yellow pages under "mortgages." Then start calling banks, savings institutions, mortgage bankers, mortgage brokers, and credit unions. Many mortgage lenders advertise in local daily newspapers.[5] Check with your state, county, or city departments of housing finance. Home builders and Realtors will also know various types of low- or nothing-down home finance programs. Sixty minutes on the telephone will help you.

In my book *The 106 Common Mistakes Homebuyers Make (and How to Avoid Them)*, I write, "Not enough money no longer serves to justify procrastination. Lack of self-discipline, yes. Lack of motivation, yes. Lack of knowledge, yes. But not lack of money. If you think 'cash short' blocks you from buying property, think again. At least one of the following 50 ideas is sure to work for you."

Although space doesn't permit a full discussion of all low or no down payment possibilities, here are 25 that are widely available:

1. *FHA 203(b).* Cash-short buyers rely on this program from the Federal Housing Administration (FHA) more than any other home finance plan. This type of loan requires a down payment of between 3 percent and 7 percent, but you need not use your own cash. You may use borrowed funds or gift money. In addition, qualifying standards (credit and income) rarely eliminate anyone who can show steady income and good-faith effort in paying bills.

2. *FHA ARM (251).* This loan sets the same down payment rules as does the FHA 203(b), but because the adjustable-rate mortgage's (ARM) qualifying interest rate typically starts out less than a fixed-rate loan, you can more easily fit within the qualifying ratio guidelines. Alternatively, the ARM may permit you to qualify for a larger amount of mortgage than FHA 203(b). As another benefit, FHA ARMs limit your annual rate increases to 1 percent (no negative amortization), and your lifetime cap is set at 5 percent.

3. *FHA GPM.* With this finance plan, you qualify for a larger mortgage than with FHA 203(b), but your payments increase gradually according to a preset schedule. In other words, compared to 203(b), the GPM (graduated payment mortgage) provides you with low monthly payments in the early years of your mortgage, which then increase later on.

---

5. For a more detailed discussion of mortgage lending, see my book *The 106 Secrets That All Homebuyers Must Learn—but Lenders Don't Tell* (Wiley, 2003).

4. *FHA/VA 203(v).* This FHA program is offered only to veterans. The down payment is less than that required for 203(b), but other qualifying standards remain the same.

5. *FHA 203(k).* This plan works well for homebuyers who want to renovate, rehab, or otherwise create value for a property. The 203(k) plan permits you to combine a home's purchase price and "fix-up" costs all in one mortgage. It has the same basic down payment and qualifying standards as the FHA 203(b). However, 203(k) also offers several possibilities for zero-down purchases by first-time buyers.

6. *FHA qualifying assumptions.* To buy with little (or maybe nothing) down *and* a below-market interest rate in a high interest rate environment, look for sellers with FHA mortgages originated when mortgage rates were in the range of 6.0 to 7.5 percent. Pay the sellers the amount of their equity (or whatever amount you both agree to) and then take over the seller's mortgage payments. Qualifying for this type of assumption is relatively easy and simple.

7. *FHA nonqualifying assumptions.* Millions of these loans were originated during the 1980s. Although most have now been repaid or refinanced, a few sellers have retained them. The nonqualifying assumption can get credit-impaired buyers into a home without going through any mortgage approval process. Also, the amount of the down payment is not subject to any rules. It's whatever amount the buyers and sellers agree to.

8. *HUD homes.* The U.S. Department of Housing and Urban Development (HUD) is the parent of the FHA. When FHA borrowers fail to make their mortgage payments, HUD often becomes the owner of these houses. Depending on market conditions, an owner-occupant may be able to buy a HUD home for as little as $300 to $1,000 down. Ask a HUD registered real estate agent for details. Also, regularly read the real estate classified and display ads in your local paper. HUD and HUD agents advertise regularly.

9. *VA mortgages.* If you are an eligible veteran, you have absolutely no "cash short" excuse for failing to own. Easy qualifying and no-cash-to-close are hallmarks of this great benefit from the Department of Veteran's Affairs (VA) for persons who have served in the U.S. military or National Guard.

10. *VA qualifying assumptions.* VA loans may be assumed by veterans or nonveterans. Find a VA seller who has built little equity in his or her home—especially someone who has bought, say, within

the past three or four years—and you can get into home owner-ship with little or nothing down.

11. *Mortgage bond programs.* For first-time buyers, nearly every state offers home mortgages with low down payments and below-market interest rates.[6] Contact your state and local housing finance agencies for the details of programs offered in your area. Unfortunately, housing finance agencies must limit the total amount of "bond money" that's available. So keep yourself informed about pending release dates for mortgage money. Quite often, the available funds run out quickly.

12. *Portfolio lenders.* Some mortgage lenders (banks, savings institu-tions, credit unions) hold the mortgages they issue in their own portfolios (rather than sell them to Fannie Mae or Freddie Mac). From time to time, these lenders offer flexible terms of financing. For example, Washington Mutual (one of the country's largest mortgage lenders) recently offered a 1-percent-down mortgage loan program. Portfolio lenders may also show more flexibility with respect to qualifying guidelines.

13. *Fannie Mae 5% Down.* This loan has relatively tighter credit and income standards, but it's widely available through participat-ing lenders all over the country.[7]

14. *Freddie Mac 5% Down.* This loan is similar to Fannie Mae's 5% Down program.

15. *Fannie Mae 97.* This is a 3-percent-down program with relaxed qualifying ratios. It is typically limited to people who have household incomes of no more than 100 (sometimes 120) percent of an area's median household income. Home buying in tar-geted neighborhoods may allow lenders to waive the income limits.

16. *Freddie Mac Discover the Gold.* This program is similar to Fannie Mae 97, both of which reflect part of Fannie's and Freddie's con-tinuing efforts to "break down barriers" and expand home own-ership to all Americans and immigrants who can responsibly manage their finances.

17. *New home builders.* As an incentive to buyers, many builders of condominiums, townhouses, and single-family homes offer low

---

6. Often, a "first-time buyer" is defined as someone who hasn't owned a home within the past three years.

7. Fannie Mae and Freddie Mac are national mortgage companies that set standards and develop loan programs for many location lenders throughout the United States.

down payments or below-market interest rates. Read the builder ads in you local paper and contact new developments directly.

18. *USDA Zero Down.* The U.S. Department of Agriculture offers nothing-down loans to homebuyers purchasing in small towns and cities—even when those "small towns or cities" are located in large urban areas such as Los Angeles County and San Bernardino County, California. These loans restrict participation to households with income equal to or less than 115 percent of an area's median household income. As with FHA, the qualifying standards are relatively easy for any first-time buyer whose credit history indicates an ability and willingness to meet obligations.

19. *CRA programs.* Under the Community Reinvestment Act (CRA), banks must reach out to serve all types of people in all types of neighborhoods. In past years, many banks did not honor this responsibility. Nor did the law provide serious penalties for noncompliance. More recently, penalties have increased, and banks (as part of the National Home Ownership Strategy) have created many different "easier-qualifying" mortgage plans with low down payments—especially for homebuyers who wish to purchase in certain areas targeted for revitalization.

   Nothing improves a neighborhood more than homeowners displacing renters—or, even better, renters displacing landlords by buying the homes they previously were previously occupying as tenants. Call your local banks. Ask them what types of CRA mortgage programs they're offering.

20. *Fannie Mae rehab loans.* This experimental program is aimed at investors (for-profit and not-for-profit) who will buy and renovate a house and then sell it on a mortgage loan assumption (low or no down payment) to first-time buyers. Fannie Mae has modeled the investor acquisition, rehab, and buyer assumption features of this program after the FHA 203(k) plan. However, Fannie Mae's maximum loan goes all the way up to $307,000.

21. *Fannie Mae cash-free loans.* Under this "flex-plan" experimental mortgage, homebuyers with excellent credit are permitted to raise their down payment of 3 percent by borrowing against their credit cards, from family members, or from their employers. In fact, the primary restrictions on this loan concern real estate agents and the sellers. Neither of these sources can lend you the down payment.

22. *Sweat equity.* With sweat equity, you provide the labor and materials necessary to increase a property's value—often in lieu of a cash down payment. Sweat equity has been used successfully in combination with lease options, lease-purchase agreements, land contracts, and new home developments.

    Say you buy a home that's worth $120,000 on a nothing-down land contract. You promise the seller that you will improve the property through sweat equity. After a year of your work and improvements, the home is worth $140,000. You now owe $119,000. Essentially, your efforts have created a $20,000 down payment—or about 15 percent of the home's market value. A lender who loans you $119,000 to pay off the seller would be secure with an 85 percent loan-to-value ratio. Apart from the amounts you spent for materials, you've acquired your home with zero cash down.

23. *Real estate owned (REOs).* At times, every mortgage lender becomes the unwilling owner of properties that it has taken back through foreclosure. Lenders vary greatly in how they market these homes and in their offered terms of financing. But as often as not, a thorough search of lenders in your area will turn up some REOs that are available with a bargain price, easy terms, or possibly both (although that combination is more difficult to find).

24. *Manufactured homes.* In days gone by, the ancestors of manufactured homes were called house trailers or prefabs. Today's manufactured homes bear little resemblance to their cheaply constructed forebears. In fact, many "prefabs" are difficult to tell from site-built houses. Even better, manufactured home dealers offer homes with good value and can arrange almost 100 percent financing for their homebuyers. If you already own (or can purchase) a lot, you can probably finance the entire price of your manufactured home. (Recently, as a result of extremely aggressive lending practices, high defaults among buyers of manufactured homes have caused banks to tighten their credit standards for financing manufactured homes with low or no down payment.)

25. *Pledged collateral.* Do you, your parents, or other close family members own a stock portfolio, retirement plan, life insurance policy, or other type of personal investment? Then you can buy a home with nothing down. Pledge the valuable asset or funds as security (in addition to the house you're buying). Make your monthly mortgage payments as scheduled, and your mortgage lender won't touch the pledged collateral. When you've accu-

mulated a 20 percent equity in the financed property, your lender will release its lien against the pledged asset.

As another benefit, when you pledge collateral in lieu of a down payment, the lender won't require private mortgage insurance (PMI). Depending on the amount of your mortgage, this exclusion could save you more than $500 to $1,000 a year. Remember, too, your home equity can accumulate through mortgage principal payments, home appreciation, and value-enhancing improvements. With growing equity from each of these sources, you can obtain a lien release for the pledged asset within just a few years.

For more discussion of home buying made easy, see not only my *106 Mistakes* book but also my *Yes! You Can Own the Home You Want* (Wiley, 1996), *Stop Renting Now* (NIHO, 1996), and my Web site at www .stoprentingnow.com. Other good Web sites on this topic include www.HUD.gov, www.VA.gov, www.FannieMae.org, www.FreddieMac .org, and www. USDA.gov.

WHAT ARE THE LOAN LIMITS?

The maximum amount you can borrow under these high-LTV programs may vary by type of loan and area of the country. However, the loan limits are high enough to finance nice homes in good neighborhoods. For example, Freddie Mac and Fannie Mae programs nationwide will lend up to the following amounts (adjusted upward each year):

Type of Residence	Loan Limits
One-family	$322,700
Two-family	413,100
Three-family	499,300
Four-family	620,500

Unlike Fannie and Freddie, FHA varies its loan limits by county. Here are several examples:

Low-Cost Areas

Type of Residence	Loan Limits
One-family	$154,896
Two-family	198,288
Three-family	239,664
Four-family	297,840

High-Cost Areas

Type of Residence	Loan Limits
One-family	$280,749
Two-family	359,397
Three-family	434,391
Four-family	539,835

For VA loans, eligible veterans may originate—and veterans and nonveterans alike may assume—up to the following amounts:[8]

Type of Residence	Loan Limits
One-family	$240,000
Two-family	240,000
Three-family	240,000
Four-family	240,000

Properties that are priced much higher than the foregoing limits seldom yield enough income to cover expenses and mortgage payments. Thus any of the loan programs described should provide adequate financing for investors who select only those rentals that will pay for themselves—even with just a relatively small down payment.

HIGH LEVERAGE FOR INVESTOR-OWNED FINANCING

Let's say you've maxed out your high-LTV (low down payment) owner-occupancy financing possibilities. Or maybe you're happy in your present home. No way will you (or your spouse) move (even temporarily) to another property. In this situation, what are some of the ways that you as an investor can avoid putting up 20 to 40 percent of the purchase price in cash from your own savings? In other words, what high-leverage (low down payment) techniques can you use to buy income properties?

High Leverage versus Low (or No) Down Payment

Before we go through various high-leverage techniques, note a subtle (but critical) distinction: High leverage does not necessarily require a low down payment. In investor lingo, high leverage means that you've been

---

8. When the veteran has contributed a down payment, these loan amounts may be higher. Also, higher limits may apply in selected high-cost areas.

able to buy a property using little cash (10 percent of the purchase price, or less) from your own funds.

Say you've found a property priced at $100,000, and your lender agrees to provide a first mortgage in the amount of $70,000. Because you can't (or don't want to) draw a full $30,000 from your savings to make the required down payment, you have to think of some other way to raise all (or part) of these funds. If successful, you will have achieved a highly leveraged transaction. You will control a $100,000 property with relatively little cash coming out of your own pocket.

In a nutshell, you gain the benefits (and risks) of high leverage in either of two ways: (1) Originate or assume a high-LTV first mortgage, or (2) originate or assume a lower-LTV mortgage. Then, to reduce (or eliminate) your own cash input, use other sources of funds (loans, equity partners) to cover much of the difference between the amount of the first mortgage and the purchase price of the property.

Creative Finance Revisited

Creative finance means running through multiple financing alternatives. The term gained wide popularity when housing prices shot up and millions of Americans felt shut out of the real estate market because they lacked sufficient cash, credit, or both. "The central theme of my course," wrote Ed Beckley in *No Down Payment Formula* (Bantam, 1987), "is to teach you how to acquire as much property as you can without using any of your own money. . . . Starting from scratch requires that you become extremely resourceful. You need to *substitute ideas for cash*" (p. 69).

Okay, then, how might investors use creative thinking and resourcefulness to substitute for cash? Here are some of the most popular ideas and techniques.

Look for a Liberal Lender.   Most banks and savings institutions will only loan 70 to 80 percent of a (non-owner-occupied) income property's value. However, some financial institutions will make 90 percent LTV loans. In addition, some wealthy private investors provide high-LTV mortgages. You can often find these private investors through newspaper classified ads: Either you can advertise in the "Capital Wanted" section, or you can telephone those who list themselves in the "Capital Available" section.

You can also call mortgage brokers who may have contacts with as many as 20 to 100 sources of property financing. Through their extensive roster of lenders, mortgage brokers may be able to find you the high LTV you want.

Second Mortgages.   Some income property lenders will permit what are called 70–20–10 loans, or some other variation such as 75–15–10, or maybe even 80–15–5. The first figure refers to the LTV of a first mortgage; the second figure refers to the percentage of the purchase price represented by a second mortgage; and the third figure refers to out-of-pocket cash contributed by the buyer. A 70–20–10 deal for the purchase of a $100,000 house would require the following amounts:

First mortgage	$70,000
Second mortgage	$20,000
Buyer cash	$10,000

Typically, the property seller is the favored source of second mortgage loans. Often called "seller seconds" or seller "carrybacks," such loans require little red tape, paperwork, or closing costs. Plus you can often persuade a seller to accept an interest rate that's lower than what a commercial lender would charge. At a time when first mortgage rates were at 11 percent, and commercial second mortgage rates were at 16 percent, I was able to get a seller to carry back a $25,000 interest-only seller second at a rate of 8 percent.[9] The deal looked like this:

Purchase price	$106,500
First mortgage at 11%	$ 60,000
Seller second at 8%	$ 25,000
Cash from buyer	$ 21,500

If sellers won't cooperate, and the deal still makes sense, look to private investors, mortgage brokers, banks, and savings institutions. Before you do turn to "loan-sharking" commercial second mortgage lenders, though, think of friends or family members who might like to earn a relatively safe return of 7 to 10 percent (more or less) on their money. Compared to certificates of deposit and passbook savings that typically pay 2.5 to 5.0 percent, a 7 to 10 percent rate of interest could look pretty good.

Borrow against Other Assets.   If you're a homeowner with good credit, you can raise seed money for investment real estate by taking out a home equity loan (i.e., second mortgage) on your home. With many lenders pushing 125 percent LTV loans for homeowners, you may be able to raise a fair amount of cash—even if you haven't yet accumulated

---

9. In this case, the seller second primarily served to reduce my overall cost of borrowing thanks to its low interest rate.

substantial equity. Alternatively, consider a high-LTV refinance of your first mortgage.

What other assets can you borrow against? Retirement accounts, cars, jewelry, artwork, coin collection, life insurance, or vacation home? List everything you own. You may surprise yourself at what you discover.

Convert Assets to Cash (Downsizing).   Rather than borrow against your assets, downsize. Friends of mine recently sold their 6,000-square-foot Chicago North Shore residence for $1,050,000. With those proceeds they bought a vacation home, a smaller primary residence, and an in-town condominium. Could you, too, live comfortably in a smaller or less expensive home? Are you wasting money on unproductive luxury cars, jewelry, watches, or clothing? Are you one of the many Americans who live the high life—for now—but are failing to build enough wealth to really support the twin goals of financial security and financial independence?

In their study of the affluent, Thomas Stanley and William Danko *(The Millionaire Next Door)* interviewed many high-income professionals whom the authors named UAWs (underaccumulators of wealth). In contrast were the PAWs (prodigious accumulators of wealth)—who worked in less prestigious jobs and earned less income. Yet because of wise budgeting and investing, the PAWs' net worths far surpassed those of the high-income prodigious spenders. Downsizing now will pay big dividends later.

Wraparound Mortgage.   Wraparound mortgages can help buyers achieve a high LTV while providing a seller with a good yield. In reality, the wraparound is a second mortgage granted by a seller to a buyer, but the buyer makes only one loan payment.

The wraparound loan is commonly used when the buyer of a property doesn't want to completely lose the benefits of existing low interest rate financing. So he or she "wraps" the existing loan with a new wraparound loan at a slightly higher interest rate. The seller continues making payments on the existing low-interest loan while the buyer makes payments to the seller on the new wraparound loan. The seller would then earn a profit on the spread in interest rates. The wraparound works best during periods when interest rates shoot up. Figure 2.1 provides an example.

In Figure 2.1, the seller creates and carries a new loan of $210,000 at 9.0 percent. Payments on the seller's existing first mortgage total $1,077 per month. Payments on the new wraparound loan are $1,691 per month. Therefore the seller earns a $614 per month profit. As a return on the $60,000 the seller has left in the deal, he or she earns a return of 12.28 percent ($12 \times 614 \div 60,000 = 12.28$). Usually, the buyer gains in this transaction because the interest rate charged by the seller still falls below the

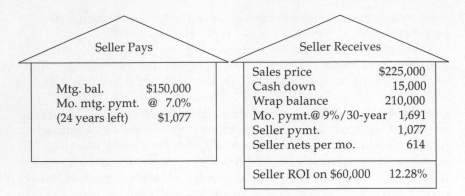

Seller Pays	Seller Receives	
Mtg. bal. $150,000	Sales price	$225,000
Mo. mtg. pymt. @ 7.0%	Cash down	15,000
(24 years left) $1,077	Wrap balance	210,000
	Mo. pymt.@ 9%/30-year	1,691
	Seller pymt.	1,077
	Seller nets per mo.	614
	Seller ROI on $60,000	12.28%

Figure 2.1   Wraparound Loan Example

prevailing market interest rate. (Note, though, that if you "wrap" a nonassumable mortgage, the seller's underlying mortgage lenders may choose to exercise its "due-on-sale" clause. If that happens, you and the sellers would have to work out some other type of financing arrangement.)

Use Credit Cards.   Although this is one of the more risky techniques of creative finance, some investors take advantage of every credit card offer they receive in the mail. Then when they require cash to quickly close a deal, they raise $5,000, $10,000, or even $50,000 from cash advances. Investors have been known to pay all cash for a property with the entire sum raised from credit cards.

Naturally, no one should use cash advances for long-term financing. On occasion, though, you might find plastic a good source to cover short-term needs. You may, for example, find a "steal" that you can renovate and immediately flip (resell) at a great profit.

Personal Loans.   In the days before credit card cash advances (which are now the most popular type of personal loan), personal loans were called signature loans. As you build your wealth through growing real estate equity, you'll find that many lenders will gladly grant you signature loans for $10,000, $25,000, or even $100,000, if your credit record and net worth can support repayment. You can use the money from these signature loans to buy more real estate. (Signature loans charge substantially lower fees and interest rates than credit card cash advances.)

Although many banks and savings institutions set rules against using personal loans for down payments, beginning and experienced investors alike routinely find ways over or around those rules. OWC (owner will carry) sellers who finance property sales seldom inquire about where you're getting your down payment money. So if you're short on cash, don't let that block you from buying rental properties. Weigh the risks and benefits of using a cash advance or signature loan to raise money for your down payment.

But again, do weigh the risk factors. Ill-conceived borrowing can easily push you into those ugly toss-and-turn, sleepless nights, if not financial ruin. Make sure your plan of repayment does not depend on any type of speculative (uncertain or unpredictable) contingency.

Land Contracts.   A land contract—sometimes referred to as a contract for deed, contract of sale, or agreement of sale—permits buyers to pay sellers for their property in installments. Under a land contract, a buyer agrees to buy a property and pay principal and interest to the seller. Unlike mortgage financing, most often, title to the property remains in the seller's name until conditions of the contract are fulfilled. The buyer, though, does gain possession of the property. If a buyer defaults on the agreement, the seller can typically repossess (not foreclose) the property. Sellers favor repossessions because they're quicker, easier, and less costly than foreclosure.

Land contracts may be useful in "wrapping" existing low interest rate financing (see the previous discussion of wraparounds). Caution must prevail when structuring buyer and seller terms and conditions in a land contract. These contracts include pitfalls for buyers and sellers. Because land contract sales are governed by state law, consult a competent real estate attorney before accepting this form of financing.

Often, properties sold on land contract are "nonconforming" properties such as storefronts with living quarters in the rear or above, farmhouses with acreage, older properties in need of repair, or various types of larger homes that have been cut up into apartments. My first property was a five-unit property—an old large house split into four one-bedroom apartments and a one-bedroom, one-bath carriage house that sat on the rear of the lot. I paid $1,000 down, and the seller (an elderly widow) financed the balance at 5 percent interest. She said that's the same rate she could get on a savings account in a bank so she didn't think it would be right to charge more than that. (I would sure like to find more sellers like her today.)

In the present market, land contracts still serve the same purposes they always have (nonconforming properties or subpar buyers). Yet it's also true that today many traditional mortgage lenders are reaching out to more diverse homebuyers and neighborhoods. As a result, many people and properties that may not have passed lender scrutiny in the past can

now qualify at credit unions, banks, and other types of mortgage companies. In addition, two types of seller-assisted financing have become popular: lease-purchase and lease-option agreements (see Chapter 9). To
some extent, these alternative types of seller-assisted financing have
reduced the use of land contracts.

All things considered, land contract real estate sales can play a role in
your property acquisition strategy. (For example, the VA often finances buyers of its REOs with land contracts.) Properly written, land contracts are low
cost and relatively easy to complete; they offer maximum flexibility in price
and interest rate; and they can give sellers quick remedies for borrower
default while they protect homebuyers against unfair forfeiture and future
title problems. If you can find (or create) a good deal using a land contract,
don't pass it up without fair consideration (and informed legal advice).

Sweat Equity (Creating Value through Renovations).   You might be able
to buy some properties with 100 percent financing if you can enhance their
value through improvements and renovations. Find a property that should
sell (in tip-top condition) for around $100,000. Yet because of its sorry state
of repair, as well as an eager seller, you can buy the property for $60,000
with short-term no-money-down owner financing. You then contribute
labor and $10,000 in materials that you pay for with a credit card.

Once you complete your work and bring the house up to its $100,000
market value, you arrange a 70 percent LTV mortgage with a lender. Then
with the loan proceeds of $70,000, you pay off the seller and your credit
card account. Voilà—you have not only achieved 100 percent financing for
your acquisition price and rehab but also created $30,000 of instant equity
(wealth).

Use Your Imagination.   The number of ways that you might use to help
fund your real estate purchases is limited only by the power of your imagination, education, and persuasion. In addition to the techniques just discussed, here are others:

- *Bring in partners.* If you can't (or don't want to) draw on your own
  cash or borrowing power, find a good deal and then show potential money partners (friends, family, contractors, wealthy
  investors) how they will benefit if they join you in the transaction.
- *Agree to swap services or products.* Does the seller need some service
  or expertise that you can render? Inventory your skills (law, med-
  icine, dentistry, writing, advertising, carpentry, accounting, landscaping, architecture, etc.). Include all areas of profession, trade,

and avocation. How about products? Say you own a radio station or newspaper. Trade off advertising time or space for a down payment. Anything you can produce, deliver, or sell wholesale (at cost) might work.

♦ *Borrow (or reduce) the real estate commission.* Although most brokers and sales agents generally hate this technique, on occasion, buyers and sellers do ask the agents involved in a transaction to defer payment until some later date. Some agents actually prefer to have their commissions in the deal. In doing so, they avoid paying income taxes on these fees, and at the same time they build wealth through interest payments or their receipt of a "piece of the action" (future profits from a sale).

♦ *Simultaneously sell off part of the property.* Does the property include an extra lot, a mobile home, or timber, oil, gas, air, or mineral rights? If so, find a buyer who will pay you cash for such rights. In turn, this money will help you close the deal.

♦ *Prepaid rents and tenant security deposits.* When you buy an income property, you are entitled to the existing tenants' security deposits and prepaid rents. Say you close on June 2. The seller (of a fourplex) is holding $4,000 in deposits and $3,800 in rent money that applies to the remaining days in June. Together, the deposits and prepaid rents amount to $7,800. In most transactions, you can use these monies to reduce your cash-to-close.

♦ *Create paper.* You've asked the seller to accept owner financing with 10 percent down. She balks. She believes the deal puts her at risk. Alleviate her fears and bolster her security. Offer her a lien against your car or a second (or third) mortgage on another property you own. Specify that when your principal paydown and the property's appreciation lift your equity to 20 percent (LTV of 80 percent), she will remove the security lien she holds against your other pledged asset.

♦ *Lease options.* No discussion of creative finance would be complete without mention of lease options. However, because of their wide usage and popularity, the pros and cons of this technique are covered in Chapter 9.

Are High-Leverage Creative-Finance Deals Really Possible?

Absolutely! I have used some type of creative finance in more than one-half of the property transactions in which I've been involved. To make creative finance work, however, you must know what you are doing. Keep a clear perspective. Stay calm. Avoid becoming so excited to make the deal that you concede too much. Low down, creative-finance deals tempt new investors into buying troubled properties or paying excessive prices. Make sure you can honor your commitments—and that those commitments are worth honoring.

Fewer Sellers.   Because creative finance violates so-called standard operating procedures, your property choices will diminish. While nearly every seller will accept all cash, far smaller numbers are willing to provide financing with little or nothing down.

Nevertheless, if you look for high-leverage creative-finance deals, you will find them. Many sellers who at first claim they're not interested will soften their attitude once you persuasively explain what's in it for them and then hand them your signed offer.

Lower-Quality, Overpriced Lemons.   Keep a sharp eye out for property owners who want to entice you into buying an overpriced lemon. Many of these sellers have read the nothing-down books. They know that advertising come-ons like "owner financing," "nothing down," "no qualifying," "make offer," and "EZ terms" will bring tons of calls from the latest "graduates" of the Carlton Sheets School of Creative Finance.

Just waiting to fleece the sheep, these sellers surreptitiously lead eager buyers into ill-advised purchase contracts. Maintenance and repair problems, disappearing tenants, phantom leases, illegal units, neighborhood crime, short-term balloon mortgages, troublesome neighbors, and undisclosed liens represent just a few of the setbacks naive buyers may run into. (For many other types of potential problems, see my book *The 106 Common Mistakes Homebuyers Make (and How to Avoid Them)*. In other words, don't let the siren call of creative finance crash your boat into the shoals soon after leaving port.

WHAT UNDERWRITING STANDARDS DO LENDERS APPLY?

Before you originate any type of new financing from an institutional mortgage lender (bank, credit union, mortgage banker, etc.), you'll complete a mortgage loan application.[10] To evaluate your loan request, lenders apply a variety of mortgage underwriting guidelines. The more you can learn about

---

10. For a much more extensive discussion of financing properties, see my book *The 106 Mortgage Secrets That All Homebuyers Must Learn—but Lenders Don't Tell* (Wiley, 2003).

these guidelines, the greater the chance that you'll locate a lender who will approve the loan you want. In addition to owner occupancy and loan-to-value ratios, here are six other underwriting standards:

1. Collateral (property characteristics)
2. Amount and source of down payment and reserves
3. Capacity (monthly income)
4. Credit history (credibility!)
5. Personal characteristics
6. Compensating factors

Collateral (Property Characteristics)

All financial institutions set standards for the properties that they will accept as collateral for their mortgage loans. Some lenders won't finance properties larger than four units. Some won't finance properties in poor condition or those located in run-down neighborhoods. Many lenders verify that a property is serviced by all utilities (e.g., some lenders avoid properties with septic tanks instead of sewer lines). Lenders may also set standards that apply to paved streets, conformance with zoning and building regulations, and proximity to schools, public transportation, shopping, and job centers.

Before you look at properties and write up an offer to buy, check whether that property meets the criteria of the lender and loan program that you intend to use. Otherwise you may waste time and money (loan application costs, appraisal, and other miscellaneous fees). Often, lenders will not refund these prepaid expenses.

Amount and Source of Down Payment and Reserves

Assume that your lender sets a 70 percent LTV for its first mortgage. Plus you're working with a seller who will carry back a second mortgage for the remainder of the purchase price. Will the financial institution approve your loan application? Maybe, maybe not.

Regardless of LTV, lenders like to see their borrowers put at least some of their own cash into their properties at the time they buy them. Moreover, the lender will probably ask you where you're getting the cash. The best source is ready money from a savings account (or other liquid assets). In contrast, most lenders would not want to hear that you're taking a $10,000 cash advance against your credit card.

Similarly, most lenders will want to know how much cash (or near cash assets) you will have on hand after you close your loan. Ideally, they would like to see enough money in reserve to cover two or three months of mortgage payments.

Capacity (Monthly Income)

As another underwriting guideline, mortgage lenders will evaluate your monthly income from employment and other sources, as well as the expected NOI of the property you're financing. For owner-occupied properties, a lender will (directly or indirectly) emphasize "qualifying ratios." A qualifying ratio is the percentage of your income that you can safely allocate to mortgage payments (principal, interest, property taxes, and insurance, or PITI). For example, if a lender sets a 28 percent housing-cost qualifying ratio and you gross $4,000 a month, the lender may limit your mortgage payments (PITI) to $1,120 a month.

In terms of rental property income and expenses, lenders may apply a debt coverage ratio (DCR). A debt coverage ratio shows the lender that the property can be expected to produce enough income to cover expenses and debt service (principal and interest). Here's a simple example for a fourplex whose units rent for $750 a month:

Gross annual income (4 x $750 x 12)	$36,000
less	
Vacancy	2,160
Operating expenses and upkeep	7,200
Property taxes and insurance equals	2,360
Net operating income (NOI)	$24,280

If a lender wants to see a 25 percent safety margin of income over debt service, calculate your maximum allowable mortgage payment by dividing the property's annual NOI by a debt coverage ratio (DCR) of 1.25:

$$\frac{NOI}{DCR} = \text{Annual mortgage payment}$$

$$\frac{\$24,280}{1.25} = \$19,424$$

To check, we reverse the calculations:

$$\frac{NOI}{\text{Debt Service}} = \text{Debt coverage ratio}$$

$$\frac{\$24,280}{\$19,424} = 1.25$$

Table 2.1   Monthly Payment Required per $1,000 of Original Mortgage Balance

Interest (%)	Monthly Payment	Interest (%)	Monthly Payment
2.5	$3.95	7.5	$ 6.99
3.0	4.21	8.0	7.34
3.5	4.49	8.5	7.69
4.0	4.77	9.0	8.05
4.5	5.07	9.5	8.41
5.0	5.37	10.0	8.77
5.5	5.67	10.5	9.15
6.0	5.99	11.0	9.52
6.5	6.32	11.5	9.90
7.0	6.65	12.0	10.29

Note: Term = 30 years.

From these calculations, you can see that with a 1.25 DCR, the property will produce enough income to support a monthly mortgage payment of $1,619 ($19,424 annual mortgage payment ÷ 12). To figure how much loan a mortgage payment of $1,619 a month will pay off (amortize) over a 30-year term, refer to Table 2.1.

At mortgage interest rates of, say, 6.0, 7.5, or 9.0 percent, the lender would consider loaning you up to $270,284, $231,617, or $201,118, respectively. Here are the figures:

6.0% Mortgage Interest Rate

$$\frac{\$1,619}{\$5.99} = \$270,284 \text{ loan amount}$$

7.5% Mortgage Interest Rate

$$\frac{\$1,619}{\$6.99} = \$231,617 \text{ loan amount}$$

9% Mortgage Interest Rate

$$\frac{\$1,619}{\$8.05} = \$201,118 \text{ loan amount}$$

As these figures show, once the lender sets a maximum amount for your monthly mortgage payment, lower interest rates dramatically boost your borrowing power. So, considered together, the interest rate and debt coverage ratio will determine how much a lender will loan you.

Credit History (Credibility!)

Do you need good credit to buy rental homes and apartments? No! But good credit certainly expands your possibilities. Without good credit, you'll be limited to buying properties with seller financing, nonqualifying assumable mortgages, or "B," "C," or "D" loans that carry high origination fees and high interest rates. If you do have an excellent credit record, though, lenders will roll out the red carpet for you. You're a desirable customer. Do all that you can to strengthen your credit record and build your reputation for meeting all credit obligations on or before their due dates.

However, "good credit" today doesn't necessarily mean what it used to mean. In today's highly competitive mortgage market, some mortgage lenders will accept borrowers who have experienced foreclosure, repossession, and bankruptcy. To qualify with these lenders, you (1) must have clean (preferably spotless) credit for the past 18 to 24 months; (2) should be able to attribute any adverse credit to divorce, unemployment, accident, illness, or other calamity; and (3) must persuade the lender that you're now firmly in control of your present and future financial well-being.

Just because you've faced serious credit problems in the past, you need not wait 5, 7, or 10 years before you can qualify for a new mortgage—especially if you're planning to live in the property you buy. (Remember, lenders give their easiest and best terms to owner occupants.)

Personal Characteristics

Although lenders cannot legally consider your age, race, religion, sex, marital status, or disability when they evaluate your loan application, they can and do look at other personal characteristics such as the following:

- ◆ Education level
- ◆ Career advancement potential
- ◆ Job stability
- ◆ Stability in the community
- ◆ Experience in property ownership
- ◆ Saving, spending, and borrowing habits
- ◆ Dependability
- ◆ Dress and mannerisms

A mortgage lender probably won't turn you down for a loan just because you dropped out of high school, dyed your hair purple, wear a silver nose ring, change jobs every six months, or don't have a telephone in your own name. Nevertheless, subtle (and not so subtle) influences still count—especially for investors.

Owning and managing income property is a serious business. Lenders want to make sure that they can trust you to fulfill these responsibilities. Do everything you can to convince the lender that you are a solid and dependable worker, investor, and borrower. As the legendary banker J. P. Morgan once told a U.S. congressional committee, "Money cannot buy credit. Because a man I do not trust could not get credit from me on all the bonds of Christendom." As J. P. Morgan affirms, character does count.

Compensating Factors

As you evaluate yourself and a property in terms of the preceding underwriting guidelines, remember, these are *guidelines*. Most lenders do not rotely evaluate their mortgage loan applications from investors. Instead, lenders weigh and consider. Because of such deliberating, you can subjectively influence the lender to approve your loan. Emphasize your positives and play down or explain away negatives.

If your debt coverage ratio is low, show the lender how you plan to improve the property and increase rents. If you have blemished credit, offset it with a higher down payment or pledged collateral. If you've frequently changed jobs, point out the raises and promotions you've received. If you lack experience in property ownership or property management, tell the lenders how you've educated yourself by reading real estate books and how you've developed a winning market strategy (see Chapter 11).

Use employer letters, references, prepared budgets, a business plan, or any other *written* evidence that you can come up with to justify your loan request. Anything in writing to persuade the lender that you are willing and able to pay back the money you borrow as agreed may help. In close (and not so close) calls, compensating factors can make the deciding difference in your favor.

Remember, too, that lenders differ—especially in the specific criteria they apply to investors. What one rejects, another accepts. Don't give up on getting the loan you want until you've knocked on many doors (or visited a number of mortgage Web sites).

Automated Underwriting

In recent years, mortgage lenders have increasingly turned to automated underwriting. Using this system, a loan representative gathers pertinent facts and enters them into a computer program. Within minutes, out pops a loan decision. Although each of the underwriting items discussed in this chapter still counts toward the approval (or rejection), many loan reps (especially new ones) don't understand the actual underwriting criteria. As a result, they simply accept the verdict of the computer output.

If your credit profile matches the acceptable profile in the computer program, that's great. It means a faster, less costly path to closing with a shorter stack of paperwork. On the other hand, if your personal situation needs "outside-the-box" personal consideration, many of today's loan reps (computer clerks) won't be willing or able to move the computer decision from a no to a yes.

If you find yourself facing rote rejection, you locate a savvy rep from the "old school" who can apply the skill and knowledge necessary to get your loan approved—or at least tell you the reasons why your application falls short and how you can work to remedy any deficiencies.

As a starting point, to see how you might fare with automated underwriting, go to www.myfico.com. From this site, you can learn your automated credit score and general pointers on how to improve it. Nevertheless, especially when applying for investor financing, get a savvy loan rep who not only knows how to improve the look of your application but also knows the right lender and loan product for your needs.

3

APPRAISAL: HOW TO
DISCOVER GREAT PROPERTIES

Nearly everyone can figure out some way to buy and finance real estate. But to buy *profitably*, you must understand how to value property.

In the past, many real estate investors, to their regret, lost sight of this critical point. Even today most popular how-to books on real estate investing give short shrift to valuing properties. Why? Because in days gone by, authors and investors believed that "inflation cures all mistakes." People got the foolish notion that to make money in real estate, all you had to do was to buy it. Even if you paid too much, rising prices would eventually bail you out. For example, here's what David Schumacher has written:

> The amount I paid for this property is inconsequential because of the degree to which the property has appreciated in value . . . . In my opinion, it is ridiculous to quibble over $5,000 or even $50,000 in price if you are buying for the long term. . . . In 1963, I bought a four-unit apartment building for $35,000. Suppose I had paid $100,000 for it. It wouldn't have made any difference because the property's worth $1.2 million today. (*The Buy and Hold Real Estate Strategy*, Wiley, 1992)

Other top-selling real estate books advise would-be investors to tell sellers, "You name the price, I'll name the terms." If the property owner agrees to sell on easy terms (usually little or nothing down), the buyer will agree to the seller's price. "Who cares what you pay today? What's important is all that money you're going to make when you sell." (You saw in Chapter 2 where that belief can lead.)

MAKE MONEY WHEN YOU BUY, NOT JUST WHEN YOU SELL

Yes, long-term appreciation will boost a property's value. Nevertheless, if you overpay, you may wait five years (or more) for the market to catch up. During that time you could have been building wealth. Even worse, the more you pay (especially with high loan-to-value [LTV] financing), the larger your mortgage payments, and the less your positive cash flow.

Whenever possible, make money when you buy a property, not just when you sell. You reduce risk and increase your chance for great returns when you buy properties at or (preferably) below their market values. But this tactic also requires that you fully understand the meaning of the term "market value."

WHAT IS MARKET VALUE?

To the naive, terms such as "appraised value," "sales price," and "market value" all mean the same thing. But they don't. "Appraised value" could refer to an insurance appraisal, a property tax appraisal, an estate tax appraisal, *or* a market value appraisal. Sales price, itself, merely refers to the nominal price at which a property has sold. That sales price could equal, exceed, or fall below market value. Market value equals sales price only when a property is sold under the following five conditions:

1. Buyers and sellers are typically motivated. Neither is acting under duress.
2. Buyers and sellers are well informed about the market and are acting in their own best interest.
3. The marketing period and sales promotion permit reasonable exposure of the property to potential buyers.
4. No special terms of financing apply.
5. Neither the sellers nor the buyers offer any out-of-the-ordinary concessions.

To illustrate: Let's say that two properties recently sold in a neighborhood where you're interested in buying: 37 Oak sold at a price of $158,000, and 164 Maple sold at a price of $155,000. Each of these three-bedroom, two-bath houses was in good condition, with around 2,100 square feet. You locate a nearby house of similar size and features at 158 Pine. It's priced at $134,750. Is that a bargain (below market value) price? Maybe, maybe not. Before you draw a conclusion, you must investigate the terms and conditions of the other two sales.

What if the sellers of 164 Maple had carried back a nothing-down, 6 percent, 30-year mortgage for their buyers (special financing)?

What if the buyers of 37 Oak had just flown into Peoria from San Francisco and had bought the first house they saw because "It was such a steal. You couldn't find anything like it in San Francisco for less than $800,000" (uninformed buyers)?

What if the sellers of 37 Oak had agreed to pay all of their buyer's closing costs and leave their authentic Chippendale buffet because it was too big to move into their new retirement condominium in Florida (i.e., out-of-the-ordinary sales concessions)?

Sales Price Doesn't Necessarily Equal Market Value

When you're shopping properties, it's not enough to know the prices at which other similar homes have sold. You must also learn whether the buyers or sellers acted with full market knowledge, gave any unusually favorable (or onerous) terms of financing, bought (or sold) in a hurry, or made any concessions that might have pushed the sales price up or pulled it down. Should you find that the sales of any comparable properties do not meet the criteria of a "market value" sale, duly weigh that information before you decide on a bid price for any of the properties that you are considering.

In other words, before you value a property from the comp sales prices, (1) verify the accuracy of your information, (2) verify the date of sale, and (3) verify the terms and conditions of the sale. Incorrect or incomplete sales price information can make bad deals look good (or vice versa).

Lenders Only Loan against Market Value

Lenders loan against market value, not purchase price. When you apply for a mortgage, you may tell the lender that you've agreed to a price of $200,000 and would like to borrow $160,000 (an 80 percent LTV). The lender, though, will not necessarily agree that this price fairly reflects the property's market value.

First, the lender will ask you about special financing terms (e.g., a $20,000 seller second) and sales concessions (e.g., the sellers plan to buy down your interest rate for three years and pay all closing costs). If your transaction violates market value norms, the lender won't loan 80 percent

of your $200,000 purchase price—even if it routinely does make 80 per-
cent LTV loans. The lender may find that easy terms of financing or sales
concessions are worth $10,000. Therefore the lender may base your 80 per-
cent LTV on $190,000, not the $200,000 purchase price.

Second, to verify that your sales price of $200,000 matches market
value, the lender will order an appraisal. If the appraisal report comes
back with a figure that's less than $200,000, the lender will use the lesser
amount to calculate an 80 percent LTV loan. Be aware, however, that you
don't have to passively accept a low appraisal. You critique the original,
or you can ask the lender to order a new appraisal with another firm. The
lender primarily wants a file document (appraisal) to justify its lending
decision. If you provide an acceptable (revised or remade) appraisal of a
satisfactory amount, you'll often get the loan you want.

On the other hand, just because a lender's appraiser comes up with
a market value estimate that matches your purchase price, don't jump to
the conclusion that the appraisal is accurate. You must still accept responsibility for your offering price. Lenders routinely tell their appraisers the
value they need to make a deal work. In return, appraisers know that if
they fail to give the right figure, lenders will select another, more accommodating firm to prepare their reports.

If you're a good customer of the bank (or if the bank would like you
to become a good customer), the loan officer may encourage the appraiser
to issue an MAI ("made as instructed") appraisal. I know of many
instances where appraisers have acquiesced to not-so-subtle hints from a
bank executive and submitted appraisals that materially overstated a
property's value.

When you invest in real estate, you'll have to work with appraisers,
and you may want to solicit their opinions, but never accept those opinions as the final word. To protect yourself against erroneous appraisals
(your own, as well as those of others), you must understand the full
details of the appraisal process.

THE THREE APPROACHES TO VALUE

Knowledgeable investors, lenders, and appraisers typically value properties from three different perspectives.

1. *Cost approach.* To apply the cost approach, investors calculate
   how much it would cost to build a subject property at today's
   prices, subtract accrued depreciation, and then add the depreciated cost figure to the current value of the lot.

2. *Comparable sales approach.* To apply the comparable sales approach, investors compare a subject property with other similar (comp) properties that have recently sold. Then they adjust the prices for each positive or negative feature of the comps relative to the subject property. Through this detailed and systematic comparison, they can get a pretty good idea of a subject property's market value.
3. *Income approach.* To apply the income approach, investors estimate the rents a property can be expected to produce and then convert those rents (income stream) into a capital (market) value amount.

When you evaluate a property from three perspectives, you check each of your value estimates against the others. You gain confidence concerning a property's value. If, however, your three value estimates deviate from each other by more than roughly 5 percent, you know that you've made a mistake, the data you're working with are inaccurate, or the market is acting "crazy" and property prices are about to head up (or down).

Figure 3.1 shows a sample appraisal form for a single-family house. Refer to this form as you read the following pages, and you'll see how to apply these appraisal techniques to the properties you look at. You might also photocopy this form (or pick up originals at a local appraisal office). Use the forms to record property and market information as you shop for your investments.

PROPERTY DESCRIPTION

To accurately estimate the value of a property, you must describe the features of the property and its neighborhood in detail. Not surprisingly, novice investors frequently err in their market valuations because they casually inspect rather than carefully compare. Focus on each of the neighborhood and property features listed on an appraisal form, and you will make better decisions.

Subject Property Identification

The subject property identification seems self-explanatory, but you must still investigate and verify. For example, the street address for one of my previous homes was 73 Roble Road, Berkeley, California 94705. However, that property did not sit in Berkeley. It was located in Oakland. The house sat back from Roble Road (which is in Berkeley) about 100 feet—just far enough to put it within the city limits of Oakland. As a result, the city laws

Property Description   **UNIFORM RESIDENTIAL APPRAISAL REPORT**   File No.   SAMPLE

Property Address	City State Zip Code
Legal Description	County
Assessor's Parcel No.	Tax Year R.E. Taxes$ Special Assessments $
Borrower Current Owner	Occupant ☐ Owner ☐ Tenant ☐ Vacant
Property rights appraised ☐ Fee Simple ☐ Leasehold Project Type ☐ PUD	☐ Condominium (HUD/VA only) HOA$ /Mo.
Neighborhood/Project Name	Map Reference Census Tract
Sale Price $ Date of Sale	Description and $ amount of loan charges/concessions to be paid by seller
Lender/Client	Address
Appraiser	Address

NEIGHBORHOOD

Location	☐ Urban	☐ Suburban ☐ Rural	Predominant	Single family housing / Present land use % / Land use change
Built Up	☐ Over 75%	☐ 25-75% ☐ Under 25%	occupancy	PRICE $(000) / AGE (yrs) / One family / ☐ Not likely ☐ Likely
Growth Rate	☐ Rapid	☐ Stable ☐ Slow	☐ Owner	/ 2-4 family / ☐ In process
Property Values	☐ Increasing	☐ Stable ☐ Declining	☐ Tenant	Low / Multi-family / To:
Demand/supply	☐ Shortage	☐ In balance ☐ Over Supply	☐ Vacant (0-5%)	High / Commercial
Marketing Time	☐ Under 3 mos.	☐ 3-6 mos. ☐ Over 6 mos.	☐ Vacant (over 5%)	Predominant

Note: Race and the racial composition of the neighborhood are not appraisal factors.

Neighborhood boundaries and characteristics: _____

Factors that affect the marketability of the properties in the neighborhood (proximity to employment and amenities, employment stability, appeal to market, etc.):
_____
_____
_____
_____

Market Conditions in the subject neighborhood (including support for the above conclusions related to the trend of property values, demand/supply, and marketing time
— — such as data on competitive properties for sale in the neighborhood, description of the prevalence of sales and financing concessions, etc.):
_____
_____
_____
_____

PUD

Project information for PUDs (if applicable) - - is the developer/builder in control of the Home Owners' Association (HOA)? ☐ Yes ☐ No
Approximate total number of units in the subject project _____. Approximate total number of units for sale in the subject project _____
Describe common elements and recreational facilities:

SITE

Dimensions		Topography
Site Area	Corner Lot ☐ Yes ☐ No	Size
Specific zoning classification and description		Shape
Zoning compliance ☐ Legal ☐ Legal nonconforming (Grandfathered use) ☐ Illegal ☐ No zoning		Drainage
Highest & best use as improved: ☐ Present use ☐ Other use (explain)		View

Utilities	Public	Other	Off-site Improvements Type	Public	Private	Landscaping
Electricity	☐		Street	☐	☐	Driveway Surface
Gas	☐		Curb/gutter	☐	☐	Apparent Easements
Water	☐		Sidewalk	☐	☐	FEMA Special Flood Hazard Area ☐ Yes ☐ No
Sanitary sewer	☐		Street lights	☐	☐	FEMA Zone Map Date
Storm sewer	☐		Alley	☐	☐	FEMA Map No.

Comments (apparent adverse easements, encroachments, special assessments, slide areas, illegal or legal nonconforming zoning use, etc.):
_____

DESCRIPTION OF IMPROVEMENTS

GENERAL DESCRIPTION	EXTERIOR DESCRIPTION	FOUNDATION	BASEMENT	INSULATION
No. of Units	Foundation	Slab	Area Sq. Ft.	Roof ☐
No. of Stories	Exterior Walls	Crawl Space	% Finished	Ceiling ☐
Type (Det./Att.)	Roof Surface	Basement	Ceiling	Walls ☐
Design (Style)	Gutters & Dwnspts.	Sump Pump	Walls	Floor ☐
Existing/Proposed	Window Type	Dampness	Floor	None ☐
Age (Yrs.)	Storm/Screens	Settlement	Outside Entry	Unknown ☐
Effective Age (Yrs.)	Manufactured House	Infestation		

ROOMS	Foyer	Living	Dining	Kitchen	Den	Family Rm.	Rec. Rm.	Bedrooms	# Baths	Laundry	Other	Area Sq. Ft.
Basement												
Level 1												
Level 2												

Finished area above grade contains: Rooms;   Bedroom(s);   Bath(s)   Square Feet of Gross Living Area

INTERIOR	Materials/Condition	HEATING	KITCHEN EQUIP.	ATTIC	AMENITIES	CAR STORAGE:
Floors		Type	Refrigerator ☐	None ☐	Fireplace(s) # ☐	None ☐
Walls		Fuel	Range/Oven ☐	Stairs ☐	Patio ☐	Garage # of cars
Trim/Finish		Condition	Disposal ☐	Drop Stair ☐	Deck ☐	Attached
Bath Floor		COOLING	Dishwasher ☐	Scuttle ☐	Porch ☐	Detached
Bath Wainscot		Central	Fan/Hood ☐	Floor ☐	Fence ☐	Built-in
Doors		Other	Microwave ☐	Heated ☐	Pool ☐	Carport
		Condition	Washer/Dryer ☐	Finished ☐		Driveway

COMMENTS

Additional features (special energy efficient items, etc.): _____

Condition of the improvements, depreciation (physical, functional, and external), repairs needed, quality of construction, remodeling/additions, etc.:
_____
_____
_____

Adverse environmental conditions (such as, but not limited to, hazardous wastes, toxic substances, etc.) present in the improvements, on the site, or in the immediate vicinity of the subject property: _____

Freddie Mac Form 70 6-93   Legal Printing by WSF, Inc. 191 Lucerne Dr. Chicago, IL 60661 312-555-0000

Figure 3.1   Appraisal Report

Valuation Section   **UNIFORM RESIDENTIAL APPRAISAL REPORT**   File No.   SAMPLE

COST APPROACH	ESTIMATED SITE VALUE . . . . = $ _____	Comments on Cost Approach (such as, source of cost estimate, site value, square foot calculation and, for HUD, VA and FmHA, the estimated remaining economic life of the property):
	ESTIMATED REPRODUCTION COST-NEW-OF IMPROVEMENTS:	
	Dwelling _____ Sq.Ft. @ $ _____ = $ _____	
	_____ Sq.Ft. @ $ _____ = _____	
	Garage/Carport _____ Sq.Ft. @ $ _____ = _____	
	Total Estimated Cost New . . . . = $ _____	
	Less Physical | Functional | External	
	Depreciation _____ = $ _____	
	Depreciated Value of Improvements . . . . = $ _____	
	"As-is" Value of Site Improvements . . . . = $ _____	
	INDICATED VALUE BY COST APPROACH . . . . = $ _____	

ITEM	SUBJECT	COMPARABLE NO. 1	COMPARABLE NO. 2	COMPARABLE NO. 3
Address				
Proximity to Subject				
Sales Price				
Price/Gross Liv. Area				
Data and/or Verification Sources				

VALUE ADJUSTMENTS	DESCRIPTION	DESCRIPTION	+(-) $ Adjustment	DESCRIPTION	+(-) $ Adjustment	DESCRIPTION	+(-) $ Adjustment
Sales or Financing Concessions							
Date of Sale/Time							
Location							
Leasehold/Fee							
Site							
View							
Design and Appeal							
Quality of Construction							
Age							
Condition							
Above Grade Room Count	Total Bdrms Baths	Total Bdrms Baths		Total Bdrms Baths		Total Bdrms Baths	
Gross Living Area	Sq. Ft.	Sq. Ft.		Sq. Ft.		Sq. Ft.	
Basement & Finished Rooms Below Grade							
Functional Utility							
Heating/Cooling							
Energy Efficient Items							
Garage/Carport							
Porch, Patio, Deck, Fireplace(s), etc.							
Fence, Pool, etc.							
Net Adj. (total)		+ - $		+ - $		+ - $	
Adjusted Sales Price of Comparable		$		$		$	

Comments on Sales Comparison (including the subject property's compatibility to the neighborhood, etc.): _____

ITEM	SUBJECT	COMPARABLE NO. 1	COMPARABLE NO. 2	COMPARABLE NO. 3
Date, Price, and Data Source for prior sales within year of appraisal				

Analysis of any current agreement of sale, option, or listing of the subject property and analysis of any prior sales of subject and comparables within one year of the date of appraisal:

INDICATED VALUE BY SALES COMPARISON APPROACH . . . . $ _____
INDICATED VALUE BY INCOME APPROACH (If Applicable) Estimated Market Rent $ _____ /Mo. x Gross Rent Multiplier _____ = $ _____
This appraisal is made ☐ "as is" ☐ subject to repairs, alterations, inspections, or conditions listed below ☐ subject to completion per plans and specifications.
Conditions of Appraisal: _____

Final Reconciliation: _____

The purpose of this appraisal is to estimate the market value of the real property that is the subject of this report, based on the above conditions and the certification, contingent and limiting conditions, and market value definition that are stated in the attached Freddie Mac Form 439/Fannie Mae Form 1004B (Revised _____).
I (WE) ESTIMATE THE MARKET VALUE, AS DEFINED, OF THE REAL PROPERTY THAT IS THE SUBJECT OF THIS REPORT, AS OF _____
(WHICH IS THE DATE OF INSPECTION AND THE EFFECTIVE DATE OF THIS REPORT) TO BE $ _____

APPRAISER	SUPERVISORY APPRAISER (ONLY IF REQUIRED):	Inspect Property
Signature	Signature	☐ Did ☐ Did Not
Name	Name	
Date Report Signed	Date Report Signed	
State Certification #	State Certification # State	
Or State License # State	Or State License # State	

Freddie Mac Form 70 6-93   Laser Printing by WCA, Inc., 101 Lancelot Ct., Simpsonville, SC 29681 803-967-3922   Fannie Mae Form 1004 6-93

Figure 3.1 *(continued)*

Owner/Borrower	Property Address
Lender/Client	

DEFINITION OF MARKET VALUE: The most probable price which a property should bring in a competitive and open market under all conditions requisite to a fair sale, the buyer and seller, each acting prudently, knowledgeably and assuming the price is not affected by undue stimulus. Implicit in this definition is the consummation of a sale as of a specified date and the passing of title from seller to buyer under conditions whereby: (1) buyer and seller are typically motivated; (2) both parties are well informed or well advised, and each acting in what he considers his own best interest (3) a reasonable time is allowed for exposure in the open market; (4) payment is made in terms of cash in U. S. dollars or in terms of financial arrangements comparable thereto; and (5) the price represents the normal consideration for the property sold unaffected by special or creative financing or sales concessions* granted by anyone associated with the sale.

*Adjustment to the comparables must be made for special or creative financing or sale concessions. No adjustments are necessary for those costs which are normally paid by sellers as a result of tradition or law in a market area; these costs are readily identifiable since the seller pays these costs in virtually all sales transactions. Special or creative financing adjustments can be made to the comparable property by comparisons to financing terms offered by a third party institutional lender that is not already involved in the property or transaction. Any adjustment should not be calculated on a mechanical dollar for dollar cost of the financing or concession but the dollar amount of any adjustment should approximate the market's reaction to the financing or concessions based on the appraiser's judgment.

STATEMENT OF LIMITING CONDITIONS AND APPRAISER'S CERTIFICATION

CONTINGENT AND LIMITING CONDITIONS: The appraiser's certification that appears in the appraisal report is subject to the following conditions:

1. The appraiser will not be responsible for matters of a legal nature that affect either the property being appraised or the title to it. The appraiser assumes that the title is good and marketable and, therefore, will not render any opinions about the title. The property is appraised on the basis of it being under responsible ownership.

2. The appraiser has provided a sketch in the appraisal report to show approximate dimensions of the improvements and the sketch is included only to assist the reader of the report in visualizing the property and understanding the appraiser's determination of its size.

3. The appraiser has examined the available flood maps that are provided by the Federal Emergency Management Agency (or other data sources) and has noted in the appraisal report whether the subject site is located in an identified Special Flood Hazard Area. Because the appraiser is not a surveyor, he or she makes no guarantees, express or implied, regarding this determination

4. The appraiser will not give testimony or appear in court because he or she made an appraisal of the property in question, unless specific arrangements to do so have been made beforehand.

5. The appraiser has estimated the value of the land in the cost approach at its highest and best use and the improvements at their contributory value. These separate valuations of the land and improvements must not be used in conjunction with any other appraisal and are invalid if they are so used.

6. The appraiser has noted in the appraisal report any adverse conditions (such as, needed repairs, depreciation, the presence of hazardous wastes, toxic substances, etc.) observed during the inspection of the subject property or that he or she became aware of during the normal research involved in performing the appraisal. Unless otherwise stated in the appraisal report, the appraiser has no knowledge of any hidden or unapparent conditions of the property or adverse environmental conditions (including the presence of hazardous wastes, toxic substances, etc.) that would make the property more or less valuable, and has assumed that there are no such conditions and makes no guarantees or warranties, express or implied, regarding the condition of the property. The appraiser will not be responsible for any such conditions that do exist or for any engineering or testing that might be required to discover whether such conditions exist. Because the appraiser is not an expert in the field of environmental hazards, the appraisal report must not be considered as environmental assessment of the property.

7. The appraiser obtained the information, estimates, and opinions that were expressed in the appraisal report from sources that he or she considers to be reliable and believes them to be true and correct. The appraiser does not assume responsibility for the accuracy of such items that were furnished by other parties.

8. The appraiser will not disclose the contents of the appraisal report except as provided for in the Uniform Standards of Professional Appraisal Practice.

9. The appraiser has based his or her appraisal report and valuation conclusion for an appraisal that is subject to satisfactory completion, repairs, or alterations on the assumption that completion of the improvements will be performed in a workmanlike manner.

10. The appraiser must provide his or her prior written consent before the lender/client specified in the appraisal report can distribute the appraisal report (including conclusions about the property value, the appraiser's identity and professional designations, and references to any professional appraisal organizations or the firm with which the appraiser is associated) to anyone other than the borrower; the mortgagee or its successors and assigns; the mortgage insurer; consultants; professional appraisal organizations; any state or federally approved financial institution; or any department, agency, or instrumentality of the United States or any state or the District of Columbia; except that the lender/client may distribute the property description section of the report only to data collection or reporting service(s) without having to obtain the appraiser's prior written consent. The appraiser's written consent and approval must also be obtained before the appraisal can be conveyed by anyone to the public through advertising, public relations, news, sales, or other media.

Figure 3.1   *(continued)*

DEFINITIONS OF APPRAISAL TERMS

ACRE: A measure of land, approximately 208.7 by 208.7 feet, in area: 43,560 square feet, or 4,840 square yards.

ADJUSTMENT: Increase or decrease in the sales price of a comparable property to account for a feature that the property has or does not have in comparison to the subject property.

APPRAISAL: An estimate of value; the process through which conclusions of property value are obtained; also, the report setting forth the process of estimating value.

APPRAISED VALUE: An estimate by an appraiser of the amount of a particular subject value, such as market value, based upon the particular assignment.

CODE OF ETHICS: Rules of conduct that govern the actions of members of a professional appraisal group.

COMPARABLES: Properties that are substantially equivalent to the subject property.

CONVENTIONAL MORTGAGE: A mortgage that is not insured by a government agency such as FHA or VA.

DEPRECIATION: Loss of value from any cause; this includes physical deterioration, functional obsolescence, and economic obsolescence.

ECONOMIC LIFE: The total number of useful years that may be expected from a particular structure.

EQUITY: The value an owner has in real estate over and above any debt or mortgage against it.

GROSS RENT MULTIPLIER: The factor used as a multiplier of the gross rental income of a property to produce an income approach estimate to value.

HIGHEST AND BEST USE: The use of land that produces the highest property value.

LEGAL DESCRIPTION: A statement describing a particular property by a standard method determined by law.

NEIGHBORHOOD: A residential or commercial area encompassing similar real properties which is defined by specific natural, land use, or typical age boundaries.

PERSONAL PROPERTY: Items which are removable and not part of the real property.

PRICE: The amount of money predetermined or paid in return for a particular item at a particular time.

REAL ESTATE: Land; a well-defined portion of the earth's surface which includes everything below the surface to the center of the earth and everything above the surface into space and all things natural or man-made permanently fixed to it.

REPLACEMENT COST: The current cost of replacing a subject property with another property having the same functional utility.

REPRODUCTION COST. The current cost of reconstructing an exact duplicate of the subject property.

TITLE: Documents or physical evidence showing an individual's right of ownership to particular real estate.

Figure 3.1 *(continued)*

governing the property (zoning, building regulations, permitting, rent controls, school district, etc.) were those of Oakland, not Berkeley.

Similarly, Park Cities (University Park and Highland Park) are high-income independent municipalities located within the geographic boundaries of Dallas, Texas. Among other amenities, Park Cities have been noted for their high-quality schools. Yet if you lived in Park Cities on the west side of the North Dallas Tollway, your children would attend the lesser-regarded schools of the Dallas Independent School District.

The lesson: Street and city addresses don't always tell you what you need to know about a property. Strange as it may seem, a property may not be located where you think it is.

Neighborhood

As the appraisal form shows, your neighborhood investigation should note the types and condition of neighborhood properties, the percentage that are owner occupied, vacancy rates, housing price (and rental) ranges, the quality of government services, and convenience to shopping, schools, employment centers, parks and recreational areas, and its overall appeal to the market.

Most important, envision the changes in the neighborhood that you see occurring over the next three to five years. Is the neighborhood stable? Is it moving toward higher rates of owner occupancy? Are property owners fixing up their properties? Do neighborhood residents and local merchants take pride in their properties and the surrounding area? Is a neighborhood (or homeowners') association working to improve the area? If not, could such an association make the neighborhood a better place to live, shop, work, and play?

When you invest in a property, you're not just buying the here and now. You're buying the future. The questions you answer shouldn't focus exclusively on what you see today. Close your eyes. Imagine how the neighborhood will (or could be made to) look five years from now.

Site (Lot) Characteristics

Many beginning real estate investors fail to realize how important the size and features of a lot may be to a property's current and future value. Depending on the neighborhood, lot value can count for less than 10 percent to more than 90 percent of a property's selling price. Smart investors pay as much attention to the lot as they do to the structure.

In addition to a lot's physical size and features (see appraisal form), check the types of government regulations that apply. As a minimum, determine whether the buildings conform to all zoning, occupancy, environmental, and safety regulations. Many two- to four-unit (and larger) properties have been modified (rehabbed, cut up, added to, repaired, rewired, reroofed, etc.) in ways that violate current laws and regulations. Plus, laws change. Even if in the past the property did conform, it may violate today's tougher legal standards.

Along these lines, the law classifies properties as (1) legal and conforming, (2) legal and nonconforming, and (3) illegal. When a property meets all of today's legal standards, it's called legal and conforming. If it met past standards that don't meet current law, but have been "grandfathered," the property qualifies as legal but nonconforming. And if the property includes features or uses that violate standards not grandfathered as permissible, those features or uses remain illegal.

If you buy a property that fails to meet current law, buy with your eyes wide open. Lower your offering price to reflect risk. At some future time, inspectors may require you to bring the property up to code. Just as important, health, safety, and environmental violations may

- subject your tenants to injury,
- stimulate a rent strike,
- expose you to a lawsuit,
- expose you to civil or criminal penalties (fines, prison).

Before you decide how much to pay for a property, verify code compliance. Bringing a nonconforming property up to code might cost thousands (or even tens of thousands) of dollars.

Improvements

After thoroughly investigating lot size, features, and improvements (e.g., parking, driveways, fencing, landscaping, utilities, sewage disposal), fully detail the size, condition, quality, and appeal of the house or apartment units located on the site. Building size itself ranks as one of the most important determinants of value. Measuring size (room count, square footage), however, requires detailed inspection.

When you shop for properties, you'll find converted basements, garages, and attics; you'll find heated/cooled and unheated/uncooled living areas; you'll find "bedrooms" without closets and "dining areas" without space for a family-size table and chairs, let alone a buffet or china cabinet; you'll find rooms with 6-foot ceilings or lower, and rooms with 12-foot ceilings or higher; you'll find some storage areas that are easily accessible and some that you can reach only while crawling on your hands and knees or standing on a ladder.

You'll find that all rooms and living areas are not created equally. You can't merely compare raw size or space. Closely inspect the quality and livability of the rooms, traffic patterns, and storage areas within the property.

Even more confusing, not everyone measures square footage in the same way: A builder recently asked five appraisers to measure one of his new homes. In sales promotion literature, the builder listed the home as 3,103 square feet. One appraiser came up with a square-footage count of 3,047 square feet. The other appraisers came up with measures that ranged between 2,704 square feet and 3,312 square feet. Differences like these occur not just because of mistakes but also because there are no "square-footage police" who prescribe or enforce measurement methods.

When someone tells you a property's room count or square footage, don't casually accept that information. Learn exactly how that figure was calculated and what living or storage space is included (and omitted). In the end analysis, you must judge the quality and measure the space for yourself.

THE COST APPROACH

The cost approach assumes that investors can build a new property or buy an existing one. Replacement cost typically sets the upper limit to the price someone should pay for a property. If you can build a new property for $180,000 (including the cost of a lot), then you shouldn't pay $210,000 for an older property located just down the street. In fact, you shouldn't even pay $180,000 for that existing property, because it has suffered depreciation.

Calculate Cost to Build New

Now refer to the appraisal form and follow the logic of the cost approach. First, calculate the cost to build the property using dollars per square foot. Use a figure that would apply in your area for the type of property you're valuing. To learn these per-square-foot costs, talk with local contractors or consult the construction cost manuals in the reference section of your local library.

Because replacement costs correlate directly with the size and quality of buildings, an accurate property measurement must precede accurate valuation. Notice, too, that the cost of upgrades and extras (crystal chandelier, high-grade wall-to-wall carpeting, high-end appliances or plumbing fixtures, sauna, hot tub, swimming pool, garage, carport, patios, porches, etc.) must be figured separately and added to the cost of the basic construction.

Subtract Depreciation

After calculating the cost to rebuild the subject property at today's construction prices, subtract an amount for three types of depreciation: (1) physical, (2) functional, and (3) external. As a building ages, it becomes less desirable than new construction because of *physical* depreciation (wear and tear). As a property is exposed to time, weather, people, use, and abuse, it deteriorates. Frayed carpets, faded paint, cracked plaster, rusty plumbing, and leaky roofs bring down a property's value when compared with new construction. Exactly how much remains a judgment call. But to fill in a number for a building in good condition, estimate, say, 10 percent or 20 percent; if the property is really run-down, even 50 percent depreciation or greater might be warranted. Or instead of applying a percentage depreciation figure, itemize the costs of the repairs and renovations that would put the property in top condition.

Usually, though, itemized repairs don't work as well as percentage estimates, because you can't feasibly upgrade an eight-year-old roof, four-year-old carpeting, or a nine-year-old furnace to like-new condition. Nevertheless, in some way, you must estimate how much the subject property has physically depreciated as contrasted to a newly built property of the same size, quality, and features.

Next, estimate the dollar amount of *functional* depreciation. Unlike wear and tear, which occurs naturally through use and abuse, functional depreciation refers to loss of value because of problems such as outdated dark wood paneling, poor floor plan, low-amperage electrical systems, or even out-of-favor color schemes or architectural design. A property may show little wear and tear (physical depreciation) but still suffer large functional depreciation because the features of the property no longer appeal to a majority of potential buyers or renters.

External (locational) depreciation occurs when a property no longer reflects the highest and best use for a site. Say you find a wonderfully well kept little house located in an area now dotted with offices and retail stores. Zoning of the site has changed. More than likely, the house would as is add little or nothing to the site's value. When someone buys the "house," they will probably tear it down (or renovate it) to make way for another retail store or office building.

For duck-out-of-water properties such as this one, external (locational) factors make the buildings obsolete. External depreciation approaches 100 percent. With or without the house, the site should sell at approximately the same price. This principle also applies when neighborhoods move upscale, and well-kept three-bedroom, two-bath houses of 2,000 square feet are torn down and replaced with 6,000-square-foot McMansions. These smaller existing houses are referred to as "teardowns."

Lot Value

Because land isn't manufactured, you can't calculate its cost in the same way that you can calculate the cost to construct a house or an apartment building. To estimate lot value, find similar (vacant) lots that have recently sold, or lots that have sold with teardowns on them. When evaluating similar sites, closely compare all features such as size, frontage, views, topography, government regulations, subdivision rules, and other features that would affect the values of the respective sites.

Estimate Market Value (Cost Approach)

As you can see on the appraisal form, after you've gone through the three steps just discussed (calculated a property's construction cost if newly built, subtracted depreciation, and added in site value), you have arrived at an *estimated* market value. Because you can't precisely measure construction costs, depreciation, or site value, the cost approach won't give you a perfect answer. But it will give you a figure to use as a check against the comparative sales and income approaches. Here's a simple example of the cost approach:

Property description: Six-year-old, good-condition, single-family house of 2,200 square feet. The house includes a two-car, 500-square-foot garage, a deck, in-ground pool, sprinkler system, and premium carpets, appliances, and kitchen cabinets. Nearby vacant lots have recently sold for $40,000.

Dwelling (2,200 x $72 per-square-foot base cost of new construction)	$158,400
Upgrades	9,000
Deck, pool, sprinklers	14,500
Garage (500 x $22 per square foot)	11,000
Total	$192,900
less	
Physical depreciation at 10%	(19,290)
Functional depreciation at 5%	(9,625)
Depreciated building value plus	$163,985
Site improvements (sidewalks, driveway, landscaping)	12,500
Lot value	40,000
equals	
Indicated market value, cost approach	$216,485

Typically builders build only when they think they can create properties that will sell (or rent) at a price high enough to cover their construction costs. Thus you can usually expect sales prices to go up when construction costs greatly exceed the market values of existing properties. Why? Because supply falls due to the lack of profits for builders. When growing demand pushes against constrained supply, market prices go up. Eventually builder profits return. The real estate construction cycle begins its next round.

THE COMPARABLE SALES APPROACH

For houses, condominiums, co-ops, townhouses, and small rental apartment buildings, the comparable sales approach generally gives the most accurate estimate of market value. If you want to know the probable price at which a specific property will sell, find out the selling prices, terms, and features of other similar properties.

Select Comparable Properties

The accuracy of the comparable sales approach depends on your ability to find recently sold properties that closely match a subject property. Ideally, the comp sales should be located in the same neighborhood or development and conform in size, age, features, condition, quality of construction, room count, and floor plan. Unfortunately, finding perfect matches usually proves quite difficult (if not impossible) because every property displays unique characteristics.

Nevertheless, you don't need perfection. When you find comp sales that reasonably match a subject property, you can ballpark a value estimate by comparing price per square foot of gross living area.

You locate three comp sales: (1) 1,680 square feet, (2) 1,840 square feet, and (3) 1,730 square feet. These homes sold recently for the respective prices of $112,560, $106,720, and $105,530. To figure the selling price per square foot of living area for these homes, divide the sales price of each house by its total square footage.

Comp 1

$$\frac{\$112{,}560}{1{,}680} = \$67$$

Comp 2

$$\frac{\$106{,}720}{1{,}840} = \$58$$

Comp 3

$$\frac{\$105{,}530}{1{,}730} = \$61$$

If the house you're interested in has 1,796 square feet of living area, it will probably sell in the range of $60 to $65 per square foot, or $107,760 to $116,740.

Approximate Value Range—Subject Property

$$\$60 \times 1,796 = \$107,760$$

$$\$65 \times 1,796 = \$116,740$$

Sales price per square foot helps you ballpark value, but to gain more confidence, carefully contrast the comparable properties to your subject property on a feature-by-feature basis.

Adjusting for Differences

After you, your real estate agent, or an appraiser finds appropriate comparables, their sales prices are adjusted up or down to compensate for the features that may be inferior or superior to a subject property. Here's a brief example of this adjustment process:

Adjustment Process (Selected Features)

	Comp 1	Comp 2	Comp 3
Sales price	$112,560	$106,720	$105,530
Features			
Sales concessions	0	–5,000	0
Financing concessions	–7,500	0	0
Date of sale	0	+5,000	0
Location	0	0	–10,000
Floor plan	0	+2,500	0
Garage	+5,500	0	+8,500
Pool, patio, deck	–4,500	–6,500	0
Indicated value of subject	$106,060	$102,220	$104,030

Detailed adjustments help you detail an answer to this question: Based on the selling prices of similar houses, what is the market value of the subject property? Although our preliminary price-per-square-foot estimate of market value showed the subject to be worth between $107,760 and $116,740, after adjustments, a price range between $102,000 and $106,000 appears to be more accurate.

Explaining the Adjustments

When you adjust for differences in size, quality, or features, you're trying to equalize a subject property and its comparable. You're asking, "At what price would the comparable have sold if it had been *exactly* like the subject property?" For example, consider the $7,500 adjustment to Comp 1 for financing concessions.

In this sale, the sellers carried back a 90 percent LTV mortgage (10 percent down) on the property at an interest rate of 7 percent. At the time, investor financing usually required a 75 percent LTV (25 percent down) and an 8.5 percent interest rate on this type of property. Without this favorable owner financing, Comp 1 would probably have sold for $7,500 less than its actual sales price of $112,560. Because the definition of market value requires financing on terms typically available in the market, the premium created by this OWC (owner will carry) financing had to be subtracted from Comp 1's actual selling price. Here are the explanations for several other adjustments:

Comp 1 garage at (+) $5,500. The subject property has an oversize double-car garage, but Comp 1 has only a single-car garage. With a better garage like the subject's, Comp 1 would have brought a $5,500 higher sales price.

Comp 1 pool, patio, and deck at (–) $4,500. Comp 1 is superior to the subject property on this feature because the subject lacks a deck and tile patio. Without this feature, Comp 1 would have sold for $4,500 less.

Comp 2 sales concession at (–) $5,000. The $106,720 sales price in this transaction included the seller's custom-made drapes, a washer and dryer, and a storage shed. Because these items aren't customary in this market, the sales price had to be adjusted downward to equalize this feature with the subject property, whose sale will not include these items.

Comp 2 floor plan at (+) $2,500. Unlike the subject property, Comp 2 lacked convenient access from the garage to the kitchen. The garage was built under the house and residents had to carry groceries up an outside stairway to enter the kitchen. With more conventional access, the selling price of Comp 2 would probably have increased by $2,500.

Comp 3 location at (–) $10,000. Comp 3 was located on a cul-de-sac, and its backyard bordered an environmentally protected wooded area. In contrast, the subject property sits on a typical subdivision street, and its rear yard abuts that of a neighbor. Owing to its less-favorable location, the subject property could be expected to sell for $10,000 less than Comp 3.

At this point, you may be asking, "How do you come up with the specific dollar amounts for each of the adjustments?" To that question, there's no easy answer. It comes from the knowledge you will gain by tracking many different sales transactions over a period of months, or even years. Until that time, you draw on the knowledge of professionally competent and informed realty agents and appraisers.

Nevertheless, regardless of your experience, always weigh the opinions of others against your own judgment. Ask questions. Explore their reasoning. Verify their facts. As you look at properties, train yourself to detail and list all features that make a difference. Before you attach adjustment numbers to each property's unique features, you must first take note of those differences.

THE INCOME APPROACH

Near the bottom of page 2 of the appraisal form, you can see a line labeled "Indicated Value by Income Approach (If Applicable)." As shown there, the income approach refers to an appraisal technique called the gross rent multiplier (GRM).

To calculate market value using the GRM, you need to know the monthly rents and sales prices of similar houses or apartment buildings. You learn of the following sales of rental houses: (1) 214 Jackson was rented at $950 a month and sold for $114,000; (2) 312 Lincoln was rented at $875 a month and sold for $120,000; and (3) 107 Adams was rented at $1,050 a month and sold for $128,100. With this information, you can calculate a range of GRMs for this neighborhood:

$$GRM = \frac{\text{Sales price}}{\text{Monthly rent}}$$

Property	Sales Price		Monthly Rent		GRM
214 Jackson	$114,000	÷	$950	=	120
312 Lincoln	120,000	÷	875	=	137
107 Adams	128,100	÷	1,050	=	122

Now, if the house you are valuing could rent for $925 a month, you can calculate a value range using the GRMs indicated by these other neighborhood rental houses:

Subject House (Estimated Value Range)

GRM		Monthly Rent		Value
120	×	$925	=	$111,000
137	×	925	=	126,725
122	×	925	=	112,850

The value range would then be $111,000 to $126,725.

Because the GRM method does not directly adjust for sales or financing concessions, different features, location, property condition, or property operating expenses, this technique yields a general answer. However, many real estate investors routinely use it as a first-pass indicator. Like the comp sales approach, the GRM works best when you can find very similar properties in the same neighborhood.

For multiple-unit income properties, the gross rent multiplier is usually based on *annual* rent collections rather than monthly rents. For example:

Multiple-Unit Income Properties

Property	Sales Price		Total Annual Rents		GRM
2112 Pope(fourplex)	$280,000	÷	$35,897	=	7.8
1806 Laurel (sixplex)	412,000	÷	56,438	=	7.3
1409 Abbot (sixplex)	367,000	÷	53,188	=	6.9

The GRMs shown in these examples *do not necessarily* correspond to the GRMs that would apply in your city. Even within the same city, different neighborhoods will show wide differences in their typical GRMs. In the San Diego area, GRMs for single-family homes in La Jolla can easily surpass 200; in nearby Clairemont, you may find GRMs in the 150 to 200 range; and in National City, GRMs sometimes drop below 150. Even within the same neighborhood, GRMs for single-family houses will often run significantly higher than those of condominiums. Therefore, as with all appraisal methods, seek out the most closely relevant *local* data before you calculate and apply gross rent multipliers.

INCOME CAPITALIZATION

Another income valuation approach that's used for multiple-unit income properties (but may also be used to value smaller properties) is called direct capitalization. To calculate market value with the direct capitalization method, use the following formula:

$$V = \frac{NOI}{R}$$

V represents the value to be estimated, NOI represents the net operating income of the property, and R represents the overall rate of return on capital that buyers of similar income properties typically require.

Net Operating Income

Investors define net operating income as annual gross potential rental income from a property less vacancy and collection losses, operating expenses, replacement reserves, property taxes, and property and liability insurance. Here's how a net income statement might look for an eight-unit apartment building where each apartment rents for $725 a month:

Income Statement (Annual)

1. Gross annual potential rents ($725 x 8 x 12)	$69,600
2. Income from parking and storage areas	6,750
3. Vacancy and collection losses at 7%	(5,345)
4. Effective gross income	$71,005
Less operating and fixed expenses	
5. Trash pickup $1,440	
6. Utilities	600
7. Registration fee	275
8. Advertising and promotion	1,200
9. Management fees at 6%	4,260
10. Maintenance and repairs	4,000
11. Yard care	650
12. Miscellaneous	3,000
13. Property taxes	4,270
14. Property and liability insurance	1,690
15. Reserves for replacement	2,500
Total operating and fixed expenses	$23,885
16. Net operating income (NOI)	$47,120

The following list explains each of the lines in the net income statement:

1. *Gross annual potential rents.* This amount is the largest possible sum of rents that you could theoretically bring in at current market rent levels and 100 percent occupancy.
2. *Income from parking and storage areas.* This property has a 16-car parking lot. Because of an extreme shortage of on-street and off-street parking in the neighborhood, the owner rents out the parking spaces separately from the apartment units. Also, the owner has built storage bins in the basement of the building that are available for rental to tenants.
3. *Vacancy and collection losses.* Market vacancy rates in the area typically range between 5 and 10 percent. Currently, all units in this building are rented. But even the best-managed apartments experience some vacancies when apartments turn over. As a practical matter, you should also figure some losses for tenants who move out owing rents that exceed the amounts of their security deposits.
4. *Effective gross income.* This term refers to the actual amount of cash that an owner receives net of vacancy and collection, but before operating and fixed expenses.
5. *Trash pickup.* Self-explanatory.
6. *Utilities.* In this property, tenants pay their unit utilities, but the property owner pays for lighting in the hallways, basement, and parking area.
7. *Licenses and permit fees.* Apartment building owners must sometimes pay for business licenses and other fees. For this property, the owner pays a rental property registration fee.
8. *Advertising and promotion.* These units generally rent by word of mouth or a For Rent sign that's posted on the property. However, as a precaution, an advertising and promotion expense of $150 per year per unit is allocated to the operating budget.
9. *Management fees.* The owner of these apartments manages the property. Nevertheless, he should pay himself the same amount he would otherwise have to pay a property management firm. Returns for labor should be kept separate from returns on investment.
10. *Maintenance and repairs.* The owner and her husband typically clean, paint, and make small repairs around the property. These labors, too, deserve payment from the property's rent collections.
11. *Yard care.* The owner pays this amount to one of the tenants to keep the grass cut, rake leaves, and shovel snow off the walks.
12. *Miscellaneous.* This expense covers legal fees, supplies, snow removal from the parking lot, municipal assessments, auto

mileage to and from the property, and other items not accounted for elsewhere in the income statement.

13. *Property taxes.* This item includes city, county, and state taxes annually assessed against the property.

14. *Property and liability insurance.* This insurance reimburses for property damage caused by fire, hail, windstorms, sinkholes, hurricanes, and other perils. It also pays to defend against, and compensate for, lawsuits alleging owner negligence (e.g., slip-and-fall cases).

15. *Reserves for replacement.* Building components subject to wear and tear such as the roof, plumbing, appliances, and carpeting must be replaced periodically. For the purposes of the income statement, these replacement costs should be averaged out annually.

16. *Net operating income (NOI).* After you itemize and total all operating expenses, subtract this amount from the effective gross income. The resulting figure equals net operating income (NOI).

When you calculate NOI, make sure you include all expenses for the coming year. Never accept a seller's income statement as accurate. Sellers notoriously omit and underestimate expenses. (Corporate CEOs aren't the only ones who try to dress up their numbers to make a pretty picture.)

Ask to see the seller's tax return IRS Schedule E for the subject property. The truth will probably sit somewhere between the owner-prepared income statement for sales purposes (where income is likely to be overstated and expenses understated) and a tax return (where income may be understated and expenses overstated). Even if the seller is perfectly truthful in reporting *last* year's income and expenses, you must still determine how each of those figures might move up or down in the coming years. You're buying the future, not the past.

Are property tax assessments headed up? Are vacancy rates (or rent concessions) increasing? Have the utility companies scheduled any rate increases? Has the seller deferred maintenance on the property? Has the owner allocated enough expense to cover replacement reserves? Has the seller self-managed or self-maintained the property and therefore omitted listing these items as cash expenses? When it comes to calculating NOI, accept nothing on faith. Verify the accuracy of every number.

Estimating Capitalization Rates (R)

After figuring out NOI, investors must decide what capitalization rate (R) to use to convert the property's expected income stream into a capital (market) value (present value dollar amount).

In other words, when you buy a rental property, you're actually paying now for the right to receive rents over the next 20, 30, or 40 years (or for however long you plan to own the property). The question comes how much these future rents are worth in today's dollars (i.e., the property's market value). If the appropriate capitalization rate is 10 percent, then the market (capital) value of this eight-unit apartment building equals $471, 210:

$$\frac{\$47,121 \ (NOI)}{.10 \ (R)} = \$471,210 \ (V)$$

But where does that 10 percent "cap rate" come from? You estimate it from the cap rates that other investors have applied to buy similar properties. Say a real estate agent gives you NOI and sales price data on four similar properties that have sold recently:

Market Data

Property	Sales Price	NOI	R
Hampton Apts. (8 units)	$452,900	$43,211	9.54%
Woodruff Apts. (6 units)	360,000	35,900	9.97
Adams Manor (12 units)	660,000	63,200	10.44
Newport Apts. (9 units)	549,000	53,700	9.78
Subject (8 units) (estimated)	471,210	47,121	10.0

From these data, you can estimate a market cap rate for those properties (provided those sales meet the criteria of a market value transaction). As you can see, when buying small income properties similar to the subject property, investors have been using cap rates between 9.54 percent (.0954) and 10.44 percent (.1044). So it appears that a 10 percent (.10) cap rate for the subject property is about what the market indicates.

Comparing Cap Rates

In real life you may not be able to discover enough similar properties with such a narrow range of cap rates. More likely, you'll find that some properties have sold with cap rates of 7 or 8 percent (or lower) and others have sold with cap rates of 12 or 14 percent (or higher). Why such large differences?

Investors aren't just buying a *quantity* of future rental income. They also pay for *quality*. In addition, they pay for expected appreciation potential. Therefore the lower the quality of the income stream, and the lower the expected rate of appreciation, the higher the capitalization rate (or the

higher the quality of the property's income and appreciation potential—
in the eyes of the market—the lower its cap rate).

You're comparing two fourplexes. One is a relatively new property
located in a well-kept neighborhood near a city's growth corridor. The
other is located in a deteriorating part of town where some factories and
other employers have either moved out, closed, or laid off workers. Crime
rates, too, are on the increase in this area.

If the annual NOIs for the two fourplexes are, respectively, $24,960
and $12,480, how much would investors pay for each property? If
investors applied a 10 percent cap rate to each property's income stream,
they would value the properties as follows:

$$\frac{\$24,960 \text{ (NOI)}}{.10 \text{ (R)}} = \$249,600 \text{ (V)}$$

$$\frac{\$12,480 \text{ (NOI)}}{.10 \text{ (R)}} = \$124,800 \text{ (V)}$$

But more than likely, investors would not apply the same cap rate to
these very different properties because the quality of their income streams
differs. The better-located property offers more stable rents, less neighborhood risk, and possibly greater appreciation potential. We might see the
actual NOIs of these two fourplexes capitalized at rates of say, 8 percent
and 14 percent, respectively.

$$\frac{\$24,960 \text{ (NOI)}}{.08 \text{ (R)}} = \$312,000 \text{ (V)}$$

$$\frac{\$12,480 \text{ (NOI)}}{.14 \text{ (R)}} = \$89,143 \text{ (V)}$$

Because most investors would rather own a property in a growing
area as opposed to a declining area, they are usually willing to pay significantly more for each dollar of income produced by such a property.

The Paradox of Risk and Appreciation Potential

Odd as it may seem, the higher-priced "low-risk, high-appreciation-
potential" property may actually produce more risk and less appreciation
potential than its lower-priced cousin in another part of town. An analogy
from the stock market will illustrate this paradox: In 1989, Sears was hitting

hard times. Its sales growth was stagnant. The company was losing its loyal base of customers, and its merchandise was losing its reputation for high quality and fair price. On the other hand, Wal-Mart was on a roll. Year after year, it was chalking up sales growth of 15 percent per year. In retailing, Sears was a "has-been," and Wal-Mart was the wave of the future.

The stock market reflected this outlook. Sears stock sold for a price-to-earnings (P/E) ratio of 8. Wal-Mart stock sold for a P/E of 30. Translating these P/E ratios into capitalization rates, we could say that the R for Sears was 12.5 percent ($1 \div 8$), and the R for Wal-Mart was 3.33 percent ($1 \div 30$). Obviously, stock market investors believed that because of Wal-Mart's "lower-risk" and "higher-growth" potential, its stock (per $1 of company earnings) was valued far more than that of Sears. But the market was proved wrong.

Within several years, the price of Sears stock had doubled, and the price of Wal-Mart stock had faltered. As it turned out, investors had overoptimistically bid up the price of Wal-Mart stock and had valued the Sears stock too pessimistically. A good company—just like a good property—can still be priced too high. Of course, the tech wreck of the early 2000s illustrates the same principle. Microsoft, Intel, Dell, and Cisco—all great companies—still became overvalued relative to, say, Procter & Gamble and JCPenney.

Always Compare Relative Prices

If you could buy a quality, high-growth company's stock at a P/E of 10 or a low-growth company's stock at a P/E of 10, by all means invest in the high-growth company. If you could buy a low-risk, high-appreciation-potential property with a cap rate of 10 percent or a higher-risk, lower-appreciation property with a cap rate of 10 percent, by all means buy the low-risk, high-appreciation property. However, that's not how the market works.

In the real world, investors bid up prices for high-quality growth-area properties and bid down the prices of so-called high-risk properties in less desirable neighborhoods. To figure out which type of property actually offers the most profit potential, you must compare their relative prices.

When investors optimistically overprice some properties, neighborhoods, and cities relative to other properties, neighborhoods, and cities, you can profitably redirect your investment strategy. In other words, don't calculate market cap rates for just one type of property or neighborhood. Learn as much as you can about a variety of submarkets and areas of the country.[1]

---

1. For instance, do you believe that San Francisco apartments can continue to command a four- to eightfold price premium over those of Orlando, Florida?

You can overpay for a property in two ways: (1) you apply a cap rate that's too low for the property and neighborhood you're buying into, or (2) you fail to realize that market cap rates themselves may sit too low relative to other types of properties or locations. In contrast, you can earn extraordinary profits when you discover out-of-favor (high cap rate) properties (locations) that yield high rents relative to the price you have to pay. (We explore these points in more detail in Chapter 4.)

VALUATION: FINAL WORDS

As emphasized earlier, "market value" does not necessarily equal "appraised value" or "sales price." Market value refers to the selling price of a property only when that sale conforms with the criteria of a market value transaction. When you estimate the market value of a property based on the sales prices of other properties, first investigate the terms and conditions under which the comparative properties were bought. A property down the street that sold for $200,000 after just three days on the market does not necessarily indicate that a similar property nearby will sell for $200,000. It depends on the terms of sale and the detailed features of each property.

Although you can use three approaches to estimate the market value of a property, you always work with imperfect data. Those three approaches do not result in the same value. You must decide in specific cases which approach best serves your purposes. Remember, too, the accuracy of a market value estimate directly relates to how well you describe the property's features. Carefully identify the differences (positive or negative) that make a difference. To make profitable investment decisions, investors must know features, properties, neighborhoods, construction costs, and lot values. Technique alone cannot substitute for knowledge and judgment.

Other Limiting Conditions

To prepare their estimates of market value, real estate appraisers list numerous limiting conditions. Especially relevant are limitations 1, 2, 6, and 7 from the sample form shown as Figure 3.1:

- ◆ Appraisers do not investigate title. They simply assume a property's bundle of rights is good and marketable. For a legal guarantee of property rights, consult a title insurance company.

◆ Appraisers do not survey the boundaries of a site, nor do they necessarily note encroachments or other potential site problems. To precisely identify site dimensions, encroachments, and some easements, you need to employ a surveyor.

◆ Appraisers only assess the condition of a property that is visible through casual inspection. To thoroughly assess the soundness of a property and its systems (heating, cooling, electrical, plumbing), always have a property inspected by professionally competent building inspection services or skilled tradespersons.

◆ Appraisers gather much of their market information from secondhand sources (real estate agents, public records, mortgage lenders, and others). For example, appraisers seldom see the interiors of the comparable properties that they include in their appraisal reports. Naturally, reliance on nonverified secondhand data means that appraisals often err in fact and interpretation. Consequently, accept a professionally prepared appraisal as "for-what-it's worth" information. Never give it more weight than it deserves. (I always check and verify the appraiser's data before I rely on his or her estimate of value.)

Valuation versus Investment Analysis

Never buy a property without an accurate understanding of its market value. Nevertheless, market value does not tell all you need to know to make profitable investment decisions. Besides figuring out what a property is worth today, you need to determine the following:

◆ Will the property generate adequate cash flows?
◆ Can you expect the property to appreciate?
◆ Can you add value to the property?

To answer these questions, we now turn to the following chapters.

4

MAXIMIZE CASH
FLOWS AND RETURNS

To estimate market value requires close study of property sales prices, terms, rental levels, expenses, and features. The more you know, the more confidence you can place in your decision to invest. Before they write an offer, savvy investors verify value.

But here's the caveat. Just because you can buy a property at a price equal to (or less than) its market value doesn't mean you should buy that property. Before buying, run the numbers on expected cash flow and assess the property's potential for appreciation.

WILL THE PROPERTY YIELD GOOD CASH FLOWS?

To estimate market value, you will need to calculate a property's net operating income (NOI). But unless you pay cash, NOI won't tell you how much money that property will put into your pocket each year. And even if you could afford to pay cash, you probably wouldn't want to because you would lose the benefit of leverage.

For reasons of necessity as well as financial advantage, most real estate investors finance their properties. Financing, though, creates another claim against the rental property's income. With a mortgage (or other type of financing) in place, you will make monthly payments. The question becomes not just how much NOI a property can be expected to produce but how much cash (if any) will be left after you pay debt service. This remainder is called *before-tax cash flow* (BTCF) or, sometimes, *cash throw-off*.

As you may recall from Chapter 2, you calculate BTCF (cash throw-off) as follows:

NOI less debt service (principal/interest, or P/I) equals BTCF

Now, let's reprise the eight-unit apartment building example introduced in Chapter 3, where we calculated NOI for that property at $47,121. Using a 10 percent cap rate, we then figured the property's value at $471,210:

$$\$471,210 \ (V) = \frac{\$47,121 \ (NOI)}{.10 \ (R)}$$

If you finance this property with a mortgage having a loan-to-value (LTV) ratio of 80 percent (20 percent down) at 9.5 percent interest, amortized over a term of 25 years, you figure your annual mortgage payments as follows:

$47,210 (V)   25.6%

.80 LTV

$376,968   Loan amount

Given mortgage terms of 9.5 percent for 25 years, the monthly mortgage factor equals $8.74 per $1,000 borrowed. Because your original loan balance is $376,968, your monthly mortgage payments would equal $3,294 for an annual total of $39,536:

$$\$376,968 \div 1,000 = 376.968$$
$$376.968 \times \$8.74 = \$3,294$$
$$12 \times \$3,294 = \$39,536$$

Based on these mortgage terms, this eight-unit property would yield a first-year BTCF of $7,585:

$47,121 (NOI)

less 39,536 (Annual debt service)

$ 7,585 (BTCF)

To calculate annual cash-on-cash return on investment (ROI), divide the down payment (original cash investment) into your annual cash return (BTCF):

$$ROI = \frac{\$7,585 \text{ (BTCF)}}{\$94,242 \text{ (Down payment)}} = 8.05\%$$

Does this first-year cash-on-cash rate of return look attractive? That would partially depend on the property's potential. Can you add value to the property through creative improvements? Is the property strategically positioned for appreciation? If you judged the property strong in either or both of these areas, you might be willing to accept relatively low cash flows. Yet for purposes of illustration, let's say that you're not happy with an annual BTCF of $7,585 and a cash-on-cash ROI of 8.05 percent. Does this mean you should cross this property off your list? Not necessarily. Before rejecting a property that fails to yield adequate cash flows, look for ways to increase those returns:

◆ Could you arrange alternative financing with lower payments?
◆ Should you decrease (increase) your down payment?
◆ Can you buy at a bargain price?

Arrange Alternative Terms of Financing

As is explained in Chapter 2, smart investors think through their financing alternatives. It's amazing how you can improve cash flows by reworking the cost or terms of the financing. In the first pass through the numbers for this eight-unit apartment building, we assumed a 9.5 percent interest rate amortized over 25 years with a 20 percent down payment. To improve the cash flows, you could do the following:

◆ Seek a lower interest rate.
◆ Lengthen the term of the mortgage.
◆ Use a nonamortizing (no or partial payments) balloon second mortgage.
◆ Combine several of these alternatives.

To obtain a lower interest rate, you could switch to an adjustable-rate mortgage, ask for seller financing, buy down the interest rate, or perhaps assume a seller's lower-interest-rate mortgage. Here's how an interest rate of, say, 8.5 percent would boost cash flows:

Monthly payment per $1,000 at 8.5% 25 years = $8.05

376.968 × $8.05 = $3,035 monthly payment

12 × $3,035 = $36,415 annual payments (debt service)

$47,121 (NOI)

less 36,415 (Debt service)

$10,706 (BTCF)

$$ROI = \frac{\$10,706 \text{ (BTCF)}}{\$94,242 \text{ (Down payment)}} = 11.36\%$$

If this BTCF and ROI still fall short of your investment goal, extend the amortization period from 25 to 40 years (with a balloon at year 10 or 15, if necessary).

Monthly payment per $1,000 at 8.5% 40 years = $7.33

376× $7.33 = $2763 per month

12 × $2,763 = $33,158

$47,121 (NOI)

less 33,158 (Debt service)

$13,963 (BTCF)

$$ROI = \frac{\$13,963 \text{ (BTCF)}}{\$94,242 \text{ (Down payment)}} = 14.8\%$$

Now let's return to the first calculation, where you borrowed mortgage money from a bank at 9.5 percent interest with a 25-year term. Say the sellers won't carry back the entire amount of the financing but will give you a $100,000 balloon second mortgage due in five years, with interest only payable at 6 percent. You borrow $276,968 from the bank on its terms, and $100,000 from the sellers on their terms. Here's what your cash flow would look like under this financing arrangement.

276.698 × $8.74 × 12 = $29,045 (to the bank)

.06 × $100,000 = 6,000 (to the seller)

Total annual debt service = $35,045 ($29,045 + $6,000)

$47,121 (NOI)

less 35,045 (Debt service)

$12,076 (BTCF)

$$ROI = \frac{\$12,076 \text{ (BTCF)}}{\$94,242 \text{ (Down payment)}} = 12.8\%$$

Although your cash flow under this financial scenario isn't quite as good as the completely seller-financed transaction, it still beats the baseline bank financing. The point here, though, is not to show which type of financing is best. Rather, you are being encouraged to calculate your returns under a variety of financing alternatives. Then you can discover which (if any) financing might make a deal work—for you and the sellers. In just the few alternatives shown here, the first-year BTCF bounced from a low of $7,585 to a high of $13,963. Changing the terms of financing can dramatically improve (or diminish) the financial performance of a property.

Decrease (or Increase) Your Down Payment

You can also influence your cash flow and ROI by decreasing (or increasing) your down payment. Say that instead of putting 20 percent down ($94,242) on this eight-unit property, you swing the deal with just a 10 percent down payment of $47,121. The seller finances the balance of $424,089 at 9.5 percent interest for 25 years:

424.098 × $8.74 × 12 = $44,478 (Debt service)

$47,121 (NOI)

less 44,478 (Debt service)

$ 2,643 (BTCF)

$$ROI = \frac{\$2,6433 \text{ (BTCF)}}{\$47,121 \text{ (Down payment)}} = 5.6\%$$

In this case, reducing your down payment gives you a thin margin of cash flow and drops your ROI to 5.6 percent. By comparison, let's see what happens to cash flow and ROI if you buy with 10 percent down seller financing at 8.5 percent interest amortized over 40 years:

$$424.098 \times \$7.33 \times 12 = \$37,302 \text{ (Debt service)}$$

$$\begin{aligned} \$47,121 \ &(\text{NOI}) \\ \text{less} \ \ 37,302 \ &(\text{Debt service}) \\ \$ \ 9,819 \ &(\text{BTCF}) \end{aligned}$$

$$\text{ROI} = \frac{\$9,819 \text{ (BTCF)}}{\$47,121 \text{ (Down payment)}} = 20.8\%$$

Now, this outcome looks attractive. When you combine the benefits of the lower interest rate with the benefits of higher positive leverage, you beat the returns realized with the hypothetical baseline bank financing (20 percent down, 9.5 percent, 25 years).

In areas of the country with generally high property prices, you may find that well-kept properties (single-family houses, duplexes, fourplexes, small apartment buildings) produce negative cash flows. Say that our eight-unit building is located in a prime neighborhood that's in high demand by both owner-occupants and investors. Instead of a market cap of 10 percent, properties in this neighborhood are typically valued with an 8 percent cap rate. Given this lower cap rate, this building commands a much higher value ($589,012 versus $471,210):

$$\$589,012 \text{ (V)} = \frac{\$47,121 \text{ (NOI)}}{.08 \text{ (R)}}$$

If you finance with an 80 percent loan, you'll put down $117,802 and secure a mortgage of $471,210. With a 9.5 percent interest rate and a 25-year term, your annual mortgage payment would total $49,420:

$$471.210 \times \$8.74 \times 12 = 49,420 \text{ (Debt service)}$$

$$\begin{aligned} \$47,121 \ &(\text{NOI}) \\ \text{less} \ \ 49,420 \ &(\text{Annual debt service}) \\ \$ -2,299 \ &(\text{BTCF}) \end{aligned}$$

In situations of negative cash flow, search for low-cost financing. If that doesn't work, then cover the negative (feed the alligator) from other income or increase the amount of your down payment. With 30 percent down ($176,703) on a price of $589,012, you would borrow $412,308 and then pay back $43,242 a year:

$$412.308 \times \$8.74 \times 12 = \$43,242 \text{ (Debt service)}$$

$$
\begin{array}{ll}
\$47,121 & \text{(NOI)} \\
\text{less} \quad 43,242 & \text{(Annual debt service)} \\
\$\ 3,879 & \text{(BTCF)}
\end{array}
$$

$$\text{ROI} = \frac{\$3,879 \text{ (BTCF)}}{\$176,703 \text{ (Down payment)}} = 2.19\%$$

At least the larger (30 percent) down payment converts your negative cash flow into a positive, but your ROI still looks anemic. Buy such a property only if you can profitably improve it, or when neighborhood property values are about to escalate. Alternatively, to combat low cap rates or negative cash flows, ferret out bargain-priced properties or move your search for properties to lower-priced geographic areas.

Buy at a Bargain Price

To increase your cash flow (or avoid a negative cash flow), locate properties that you can buy at less than market value. Although this technique requires hustle, knowledge, and creativity, you can do it. Motivated sellers, lender-owned properties (REOs [real estate owned]), foreclosures, tax sales, uninformed sellers, trade-in properties, and other sources of bargains routinely account for between 10 and 20 percent of property sales.

Each of these types of bargains is discussed in later chapters, but the purpose here is to simply show how a below-market price can lead to higher cash flows.

Return to the eight-unit example that was valued with a 10 percent cap rate at $471,210. With the hypothetical baseline bank financing of 20 percent down and 9.5 percent, 25-year terms, the property produced a first-year cash flow of $7,585. But what if you could buy that property (or a similar one) at a bargain price (say 10 percent under market)? You would pay $424,089, put $84,817 down, and borrow $339,271 (80 percent).

Your annual debt service would fall to $35,582, and your cash flow (BTCF) would increase to $11,539:

$$339.271 \times \$8.74 \times 12 = 35,582 \text{ (Debt service)}$$

$$
\begin{aligned}
&\$47,121 \quad \text{(NOI)} \\
\text{less } &35,582 \text{ (Debt service)} \\
&\$11,539 \quad \text{(BTCF)}
\end{aligned}
$$

Your first-year ROI would increase to 13.6 percent:

$$\text{ROI} = \frac{\$11,539 \text{ (BTCF)}}{\$84,817 \text{ (Down payment)}} = 13.6\%$$

In markets where properties typically fail to give you the cash flows you want, don't necessarily give up your search. Instead, try to ferret out a property you can buy at a bargain price.

Should You Ever Overpay for a Property?

Now return to the ploy where you tell sellers that you will pay their price if you can name the terms. The idea is that you will stroke the sellers' egos and give them a price they can brag about. But you'll still earn good cash flows and a high ROI because you receive liberal terms and low-cost financing.

Staying with the eight-unit example, say the sellers take you up on your offer and set a price of $525,000 ($471,210 market value). You say, "Fine, here are my terms: $25,000 down, 6.5 percent interest, and 40-year amortization period with a balloon note due in 12 years." This arrangement means that the sellers would carry back a mortgage (or contract for deed) of $500,000. Here's how the numbers work out:

$$500(000) \times \$5.85 \times 12 = \$35,100$$

$$
\begin{aligned}
&\$47,121 \quad \text{(NOI)} \\
\text{less } &35,100 \text{ (Debt service)} \\
&\$12,021 \quad \text{(BTCF)}
\end{aligned}
$$

$$\text{ROI} = \frac{\$12,021 \text{ (BTCF)}}{\$125,000 \text{ (Down payment)}} = 48\%$$

Wow! These numbers look terrific. Compared with a market value price and bank financing, you've achieved three important objectives: (1) You've reduced the cash you need to buy the property; (2) you've increased your cash flow; and (3) you've lifted your ROI into superstar territory. You can readily see why some authors encourage you to trade off concessions on price for easy, low-cost OWC financing.

Nevertheless, you've created a serious problem. You owe more than the property is worth. Absent a strong increase in value, you will not be able to sell the property. Also, if market interest rates drop, you will not be able to refinance your outstanding mortgage balance. This so-called favorable financing essentially locks you in for what could be a long period of time (especially in slow markets, when this type of deal seems to proliferate).

To protect against these downsides, ask for two other seller concessions:

1. *The right to assign.* If your buyer can assume that 6.5 percent financing, you will enhance your ability to sell the property without coming up with cash out of your own pocket.
2. *The right to prepay the mortgage at a discount.* To help you overcome the excessive mortgage problem, insert a prepayment discount clause into the mortgage contract. If you pay the seller off within the first five years (for example), the payoff balance will be discounted by, say, 5 or 7.5 percent, or some higher figure. Sellers who are eager to cash out their lien on a property may agree to this discount clause. (Also, even when a mortgage does not include a prepayment discount clause, many sellers will later accept such offers.)

The "you set the price, I'll set the terms" buying tactic can work to decrease your down payment, increase your annual cash flow, and leverage up your ROI. Yet if such prices and terms leave you with an excessive mortgage balance, you've entered a risky transaction. Explicitly calculate whether the benefits of the deal outweigh these risks. Most important, never naively assume that market appreciation rates of 6 or 8 percent a year will bail you out of the excessive mortgage problem. Maybe you will get lucky, but don't bet the ranch on it.

The Debt Coverage Ratio

Up to this point, you've seen how financing (mortgage amount, interest rate, amortization period) can increase or decrease your annual cash flows and ROI. In addition, the lender may apply a debt coverage ratio (DCR) as one of its underwriting criteria. The lender may want to see whether the property's NOI is large enough to provide a margin of safety. For example:

$$\text{DCR} = \frac{\$47,121 \text{ (NOI)}}{\$39,536 \text{ (Debt service)}} = 1.19$$

Among lenders who incorporate debt coverage ratios into their underwriting decisions, a DCR range of 1.1 to 1.3 is usually considered reasonable. If your property's NOI does fail to meet the lender's standard, go back to the drawing board. Real estate investors frequently work their deals not only to meet their own cash flow requirements but also to meet a lender's required debt coverage ratio.

Numbers Change, Principles Remain

The preceding discussions focus on the cash flows of an eight-unit apartment building with a variety of interest rates, loan balances, amortization periods, cap rates, and purchase prices. Even though the numbers used in these examples were figured from actual properties and financing arrangements, primarily they illustrate techniques and principles—not the specific numbers you should apply in your market or for your investment goals.

In the Dallas suburb of Denton, Texas, not long ago, you could buy a good eight-unit rental property for less than $300,000. In San Francisco, you can pay well in excess of $2,000,000 for a similar building. In Denton, I've seen cap rates over 12 percent. In San Francisco, I've seen them at less than 6 percent. All markets are different. Even within the same urban area, you'll find that types of properties, neighborhood quality, gross rent multipliers, and terms of financing can vary widely.

Whenever you buy condos, single-family houses, or small apartment buildings, search throughout your local area. Look at properties. Talk to well-informed realty agents, mortgage loan officers, real estate appraisers, property managers, and real estate investors.

After you learn the numbers that apply to proposed deals, work through them as demonstrated in this chapter (and in Chapter 3). To a large degree, investing profitably means *structuring* deals to yield positive cash flows and high ROIs while avoiding foolish financial risk. When you buy at a below-market price, you normally increase your odds of success. But "price" represents only one variable. Without positive cash flows and good cash-on-cash returns, even a "bargain-priced" deal can turn sour.

WILL THE PROPERTY YIELD ABOVE-AVERAGE APPRECIATION?

In addition to the amount of yearly cash flows and cash-on-cash ROI, most real estate investors expect their properties to appreciate. Over longer periods, even appreciation rates of 3 percent to 5 percent per year can add hundreds of thousands of dollars to your net wealth.

Buy just one rental unit at a price of $100,000 and finance it with a $90,000 mortgage at 8 percent interest and a 30-year term at an annual appreciation rate of 4 percent. After 15 years, that $100,000 unit would be worth $180,000. Subtract your outstanding mortgage balance of $69,102, and your $10,000 down payment has grown elevenfold to $110,898. After 30 years, your mortgage balance would drop to zero, and the value of the property (at 4 percent yearly appreciation) would total $324,340.

Buy just three or four $100,000 properties within the next several years, and at retirement (if you're under age 50), your net wealth from those houses could easily total somewhere between $400,000 and $1,000,000. With only modest increases in rents, your income from those properties could reach $6,000 to $10,000 a month. And that's from only three or four units! After 18 years, a current monthly rent of $1,000 would then equal $2,000 a month—assuming just a 4 percent average increase each year.

Note: I realize that to Californians and residents of other high-priced areas, these purchase figures look absurdly low. However, just double or triple these figures. The same principle applies. Or look for properties in lower-cost geographic areas. You can also join with others and buy multiple-unit buildings where you get lower per-unit prices and higher cash flows than those typically available with single-family houses. "Fixers," too, provide a good alternative. (See especially Chapter 8 and my new book *Make Money with Fixers, Rehabs, and Renovations,* Wiley, 2003.)

Low-Involvement versus High-Involvement Investing

An investment strategy where you buy and hold three or four properties for income and appreciation over a period of 15 to 30 years (or more) can be considered a low-involvement investment strategy. Nearly anyone can come up with the limited time and money necessary to make this modest strategy pay off. However, if your goal is to build more wealth over a shorter period, then pursue a higher-involvement appreciation strategy. Although this approach won't necessarily require more cash, it will require more time, effort, and knowledge.

To beat the market averages, identify communities, neighborhoods, and properties that are positioned for faster appreciation. To gain this knowledge, you or your real estate agent astutely research a variety of geographic areas and types of properties. In addition, within markets that show the highest potential for appreciation, search for bargain-priced units whose market values can be increased through improvements.

As most everyone should realize, short-term property appreciation is never guaranteed. However, you can count on a buy-and-hold strategy to help you build large amounts of wealth over the mid- to longer term. During the short term, local job layoffs, speculative excess, overbuilding, high interest rates, and other factors can temporarily stall housing price increases.

Yet even in perilous times, you can take steps to profit from short-term appreciation. Look for markets that signal strong potential, and you can gain even when market averages just crawl along. Here's how to find these future star performers.

Compare Relative Prices of Neighborhoods

An oft-cited cliché in real estate tells investors to "buy in the best neighborhoods you can afford; the best neighborhoods always appreciate the fastest." On closer inspection, this advice makes no sense. No neighborhood or community can persistently outperform all others. The law of compound interest proves the statement false.

Assume you can choose between a neighborhood where apartments are priced at $100,000 per unit (College Park) and a neighborhood where apartments are priced at $50,000 per unit (Modest Manor). Over the past several years, properties in College Park have jumped in value by 25 percent (say 8 percent a year). Units in Modest Manor have moved up by only 10 percent (say 3 percent a year). Can these different rates of appreciation continue indefinitely? Not likely. A look at the projected values shows why.

Future Appreciated Values: College Park
versus Modest Manor

Years	$100,000 Neighborhood at 8%	$50,000 Neighborhood at 3%
3	$125,970	$54,635
6	158,690	59,700
9	199,900	65,200
12	251,820	71,250
15	317,222	77,900
20	466,100	90,300

In one year, rental units in the better area cost twice as much as those located in the lower-priced area. But after 20 years of faster appreciation, the higher-priced units would cost more than five times as much as their "inferiors." Unless some rare market forces were at work in this example, such a situation could not occur.

Long before such exaggerated price differences could result, increasing numbers of potential investors or tenants would be priced out of College Park and would switch their buying (or renting) to Modest Manor. Appreciation rates in College Park would slow. Appreciation rates in Modest Manor would accelerate.

The intelligent investor never assumes that future neighborhood appreciation rates will mirror the past. Intelligent investors compare the prices and features of a variety of neighborhoods and communities and search for those that are comparatively undervalued.

Undervalued Neighborhoods and Communities

At any given time and in any given area, no general statement about neighborhood or community appreciation potential ever holds true. Sometimes lower-priced areas may represent a great buy. On other occasions, higher-priced neighborhoods may look best. Sometimes new developments beat established neighborhoods; sometimes established beats new. Nor can anyone speak definitively about close-in versus far-out, well-kept versus run-down, or lower-crime versus higher-crime neighborhoods. Neither racial nor ethnic composition, or household income level, or occupational status necessarily relates to neighborhood appreciation potential.

The neighborhood that offers the best appreciation potential is the neighborhood (community) where price and rent levels look good relative to the prices and benefits offered by other neighborhoods.

Beverly Hills versus Watts (South Central Los Angeles)

By 1989, property prices in prestigious Beverly Hills had shot up by 50 percent or more since 1985. During the same period, property prices in the troubled neighborhood of Watts had barely budged upward. But by 1995, $5 million (1989) properties in Beverly Hills were selling at reduced prices of $3 million to $4 million, whereas $85,000 (1989) properties in Watts were selling at the increased price of $125,000. Between 1989 and 1995, property investors who owned units in troubled South Central Los Angeles outperformed investors who owned properties in the movie star haven of Beverly Hills.

In response to this fact, here's what I wrote in 1995 in the second edition of this book: "Does this same relative potential exist today? Will

Watts outperform Beverly Hills during the coming five or six years? My guess is no. Relative to other premier neighborhoods in world-class cities, homes in Beverly Hills now stand as terrific bargains. With the California economy at last climbing out of recession, house prices and rentals in Beverly Hills may now be positioned to hit new record highs."

Looking back now, you can see that my forecast was right on target. Between 1995 and 2002, upscale property prices in California did hit record highs. As this example shows, smart investors can profit when they study neighborhood home prices relative to features, benefits, and buyer/renter demographics. Astute buyers never arbitrarily prejudge which neighborhoods or communities present the best potential for appreciation.

Apart from relative prices, what neighborhood features should you compare? Here are the most important market data to investigate:

♦ Demographics
♦ Accessibility
♦ Job centers
♦ Taxes, services, and fiscal solvency
♦ Construction and renovation
♦ Land-use laws
♦ Civic pride
♦ Sales and rental trends

Demographics

When real estate investors refer to community demographics, they're referring to the income levels, occupations, education, ages, household size, household composition, and other characteristics of the people who live in an area. These data are readily available from the U.S. Bureau of Census and commercial market research firms (see www.census.gov).

However, even more important than current neighborhood demographics, learn who is moving *into* the neighborhood. A historically lower-income area that's attracting middle- or even upper-middle-income younger residents may signal appreciation potential. Likewise, a neighborhood where many residents are moving from welfare to jobs signals turnaround.

To learn about the people in a neighborhood, get out of your car. Talk with neighborhood residents who are working in their yards or walking their dogs. Talk with Realtors, mortgage loan officers, retail merchants, schoolteachers, and anyone else who might relay their firsthand knowledge. Ask anyone and everyone how the neighborhood is changing and whether they see these changes as positive or negative. Ask the people you talk to what they like least and what they like most about the neighborhood. Evaluate what you hear, see, and research. Then form your own conclusions. Do you think the people moving into the neighborhood are likely to push up home prices and rental rates? Or does "filtering down" point to deterioration?

Accessibility (Convenience)

Neighborhoods don't change their physical position on the face of the earth. Nevertheless, they can become more or less convenient relative to other neighborhoods and relative to their own past. Several years back, I chose to buy a home in the southeast part of town rather than the more popular northwest corridor. A primary reason was easier accessibility. Because of rapid growth and development, the freeway leading to the northwest corridor was becoming increasingly congested. What had been a 15- to 20-minute drive to town was now taking 30 to 45 minutes. And congestion was even getting worse.

As a result, increasing numbers of homebuyers decided that they did not want the hassle of fighting traffic everyday. They switched their preferences to the east and southeast developments. Property prices in my neighborhood jumped 40 percent within three years.

Improved (Increased) Transportation Routes

As another accessibility factor, find out whether a neighborhood might become more convenient because of changing transportation routes. Are any new or expanded freeways or toll roads planned or under construction? What about bridges, ferries, subways, commuter trains, or bus service? Will any type of new or expanded transportation facilities or services make travel to and from a neighborhood or community easier, cheaper, or faster?

Can you recall 5, 10, or 20 years ago when some of those "outlying" developments were built in your area? Are they still outlying? More than likely they're now just minutes from shopping centers, office complexes, restaurants, and other commercial developments. Because growth and development move outward, identify how convenience might be coming to the neighborhood. Developments or communities that today sit miles from anywhere may tomorrow be located just minutes from everything.

Centers of Employment

Most people prefer to live close to their jobs. As you search for appreciation potential, discover neighborhoods that are situated near employers or employment centers that are adding jobs to their payrolls.

During the late 1970s and 1980s, when housing prices shot up in Boston, New York, Los Angeles, San Francisco, Washington, D.C., and other large cities, experts said that the price increases were caused by millions of baby boomers flooding the housing market. Although that explanation was partly true, it was not *primarily* true.

Primarily, home prices shot up because these cities lacked developable land close to the downtown areas, where millions of square feet of new office space were being built. As these new office buildings filled with workers, tens of thousands of people began looking for homes and apartments convenient to their jobs. People with money (especially two-income career professionals) bid up the prices of desirable close-in properties. People with lower pay were pushed to outlying suburbs. Housing prices in both markets accelerated, but the prices in sought-after, close-in neighborhoods increased the most. Huge increases in demand pressed against a scarce and severely constrained supply of homes. This upward push on prices has recently occurred in Silicon Valley, where modest Palo Alto houses sell for $1,000,000, and upscale homes sell for $2,000,000 to $5,000,000 or more.

In contrast, during the late 1980s and early 1990s, property prices stalled and retreated in many high-cost cities. Corporate downsizing took a toll. Not only did construction of new office space stop, but much that had been built remained vacant. Architects, mortgage lenders, leasing agents, construction workers, real estate lawyers and accountants, and others employed in fields related to construction and real estate experienced job losses and reduced incomes. Cutbacks in government defense spending, too, depressed demand in San Diego and Boston.

In looking to the future, your task as an investor is to identify where employment gains are most likely to grow against constrained supply. The greater the job growth and the less the amount of nearby developable land, the greater the appreciation potential.

Taxes, Services, and Fiscal Solvency

In the early 1990s, Orange County, California, shocked the financial world. The county had lost $1.7 billion by speculating in risky stock and bond derivatives. As a result, Orange County defaulted on the payment of its outstanding municipal bonds and filed bankruptcy. Thousands of county employees were laid off, government services were cut back, and all new county spending projects were put on hold.

Fortunately, because California's constitution limits property tax increases to about 2 percent a year, property owners in Orange County did not suffer a large spike in their property taxes. Nevertheless, the Orange County financial debacle did flash orange (no pun intended) to property owners and potential buyers throughout the United States: Governments can mismanage their finances. Governments can go bankrupt. And governments can cut back or discontinue many types of services and programs (schools, libraries, parks and recreation, public transportation, legal aid, housing assistance, trash collection, etc.).

As you ferret out neighborhoods and communities (counties) in which to invest, check their property taxes, government services, and fiscal fitness. Does the community offer a high level of services and programs? Are the public finances of the community well managed? Does the tax/benefit ratio for the community (neighborhood) compare favorably with other areas? Consider all taxes and services. Do community governments provide residents relatively good value?

Note that co-ops, condos, and other developments governed by homeowners' associations present another layer of inquiry. In a sense, a homeowners' association functions as a government within a government. It issues rules and regulations, it provides services and recreational amenities, and it charges legally enforceable monthly fees. If you plan to buy into any type of property development that's governed by a property owners' association, check out the association's "laws," services, fees, and fiscal solvency in the same way that you would check out a local government.

At one point during the early 1990s, 50 percent of the homeowners' associations in the state of Massachusetts were insolvent. When Massachusetts condo prices collapsed, many unit owners stopped paying their monthly fees. This action, in turn, caused higher fees for other unit owners. Many of the remaining owners refused to pay. A vicious cycle spun losses. Foreclosures mounted, and condo prices continued to fall.

Since then, new state laws prevent similar wide-scale fiscal disasters. Homeowners' associations in Massachusetts (and other states) have been given stronger powers to collect unpaid association fees before an association's finances sink into an abyss. Even so, don't trust your financial fate to others. Before you buy, thoroughly review the operating rules, budget, and financial fitness of any homeowners' association that will govern your property. (In most areas, you can obtain this and other important association information by asking for a copy of the homeowners' association's "resale package.")

New Construction, Renovation, and Remodeling

Are neighborhood property owners (especially those who have recently bought into the area) upgrading their houses and apartment buildings? Are they painting exteriors, remodeling interiors, building additions, or installing amenities such as central heat and air, decks, patios, hot tubs, or skylights? Do you see properties being brought back to life after years of neglect? Check with building contractors, home improvement stores, and government building inspectors. Note trends in building permits for the area. Try to learn whether spending for property improvements is increasing.

Look for new construction of housing, office buildings, manufacturing plants, retail stores, or parks and recreational facilities. New construction not only creates jobs but, if properly integrated into an area, increases the area's desirability. Note, too, the prices or rental rates of any housing that's newly built or under construction. Is the new housing noticeably more expensive than the existing homes and apartments in the area? If so, these higher prices indicate that the neighborhood is moving upscale.

Watch carefully, though. Too much new housing can temporarily pull prices and rental rates down. Although everyone thinks Oil Belt property prices fell in the 1980s because of the collapse in oil prices, that's another partial truth. In fact, *overbuilding* (especially apartments and condominiums) proved far more damaging. In Houston, during the early to mid 1980s, developers brought more than 100,000 new multifamily units to market. Apartment vacancy rates ran close to 20 percent. Rent levels for new luxury two-bedroom apartments fell to less than $300 a month. Low rents for apartments pulled down the prices of condominiums and houses. Why buy when you can rent for peanuts?

In response to that construction excess, lenders tightened development financing for new subdivisions, condominiums, and apartments. During the 1990s, fewer new rental units were built than in any other ten-year period since the 1960s. Still, no one knows what the future holds. Overbuilding always presents a risk to property owners. Before you invest, check whether new housing in competing areas is renting (selling) without difficulty and that vacancy rates aren't flying up toward 10 percent or higher.

Land-Use Laws

Land-use laws include zoning, building codes, health and safety rules, occupancy codes, rent controls, environmental protection, historical preservation, architectural review boards, and many other laws, rules, and regulations. These laws tend to restrict growth and increase costs of development.

To forecast appreciation potential for a neighborhood or community, learn community attitudes toward growth. Do current (or pending) land-use laws limit construction and drive up building costs? Is government restricting supply? While debates rage between pro-growth and no-growth forces, history shows that in desirable areas where no- or slow-growth attitudes prevail, rent levels and housing prices are pushed up. California has been adding households at twice the rate it has been building houses.

Civic Pride

Here are two critical points: (1) You're not buying a neighborhood's past, you're investing in its future, and (2) you and other property owners in the neighborhood can join together to enhance and improve the area. Civic pride, community spirit, and community action can change a neighborhood with a poor reputation into one that becomes "the place to be." Contrary to popular opinion, you can change and improve the location of a property.

To carefully evaluate appreciation *potential*, assess the civic pride of neighborhood residents. Are they working individually and collectively to make their community a better place to call home? Are they cooperating with the people responsible for government services such as schools, libraries, police, street maintenance, parks and recreation, and public health? Are residents and public officials putting a plan into action to solve problems such as crime, graffiti, school quality, traffic congestion, or unkempt public areas?

Locate a neighborhood with possibilities for improvement, and you've located a neighborhood with strong potential for appreciation. When you, other property owners, and tenants work together, civic pride and community action can make a world of difference. (For dozens of examples, see *Fixing Broken Windows,* by George Kelling and Catherine Coles [Free Press, 1996].)

Sales and Rental Trends

Among the most important leading indicators of rising (or falling) property prices are sales trends and rental trends. As you move forward to a profitable career in real estate investing, create a system for tracking and recording trend data such as unit selling prices, time on market, number of listings, rent levels, and vacancy rates. Watch these trends. You can detect market changes as they are occurring and sometimes score big short-term gains.

Sales Trends.   As prices begin to increase in a neighborhood, time-on-market data will show increasingly faster sales. In slow markets, properties can sit unsold for months (180, 270, 360 days, or longer). In contrast, as average time on market falls from, say, 270 days to 180 days to 120 days, prices are about to go up. A decreasing inventory of unsold properties also points the way to rapid advances in property prices. When the numbers of For Sale and For Rent signs dwindle, sellers soon raise their prices and rental rates.

Savvy investors track time-on-market and unsold-inventory data. A short supply of properties that sell or rent quickly signals an appreciating market.

Rental Market Trends.   Here are four important rental market trends: (1) vacancy rates, (2) time on market, (3) annual rent increases (or rental concessions), and (4) rates of owner occupancy. Review the past 12 to 24 months. Are community vacancy rates falling or increasing? How long do vacant apartments or rental houses sit vacant before they're rented? What types of units rent the quickest? How do vacancy rates differ among various neighborhoods and communities? Do some types of buildings or units enjoy waiting lists? What are their features and locations?

Are rents steady or increasing? Or are property owners giving concessions like one or two months' free rent for a 12-month lease? Are homes in the neighborhood or community primarily owner occupied or tenant occupied? In which direction is the neighborhood trending? Ideally, you would like to own rentals in neighborhoods where tenants are being squeezed out by homebuyers. Increasing numbers of homeowners signal higher property prices and higher rental rates for the relatively few rental units that remain.

Summing Up

To discover properties that will gain from higher-than-average appreciation, thoroughly track neighborhood data. Monitor changes in selling prices, accessibility, civic pride, and community action. Property prices and rent levels gallop ahead or fall behind because buyers and tenants persistently shop neighborhoods and communities to discover the best *values*— not necessarily the best features or lowest prices per se. When you discover comparatively undervalued areas, price increases will surely follow.

5

HOW TO FIND BARGAINS

In real estate—unlike the stock market—you can make money not only when you sell but also when you buy. In the stock market, it's virtually impossible to buy a stock for less than its market value; in real estate, such transactions occur every day. If Ford Motor Company is selling at $47, no one would tell Merrill Lynch to try to find a Ford stockholder who will sell 100 shares at a price of $40 a share. But if you want to buy a $250,000 house or apartment building for $200,000 to $225,000, it's possible that you or your real estate agent can locate a seller who will oblige you.

WHY PROPERTIES SELL FOR LESS (OR MORE) THAN THEIR MARKET VALUE

Recall from Chapter 3 that a market value sale must meet these five criteria:

1. Buyers and sellers are typically motivated. Neither is acting under duress.
2. Buyers and sellers are well informed and knowledgeable about the property and the market.
3. The marketing period and sales promotion efforts are sufficient to reasonably inform potential buyers of the property's availability (i.e., no forced or rushed sales).
4. There are no special terms of financing (e.g., low down payment, below-market interest rate).

5. No unusual sales concessions are made by either the seller or the buyer (e.g., sellers are not permitted to stay in the house rent-free for three to six months until their under-construction new house is completed).

As you think through these market value criteria, you will realize that owners who are in a hurry to sell may have to accept a price lower than market value. Likewise, an FSBO (for sale by owner) who doesn't know how to market and promote a property will not likely receive top dollar. Or say the sellers live out of town. They don't realize that recent sales prices have jumped up, or maybe they don't realize that their property (or the neighborhood) is ripe for profitable improvement. Also consider the following possibilities.

Owners in Distress

Every day people hit hard times. They are laid off from their jobs, file for divorce, suffer accidents or illness, experience setbacks in their business, and run into a freight train of other problems. Any or all these calamities can create financial distress. For many of these property owners, their only way out of a jam is to raise cash by selling their home (or other real estate) quickly at a bargain price.

Some investors find it distasteful and unethical to prey on the down-and-out. Yet most sellers who find themselves in financial distress are longing for the chance to get rid of their sleepless, toss-and-turn nights. If that means selling their property for "less than it's worth," then that's what they're willing to do. These people are not just selling a property; they are buying relief.

Under these circumstances, as long as the sellers believe they have gained more from the sale than they've lost, both parties win. If you help people cope with predicament—as opposed to fleecing them—then seek out distressed owners who will give you the bargain price (or favorable terms) you want.

The "Grass-Is-Greener" Sellers

One day Karla Lopez is sitting in her office, and in walks the executive vice president of her firm. "Karla," she says, "Aaron Stein in the Denver branch just quit. If you want his district manager's job, you can have it. We will pay you $25,000 more a year plus a bonus. But you have to be relocated and on the job within thirty days."

"Do I want it?" Karla says. "Of course I want it. A promotion like this is why I've been working sixty- to eighty-hour weeks for these past four years."

Think about it. In this situation, does Karla think, "Well, the first thing I must do is put my house up for sale and go for top dollar?" Hardly. More than likely, Karla will be willing to strike a deal with the first buyer who gives her any type of offer she can live with. Karla has her sights set on the greener grass of Denver. Optimistic about her career and facing a time deadline, Karla wants to get her home sold as quickly as possible.

Grass-is-greener sellers stand in contrast to the financially distressed. Whereas distressed owners sell on bargain terms or price to relieve themselves of pain, grass-is-greener sellers are willing to accept an offer of less than market value so that they can quickly grab better opportunities that lie elsewhere.

On one occasion where I was a grass-is-greener seller, I not only gave my buyers a slight break on price but, more important from their perspective, let them assume my below-market interest rate first mortgage and carried back an unsecured note for virtually all of their down payment. On at least three occasions, I've bought from sellers who were eager to pursue better opportunities elsewhere. Each time, I negotiated a good (if not great) price and favorable financing.

If looking for distressed owners doesn't appeal to you, turn your search in the opposite direction: Sellers who are moving to greener pastures (especially under a deadline of time) are frequently the easiest people to work with and the most accommodating in price and terms.

Stage-of-Life Sellers

When shopping for bargains, you can also find good deals among stage-of-life sellers. These sellers are typically people whose lifestyle now conflicts with their property. They may no longer enjoy keeping up a big house or yard, collecting rent, or dealing with tenant complaints. They eagerly anticipate their move to that condo on the 14th green at the Bayshore Country Club. Or perhaps they would rather not go through the trouble of updating and repairing their current property. Whatever their reasons, stage-of-life sellers are motivated to get on with their lives.

In addition—and this circumstance makes these sellers good prospects for a bargain price or terms—stage-of-life sellers have typically accumulated large amounts of equity in their properties. And because they're older, they may have substantial sums in savings or other investments. Stage-of-life sellers can be flexible. They don't need to squeeze every last penny out of their sale.

Because stage-of-life sellers don't face a pressing need for cash, they make excellent candidates for some type of "owner will carry" (OWC) financing. Not only will OWC terms help them sell their property more quickly, but an installment sale reduces or defers the capital gain taxes that a cash sale might otherwise trigger. As another advantage, OWC financing—even when offered at below-market rates—will bring the sellers a higher return than they could earn in a savings account, certificate of deposit, money market fund, or perhaps even stocks.

Case in point: As a college student who wanted to invest in real estate, I sought out stage-of-life owners of rental houses and small apartment buildings. These people were tired of managing their properties. At the same time, however, they preferred a monthly income and didn't want to settle for the meager interest paid by banks or deal with the risks of stocks. They also didn't want to sell their properties and get hit with a heavy tax bill for capital gains.

Their solution: Sell on easy OWC terms to an ambitious young person who was willing to accept the work of rental properties in exchange for an opportunity to start building wealth through investment real estate. This technique remains valid today. Because properly selected, well-managed rentals will pay for themselves, a buyer who is willing to work can substitute ambition and perseverance for a large down payment and high monthly wages.

Seller Ignorance

Some sellers underprice their properties because they don't know the recent prices at which similar homes have been selling. Or they may not know of a unique advantage that favorably distinguishes their property from others. I confess that as a seller, I have made the mistake of selling too low because I was ignorant of the market.

In one particular case, I was living in Palo Alto, California. The rental house I decided to sell was located in Dallas, Texas. A year earlier, the house had been appraised for $110,000, which at the time of the appraisal was about right. So I decided to ask $125,000. I figured that price was high enough to account for inflation and still leave room for negotiating.

The first weekend the house went on the market, three offers came in at the asking price. Immediately, of course, I knew I had underpriced. What I didn't know but soon learned was that during the year I'd been away, home prices in that Dallas neighborhood had jumped 30 percent. After learning of my ignorance, I could have rejected all the offers and raised my price. Or I could have put the buyers into a bidding war. But I didn't. I decided to sell to the person with the cleanest offer (no contingencies). I was making a good profit; why get greedy?

Although it's not an everyday occurrence, some sellers do mistakenly underprice their properties. Stay on the lookout for this possibility. When you spot a good deal, jump on it. Underpriced properties get snapped up quickly.

◆ ◆ ◆

Although good deals go fast, not all bargain-priced properties represent good deals. You have received a good deal only if you can sell the property for substantially more than you have put into it. Beware of underestimating fix-up expenses; beware of hidden defects; beware of environmental problems (e.g., lead paint, underground oil storage tanks, asbestos, contaminated well water); and beware of pouring so much cash into improvements that you'll have to overshoot the rent level that tenants are willing and able to pay.

Always temper your eagerness to buy a bargain-priced property with a thorough physical, financial, market, and legal analysis. Especially in cases of low- or nothing-down seller financing, many beginning investors jump at a "great" deal without first putting it under a magnifying glass. Act quickly when you must. But the less you know about a property and the more you naively assume, the greater your risk. Balance your eagerness to buy with an explicit and realistic view of potential pitfalls.

WHAT ARE YOUR SCREENING CRITERIA?

As a practical matter, you can't look at every property in an area. And even if you could, you still wouldn't want to buy every bargain-priced property that comes to your attention. Before you move to the "buy" stage of your investing decision, narrow your choices. Research and think through answers to the following questions:

- What neighborhoods look most promising?
- Do you want a single-family house, condominium, co-op, townhouse, or multiple-unit rental property? If multiple units, how large a property will you accept?
- Do you want a property for owner occupancy as well as an investment? If owner occupancy is important, how does this fact limit your choice of properties?
- How much repair, renovation, or remodeling work are you prepared to take on?
- What types of improvements are you willing to undertake? Structural? Cosmetic? Environmental? Fire damaged? Earthquake damaged? Other?
- Which is most important: a bargain price or bargain terms? Would you buy a property with negative cash flows? If no, what is your minimum cash-on-cash return on investment (ROI)?
- Would you accept a property that is occupied by problem tenants?

- How much risk are you willing to tolerate? When buying fixer-uppers, your repairs and renovation costs may exceed your estimates. If you buy into a turnaround neighborhood, the turnaround may take longer than you expect. How much cash or borrowing power can you draw on to carry you through a period of impaired rent collections (vacancies, bad tenants)?
- What's the minimum time period you would accept on a balloon mortgage or other short-term financing?
- How long do you plan to own the property? After all costs are considered, will the property command a selling price or rent level high enough to meet your profit objectives? What are your profit objectives?

By focusing on properties that match your requirements, you eliminate the wild-goose chases that steal the time of many beginning real estate investors. By asking questions to clarify your goals and circumstances, you reduce the temptation to grab a deal just because it is a deal, rather than because the property suits your abilities, finances, and inclinations.

BARGAIN SELLERS

Now that you have developed your screening criteria, how do you start finding potential sellers? Here are five techniques:

1. Networking
2. Newspapers and other publications
3. Cold calls directly to owners
4. Real estate agents
5. Information highway

Networking

Some time back, I was leaving the country for several years and decided to sell my house with a minimum of hassle. Coincidentally, the Ph.D. student club at the university where I was teaching was looking for a faculty member to host the upcoming faculty-student party. Aha, I thought, what better way to expose my house to more than 100 people? So I volunteered. In the week following the party, I received two offers and accepted one of them.

The buyers got a good price and excellent financing. I avoided the hassle of putting the property on the market and did not have to pay a real estate commission. Everyone involved was satisfied.

This personal example shows the power of networking. What's surprising, though, is that so few buyers and sellers consciously try to discover each other through informal contacts among friends, family, relatives, coworkers, church groups, clubs, business associates, customers, parent-teacher groups, and other types of acquaintances. Don't keep your search a secret. Tell everyone you know. Describe what you're looking for. Why do it alone when you can enlist dozens of others to help you?

Newspapers and Other Publications

To most people, looking for real estate means perusing the real estate classifieds with a highlighter, calling owners or Realtors, getting basic information, and, when something sounds promising, setting up an appointment. Although this method can work reasonably well, it can also fail for two reasons: (1) If a property isn't advertised, you won't learn about it, and (2) if the ad for a property you might be interested in is not written effectively, you may pass it by without serious notice.

To at least partially overcome these drawbacks, run your own advertisement in the "wanted to buy" column. When you describe the type of property and terms that you're looking for, you invite serious sellers to contact you. I have used this technique to locate about 30 percent of the properties I have bought.

As another way to use the newspaper, read through the "houses for rent," "condos for rent," and "apartments for rent" ads. Not only will this research help you gauge rent levels, but often you'll see properties advertised as "lease-option" or "for rent or sale." These kinds of ads generally indicate a flexible seller.

To search for potential bargain sellers in the newspaper, move beyond the classified real estate ads. Locate names of people from the public notices: births, divorces, deaths, bankruptcy, foreclosure, or marriage. Each of these events can trigger the need to sell real estate quickly. If you contact these potential sellers before they have listed with a sales agent, you stand a fair chance of buying at a bargain price. (In addition, you might subscribe to the "default" or "foreclosure" lists and newsletters published in your area. Buying foreclosures is discussed in Chapter 6.)

Cold Calls Directly to Owners

To learn successful cold calling, follow the techniques of Realtors. Most successful real estate agents develop listing farms. A listing farm represents a neighborhood or other geographic area that an agent consistently cultivates to find sellers who will list their properties for sale with that agent. Agent cold-call techniques typically include telephoning property owners with names gathered from a crisscross directory, walking the neighborhood, talking to residents, circulating flyers by mail or doorknob hangers, and taking part in neighborhood or community-sponsored events. By cultivating a farm, an agent hopes to become known in the area and to position himself or herself to be the first person property owners think of when they contemplate a sale.

Take a lesson out of the real estate agent's playbook. Cultivate a farm in the neighborhoods or communities where you would like to buy. Circulate a flyer, for example, that reads:

Before you list your home for sale, please call me. I am looking to buy a property in this neighborhood directly from the own- ers. Let's see if we can sit down together and work out an agreement that will benefit both of us.

When property owners learn how they can save time, effort, and money selling direct, they may be willing to offer you a favorable price or terms.

Vacant Houses and Out-of-the-Area Owners. Your farm area will include some properties (vacant or tenant occupied) that are owned by people who do not live in the neighborhood. These owners may not see your flyers, nor will they be listed in a crisscross directory. To learn how to reach these potential sellers, ask neighbors of nearby properties or talk directly with the tenants who live in the property.

If this research doesn't reveal the owners' names and addresses, you can contact the county property tax assessor's office. There you can learn where and to whom the property tax statements are mailed. It's not unusual to find that out-of-the-area property owners are actually "sleep- ing sellers." That is, they would like to sell but haven't as yet awoken to the idea. With luck and perseverance, you could become their alarm clock.

Broker Listings.   For any number of reasons, many properties listed with real estate agents do not sell during their original listing period. When this situation occurs, the listing agent will try to get the owners to relist with his or her firm. And quite likely, agents from other brokerage firms also will approach the sellers. However, here's what you can do to cut them off at the pass and perhaps arrange a bargain purchase.

When you notice a listed property that looks as if it might fit your requirements, do *not* call the agent. Do *not* call or stop by to talk to the owners. Instead write the owners a letter stating the price and terms that you would consider paying. Then ask the owners to contact you *after* their listing has expired. (If a seller goes behind his agent's back and arranges a sale while the property is listed, the owner is still legally obligated to pay the sales commission.)

Consider this possibility: The property is listed at its market value of $200,000. The listing contract sets a 6 percent sales commission. The sellers have told themselves that they will accept nothing less than $192,500, meaning that after selling expenses they would net around $180,000. You offer $175,000. Would the sellers accept it? Or would they relist, postpone their move, and hold out for another $5,000 to $10,000?

It would depend, of course, on the sellers' finances, their reason for moving, and any other pressures they may be facing. But you can see that even though your offer is low relative to the value of the house, it still provides the sellers almost as much as they could expect if their agent found them a buyer. (Naturally, your letter offer would not formally commit you to the purchase. It would merely state the price and terms that you have in mind.)

Do not conclude here that you should never use a real estate agent to help find your investment properties. A top agent provides valuable assistance in many ways. However, agents do deserve to be paid for their services. So if you're planning to buy at a bargain price or buy on bargain terms (especially with low- or no-down-payment financing), where is the agent's fee going to come from? If you want to pursue the best deal possible, at times you may have to forgo an agent's services and do your own legwork.

Agent Services

Before you go it alone, though, consider some words of experience from career real estate investor and renovator Suzanne Brangham. In her excellent book *Housewise* (HarperCollins, 1987, p. 163), Brangham writes:

> Real estate agents are invaluable. You need them as much as they need you. After you have narrowed your choice to one or two neighborhoods or towns, enlist the aid of an expert. Your real estate agent will be your guide so you can sit back, take out your notebook, ask questions, and learn . . . . Good agents know what properties are selling for, which areas are strong, and which neighborhoods are getting hot . . . .
>
> If you let your agent know that you plan to buy and sell several properties over the next few years, he (or she) will do

everything short of breaking and entering to show you the properties that are available . . . . I'd been lusting after a beautiful two-unit building, but it had never been up for sale. My agent called me the minute it was listed and I bought it in less than an hour. In fact, I soon became notorious for signing offer forms on the roof of my agent's car. When there's a race to get in your bid on a particularly juicy piece of property, a faithful agent who knows exactly what you want can make all the difference.

In addition to showing you properties and neighborhoods, a good agent can assist with at least eight other tasks:

1. Suggest sources and techniques of financing and help you run through the numbers.
2. Research comp sales and rent levels so that you can better understand values.
3. Act as an intermediary in negotiations.
4. Recommend other professionals whose services you may need (lawyer, mortgage broker, contractor, designer, architect, property inspector).
5. Handle innumerable details and problems that always seem to pop up on the way from contract to closing.
6. Clue you in about what type of interest and market activity has developed around various properties.
7. Give you an insider's glimpse into an area to let you know who's doing what and where.
8. Disclose negatives about a property or neighborhood that might otherwise have escaped your attention.

Your agent can become your trusted partner. He or she will help you sort through your neighborhood and property trade-offs, suggest possibilities for value-creating improvements, and help persuade sellers to accept your price and terms. Overall, as Suzanne Brangham points out, "A good agent, one who really listens when you explain what you want, is likely to take you directly to the buried treasure you've been looking for."

Tell Agents What You Expect.   Depending on your experiences with real estate agents, you may think this discussion of agent services is fantastically exaggerated. But it's not. Because most relatively new real estate investors don't expect much from their agents, they tend to tolerate mediocrity. Then they complain that "agents are overpaid and underworked."

To avoid this self-fulfilling prophecy, accept responsibility for specifying the types and quality of services you expect to receive. As you talk with agents, tell them the information you'll need and the types of questions you will be asking. Test them with tough inquiries. Do they rattle off answers as if they're a walking almanac of community information? Or do they lamely respond, "I don't know, but I can find that out for you if you really want me to."

No agent can know or anticipate all of the information about neighborhoods and properties that you might require. But when an agent repeatedly waits for you to ask questions before doing the necessary legwork, you need to find a more thoughtful agent who shows hustle and initiative.

Civil Rights Caveat.   Real estate agents (like everyone else) must constantly guard what they say out of fear of lawsuits. If you ask, "What's the quality of the schools in this neighborhood?" the agent may hedge an answer if, say, at one time forced school busing or racial turmoil has spurred an exodus to suburbia, and corresponding school achievement test scores have fallen.

Similarly, if a changing ethnic or racial composition of a neighborhood is affecting property values (either up or down), a sales agent would avoid discussions along those lines. The U.S. Department of Justice (DOJ) and the U.S. Department of Housing and Urban Development (HUD) have decreed that neither ethnic, religious, nor racial demographics affect property values. Hence any real estate agent (or appraiser) who disagrees with HUD or DOJ can be held civilly and criminally liable for damages.

In a fit of excess, sales agents have even been warned against using terms such as "exclusive neighborhood," "walk-in closet," "beautiful view," "master bedroom," and "walking distance to school." In Berkeley, California, HUD sued a group of neighbors for speaking against the placement of a home for the mentally retarded in their neighborhood. In today's climate of victimhood, any statement that in any way might give offense to some "protected" group can land a real estate agent in court and out of a job. Don't expect candid answers to any questions that may even remotely transgress someone's idea of civil rights.

Property Condition Caveat.   In addition to fair housing issues, most agents tread lightly in response to questions about the condition of a property. "How's the roof?" you ask. The agent answers, "As far as I know, it's eight years old and hasn't had any leaks." You buy the property, and three months later the roof begins to leak. On the basis of the agent's statement, you sue the brokerage firm for misrepresentation and fraud. Even though the agent was telling the truth as far as he or she knew it, many judges or juries would still find the agent liable.

Agents have been sued so many times for giving "to the best of my knowledge" answers concerning property condition that many avoid such questions and will refer you to appropriate specialists and inspectors. In one major precedent-setting case in California, an agent was held liable for not informing his buyers that a property was located in a mud slide area—even though the agent did not know that the area was risky. In response to this case, the California Association of Realtors convinced the California legislature to enact a *seller disclosure* law. More than 35 other states have followed California's lead.

To confirm your belief that you're buying at a bargain price, you need full and accurate information about neighborhoods and specific properties. A top real estate agent will provide you with some of this knowledge. But not all of it. You must recognize the practical and legal limitations that even top agents confront.

Experience and Professional Education. When investing in single-family houses, condos, or townhomes, rely on a knowledgeable agent who specializes in residential sales, but also look for agents who have achieved the GRI (Graduate Realtors Institute), the CRS (Certified Residential Specialist), or the CRB (Certified Residential Broker) designation. Each of these designations requires experience and advanced professional education. Although the National Association of Realtors has signed up 800,000 members, only 32,000 of these agents have met the experience and education standards required for the CRS designation.

When buying income properties of four units or more, consider using an agent who has earned the CCIM (Certified Commercial Investment Member) designation. To earn this credential, agents complete advanced courses in market analysis, economics, statistics, taxation, property exchanging, financial analysis, and other topics related to real estate investing. Most CCIMs work exclusively with buyers and sellers of apartment buildings, office buildings, and shopping centers.

Beyond professional education and experience, you want an agent "who is sophisticated, hardworking, fun, fast, and smart—someone who knows the town inside out and makes a lot of deals," advises Suzanne Brangham. I agree. My book *Yes! You Can Own the Home You Want* (Wiley, 1995) tells of agents who are skilled in "possibility analysis." These agents demonstrate a "we can make it happen" attitude. Rather than tell you what you can't do, they show you how to get over, under, or around whatever obstacles that stand in your way. These agents know how to get deals structured, financed, and closed.

Buyer Loyalty. For every real buyer they work with, most agents encounter a dozen pretenders—people who steal an agent's time and knowledge but feel no obligation to buy from that agent. Or if they do buy, the first thing they do to make a deal work is to try to cut the agent's commission. This approach does not build a lasting and mutually beneficial relationship. For best results, once you find a top agent, demonstrate buyer loyalty.

When you're loyal to your agents, they will see you as a real buyer who will give them repeat business (as well as referrals). In return, they will give you preferred treatment and make sure that you're among the first to learn of those "juicy deals" as soon as they hit the market, and sometimes even before a listing goes into the MLS (Multiple Listing Service).

Law of Agency. Until the early 1990s, the great majority of real estate agents who helped buyers find properties actually worked as agents or subagents for the sellers. This system had worked reasonably well for 100 years. More recently, though, lawyers and self-proclaimed consumer advocates have widely publicized claims that such a system cheated buyers by denying them their own representation. Furthermore, because many buyers did not know that "their" agent was really a subagent of the sellers, all too frequently these buyers unwittingly disclosed personal confidential information to an agent, who then passed it on to the sellers to use against the buyers during negotiations.

While undoubtedly some agents did abuse their buyers' trust under this subagency system, most did not. Of the tens of millions of real estate transactions that have occurred over the years, only a small percentage have resulted in serious complaining. In fact, under the previous subagency system, "seller's" agents often disclosed to buyers valuable tidbits of information such as "The sellers are asking $260,000, but they're going through a bitter divorce and are pressed to sell. They will probably accept something around $225,000. Would you be interested at that price? Let's write up an offer and see what happens."

Notwithstanding this reality, it was a 1992 buyers' class action lawsuit against Edina Realty in Minnesota that sent shock waves throughout the real estate industry. Even though Edina's agents were not proven to have acted against their buyers' interests, in 1995 Edina Realty suffered a $250 million judgment for having "insufficiently emphasized and explained their role as seller agents or subagents."

In self-defense, Realtor groups throughout the country petitioned courts and state legislatures to clarify their legal responsibilities to both buyers and sellers. Although this area of law is still murky, nearly all states have enacted mandatory agent disclosure. These laws compel buyers to explicitly choose the type of agency relationship they want to enter into with their real estate agents. Generally, you can select one of the following four possibilities:

1. You may work with an agent or subagent of the sellers.
2. You may elect a dual agency. Under this arrangement, an agent may help both buyers and sellers, but he or she also agrees not to pass along confidential information that could benefit either a buyer or a seller at the expense of the other party. (Many agents now refuse to act as dual agents because they believe the risk of liability is too great.)
3. Some agents hold themselves out as facilitators. In this role, they do not advocate or represent the interests of either the buyers or the sellers. Instead, they act as mediators helping buyer and seller structure an agreement that both parties can live with.
4. The fastest growing type of agency relationship is called "buyer's agency" or "buyer's brokerage." Although any licensed real estate agent may serve as a buyer's agent, a true buyer's brokerage firm only represents buyers. Such a firm will not accept listings from sellers.

In most situations, you will probably want to choose a buyer's agent or buyer's brokerage relationship with your agent. In that way, the agent is free to research, inquire, and discover any type of information that could be helpful to you without worrying about any conflicting duties or loyalties that he or she owes a seller.

However, two advantages might motivate you to work with the seller's listing agent. First, although I generally oppose asking agents to cut their commission, working with a listing agent presents a possible exception. If the listing agent does not have to split the sales fee with your buyer's agent, why not "split it" with you?

While the agent may not legally be able to give you a cash kickback, he or she could pass the savings along to the sellers, who would then reduce their price accordingly. Say the listing agreement sets a sales fee of 6 percent of the selling price. You have offered $97,000 tops. The seller's bottom dollar is $100,000, which, after paying a $6,000 sales fee, will leave a net of $94,000. If the agent gives up the 3 percent of that fee that would have gone to your buyer's agent, the sellers can meet your price without losing anything from their net of $94,000 because they'll now pay a sales commission of around $3,000 instead of $6,000. You, the sellers, and the agent all benefit.

A second possible reason to work with a listing agent is to obtain information about the sellers. When you're trying to negotiate a bargain price, you must learn all you can about the sellers' personal situation, their finances, their motivation for selling, and anything else that might help you structure an offer that will gain their signature. In the past, listing agents would often intentionally (or unintentionally) reveal such personal information.

In today's litigious climate, some listing agents are more tight-lipped than they used to be. Still, it doesn't hurt to ask. In many instances, it's actually in the sellers' interests for their agent to disclose at least enough information to tempt a buyer into making an offer. If the sellers really need to sell, an honest admission often sets the stage for productive negotiations.

Agents: Summing Up. Most experienced real estate investors buy their properties through real estate agents. Although they might save money dealing directly with property owners, they would lose time and valuable help. So most investors delegate the legwork to someone who knows their requirements, knows how to find properties, and knows how to push a deal through to closing. Top real estate agents are out talking to buyers, sellers, investors, lenders, politicians, merchants, employers, and government agencies, every day, all day. Put one of these agents to work, and you may learn of more good deals than you could ever turn up on your own.

The Information Highway

Today's investors not only cruise neighborhoods but also cruise the Internet to look for properties. Thousands of Web sites now list properties for sale. Property buyers (or browsers) can directly access the Realtors' multiple listing service at www.Realtor.com.

There is also a budding entrepreneurial industry of network providers who are accumulating specialized listings of everything from foreclosures to distressed properties to FSBOs. Going on-line, you can locate investors looking for money—or money looking for properties. Virtually all real estate information that in the past has been available from Realtors, public records, newspaper ads, newsletters, and other sources is now (or will soon be) accessible to anyone with access to the Internet. Nobody today knows exactly where technology will lead us tomorrow. But electronic shopping for real estate (and mortgages) has virtually made the MLS book as obsolete as a slide rule. (For a listing and links to Web sites useful to real estate investors, see the Internet Appendix at the end of this book.)

Will Realtors Become Obsolete, Too?   The continuing revolution in information technology has not escaped the attention of organized real estate groups. The question is repeatedly asked, "Since the stock in trade of real estate agents is information, will anyone need a Realtor when prospective buyers and sellers can communicate directly with each other over the information highway?" Most agents believe that the answer to that question is yes, for two reasons.

First, much of the information, knowledge, and assistance Realtors provide is personal, informal, analytical, and creative. Information technology hasn't yet been able to replace these human characteristics.

Second, Realtors aren't standing around watching the World Wide Web pass them by. Technologically sophisticated Realtors are using advanced software to prepare reports for prospective buyers that detail and map out neighborhoods, population demographics, home prices, school districts, property tax records, environmental hazards, and many other statistical and geographic data that can assist homebuyers and real estate investors. Moreover, in the future, you will be able to use video technology to do a virtual walk-through of nearly every property listed for sale.

Will the Information Highway Make Buying Easier?   In one sense, the information highway could make buying properties easier but could make buying *bargain-priced* properties more difficult. As sales and rental data become just a mouse click away and less costly to obtain, sellers will be less likely to underprice their properties (as I did with my Dallas rental house while living in Palo Alto). Also, property owners who need to cut their price to sell quickly will be able to inform millions of potential buyers simultaneously. With greater market exposure, bargain-priced houses may sell faster and with smaller discounts. From a different perspective, though, astute investors may actually find it easier to locate bargains. As the information networks homogenize market data, run-of-the-mill investors will simply act on that data as it is presented. As the stock market illustrates, a greater flow of information encourages and accents fads and volatility. The stocks of popular companies get bid up beyond reason. Other currently out-of-favor companies become undervalued.

Warren Buffett, the titan of stock market investors, built his multibillion net worth by applying the principles of *value investing*—not by following market trends and popularly held notions.[1] With or without the information highway, you can build your real estate portfolio in a similar manner.

1. See my book *Value Investing in Real Estate* (Wiley, 2002).

Always critically examine conventional wisdom. Look at market information from a variety of perspectives. Constantly ask yourself, What does this fact mean for the future? Focus on property and neighborhood details; make reasoned interpretations. Discipline your intellect to apply the valuation principles explained in Chapters 3 and 4. Remember, you find and create good deals through legwork, intelligence, and creativity. Information provides only raw material. Without effort and intelligence, information is worth no more than yesterday's newspaper. Keep these entrepreneurial principles in mind, and, like Warren Buffett, you will stand head and shoulders above most other investors who obsess over information but remain strangers to knowledge and insight.

◆ ◆ ◆

In many ways, finding bargain sellers is like panning for gold. Even when you know a stream is loaded with nuggets, you must sift through a ton of muck and rock before finding the treasure that earns the profits. Likewise, when trying to locate bargain sellers, expect to work at it. As you gain experience and reputation as a real estate investor, deals will start coming to you. But as stock speculator Gordon Gekko (Michael Douglas) tells Bud Fox (Charlie Sheen) in the movie *Wall Street*, "Kid, I look at 100 deals a day. I may choose one." As a starting point, when locating bargains, mentally prepare yourself.

Among the many properties that are promoted as bargains, most are overpriced money traps. However, through skillful negotiation and financial structuring, you can sometimes transform an apparently mediocre deal into a true winner. Except in cases of pure luck, putting gold nuggets in your pocket will require time, effort, intelligence, knowledge, and possibility thinking.

SELLER DISCLOSURES

In real estate, what you see is not all that you get. That property you bought at a bargain price won't seem like such a great deal once you learn the roof leaks, the foundation is cracking, and termites are eating away the floor joists. Moreover, if the next-door neighbors behave like an unruly mob, you may find that you can't keep your property occupied with quality, rent-paying tenants.

As a first line of defense against such unwanted surprises, thoroughly inspect the property, talk to existing tenants, walk the neighborhood, and make sure you're working with a knowledgeable and trustworthy real estate agent. As a second line of defense, get the property checked out by a property inspector, a structural engineer, a pest control expert, or other specialists who can accurately evaluate the condition of the property. And third, ask the sellers to complete a sellers' disclosure statement.

The Disclosure Revolution

Most states now require sellers to complete a seller's disclosure statement that lists and explains all *known* problems or defects that may plague a property. But even if your state doesn't yet mandate seller disclosure, you should still obtain a disclosure form (most major realty firms keep blank copies on hand) and ask the sellers to fill it out. In reviewing a completed disclosure statement, however, keep in mind the following five trouble points.

1. Sellers are not required to disclose facts or conditions of which they are unaware.
2. Disclosure reveals the past. It does not guarantee the future. By completing the statement, sellers do not warrant the condition of the property.
3. Many disclosure questions require somewhat subjective answers. Are playing children a neighborhood "noise" problem? Is a planned street widening an "adverse" condition?
4. Disclosure statements may not require sellers to disclose property defects that are readily observable.
5. Pay close attention to any seller (or agent) statements that begin, "I believe," "I think," "as far as we know," and other similar hedges. Don't accept these answers as conclusive. Make a *written* note to follow up with further inquiry or inspection.

Seller disclosure statements substantially reduce the chance for unwelcome surprise after you take possession of a property. But even so, independently check out the property to satisfy yourself that you know what you are buying.

Income Properties

Many seller disclosure laws apply only to one- to four-family owner-occupied properties. If you're buying a larger income property, the law may not require the seller to fill out a disclosure statement. If in this situation the seller refuses, offset this additional risk by scaling down the top price you're willing to pay—and enhance the rigor of your prepurchase inspections.

Additionally, when buying income properties, verify rental income and operating expenses. Ask the sellers to sign a statement whereby they swear that the income and expense figures that they have reported to you are true and factual. Beware of owners who put friends, relatives, and employees into their buildings at inflated rent levels. These tenants don't really pay the rents stated (or if they do, they get kickbacks in cash or other benefits), but their signed leases sure look attractive to unsuspecting buyers.

SUMMARY

The great majority of real estate deals involve negotiated transactions. Each buyer and seller must confront his or her own personal needs, pressures, time schedule, financial worries, capabilities, interests, knowledge, and objectives. Every property presents unique physical features, location, and potential for improvement. To make matters more complex, you can't confidently use "comp" prices as a guide without good information about the parties involved, the details of their transaction, and the precise property features.

To use the jargon of economists, these facts mean that real estate sells in an imperfect (inefficient) market. As a result, investors who buy with the best information, knowledge, perseverance, and imagination do earn superior returns. So shop carefully, systematically compare properties, seek out motivated or uninformed sellers, negotiate skillfully, and you will put together great deals that include a bargain price, bargain financing, or maybe both.

6

PROFITING FROM FORECLOSURES

Most people believe that to profit from foreclosures, you buy a property at a foreclosure auction for pennies on the dollar—then quickly resell that property for large and easy windfall gains. In fact, buying foreclosures at auction represents just one type of foreclosure possibility. And that widely promoted approach entails huge risks and uncertain profits. Consequently, experienced and successful investors usually buy *before* or *after* a foreclosure auction—not during.

THE FORECLOSURE PROCESS

The foreclosure process is triggered when a property owner fails to fulfill his or her contractual mortgage obligations. The process ends with the foreclosure sale, which often results in the mortgaged property becoming a lender (or guarantor) REO (real estate owned).

Owner's Default

When property owners default, most commonly they have failed to make their scheduled mortgage payments. But defaults may also occur when owners fail to pay their property taxes, fail to pay some related obligation (homeowners' association fees, a superior mortgage claim, special assessments), transfer a property without lender approval, or undertake renovations, remodeling, or demolition that diminish the value of the property.

Lender Tries to Resolve Problem.   In the early stages of borrower default, the foreclosing lender will encourage, coerce, or threaten the property owner through reminder letters, telephone calls, and credit counseling. If such efforts don't produce acceptable results, the lender's lawyers take over. Talking tough, the lawyers usually threaten foreclosure and warn the property owners to pay up or face dire consequences.

Depending on the lender, its total resolution efforts may continue for anywhere from one to six months, or even longer in some circumstances. If a lender thinks it has a "rush to judgment" competition among multiple parties who are suing the property owners, it may act very quickly. If it believes a loan "workout" looks promising, the lender may choose patience and cooperation.

In contrast to the late 1980s and early 1990s, most lenders today to give borrowers generous opportunity to reinstate or even refinance their delinquent mortgages. That's why even though the current number of mortgages in foreclosure has reached record levels, the number of properties sold at foreclosure auctions has not risen as fast. With more workouts, fewer properties go through a foreclosure sale—especially as compared to the huge REO buildups of 10 to 15 years ago. Nevertheless, opportunities in foreclosures abound. Mortgage lenders (or guarantors) will get the keys to several hundred thousand properties this year. And the number of borrowers who have fallen behind in their payments (and thus are in need of a workout) now totals close to 1.3 million. Given these huge volumes, serious investors can still ferret out great foreclosure bargains.

Filing Legal Notice.   When a lender does finally give up on a workout, its lawyers file either a legal "notice of default" or a "lawsuit to foreclose" (depending on the state). This legal filing and its subsequent posting of notice on the Internet or in newspapers formally announce to (1) the property owners, (2) any other parties who may have legal claims against the owners or their property, and (3) the public in general that legal action is moving forward to force a sale of the property.

At least one month passes between the date of legal filing and the foreclosure sale. More typically, this waiting period ranges between 60 and 180 days. If the property owners file a legal defense to the lender's foreclosure action (e.g., lender violated due process, fraud, consumer rights, truth in lending), the foreclosure sale date may be delayed until after full-blown litigation and trial. Those kinds of legal battles can drag on for a year, two years, or even longer.

Also, to delay a foreclosure sale for *at least* a month or two, property owners may file for bankruptcy. Any bankruptcy filing by the property owners immediately and automatically stays a foreclosure action. To proceed further in its efforts to force a sale, the lender must petition the bankruptcy trustee. Only after the trustee grants permission will the foreclosure process start running again. (In fact, in some situations, a bankruptcy trustee can even annul a foreclosure sale that has already occurred.)

The Foreclosure Sale

Eventually, when defaulting property owners run out of legal defenses or delaying tactics, the foreclosure sale date arrives. At this point, the property is auctioned to the highest cash bidder. On occasion, the winning bid is submitted by a real estate investor (foreclosure specialist), speculator, or even a homebuyer. More likely, though, the lender who has forced the foreclosure sale bids, say, one dollar more than the amount of its unpaid claims (mortgage balance, late fees, accrued interest, attorney fees, foreclosure costs) and walks away with a sheriff's deed to the property. From then on until the lender (or its realty agent) sells the property, that property remains on the lender's books as an REO.

REOs

The most important thing to know concerning foreclosure should be written in capital letters: LENDERS DO NOT WANT TO OWN REAL ESTATE. For a lender (or institutions such as the Federal Housing Administration [FHA], Department of Veterans Affairs [VA], Fannie Mae, Freddie Mac), holding onto an REO that has been acquired through foreclosure rarely seems like a good idea. No matter how much potential the property offers, owners of REOs want to sell quickly. For you, their desire to sell quickly may mean their loss and your gain.

◆ ◆ ◆

Foreclosure offers three possibilities to buy at a bargain price or bargain terms:

1. You can negotiate with the distressed property owners and, if necessary, the foreclosing lender.
2. You can bid at the foreclosure auction.
3. You can negotiate and buy directly from the lender or the "insuring" agency (FHA, VA, Fannie Mae, Freddie Mac) that owns the property as an REO. (This topic is covered in Chapter 7.)

BUYING FROM DISTRESSED OWNERS

Each year in every community, hundreds (sometimes thousands) of property owners hit the financial skids. Divorce, job loss, accident, illness, business failure, and other setbacks render people unable to make their mortgage payments. Rather than effectively deal with their problems as soon as default is imminent, most owners hang on too long, hoping for a miracle to bail them out. Since miracles are rare, most of these people end up staring foreclosure in the face.

At that point, you may be able to help them salvage their credit record and part of their home equity, and at the same time secure a bargain for yourself. Faced with pressures of time and money, distressed property owners may be willing to accept a quick, credit-rescuing sale at a price less than market value.

Approach Owners with Empathy

There's no magic system for successfully buying a property from owners facing foreclosure. These owners must contend with financial troubles, personal anguish, and indecisiveness brought on by mental depression. In addition, they have probably already been attacked by innumerable foreclosure sharks, speculators, bank lawyers, and recent attendees of get-rich-quick foreclosure seminars. These owners are living with the public shame of failure. For all these reasons, and more, they are not easy people to deal with.

But when you develop a sensitive, empathetic, problem-solving approach with someone suffering foreclosure, you may be able to come up with a win-win agreement. Just keep in mind that more than likely, you will compete with foreclosure specialists. A "Here's my offer—take it or leave it" approach will undoubtedly antagonize the owners. It will not favorably distinguish you from a dozen other potential buyers (sharks). So develop your offer and negotiations to preserve what little may be left of the owner's dignity and self-esteem. Perhaps you can share personal information about setbacks you have lived through. Above all, emphasize win-win outcomes. Dire straits or not, no one wants his or her home (property) stolen away.

Investigate, Investigate, Investigate

Although "investigate, investigate, investigate" must guide in all real estate transactions, this maxim especially applies when dealing with homeowners and properties in foreclosure. Unless you do your homework (due diligence), you will waste time and money chasing deals that can never work—or, even worse, you might put together a deal that loses you a fair-sized sum of money.

The Difficulties of Dealing Profitably with Owners in Default

The promoters of "get rich in foreclosures" seminars, tapes, and books greatly exaggerate the possibilities of profiting from property owners who face foreclosure. The enticing scenarios imagined by these promoters put you in the picture with high-equity sellers who hold a nonqualifying assumable mortgage. You offer the sellers a few thousand dollars in cash and agree to make up their past-due mortgage payments. The sellers deed you their property and move out. You then put a tenant in the property, collect rents, and pay the property expenses and scheduled mortgage payments. Or, alternatively, you fix up the property, put it on the market, and sell for a fat profit. Regardless of which strategy you choose, buying foreclosures can make you wealthy very fast—at least that's the pitch of the foreclosure gurus.

Admittedly, such simple deals are great when you can find them. Unfortunately, it's rarely that easy. When you talk with property owners in foreclosure, you're far more likely to uncover a minefield of problems that you must crisscross with skill and creativity. Here are some of them.

Mortgage Debt Exceeds Market Value.   Many homeowners in foreclosure owe more than their properties are worth. To make a deal work, you must talk the lender into a "short sale"; that is, the lender voluntarily reduces the amount of its outstanding claim so that you receive a "fair" profit for agreeing to make up past-due payments and take over the loan. It happens, but you face a tough sell.

Nonquals Are Tough to Find.   Most mortgages today do not automatically permit assumptions. Finding a homeowner in foreclosure who actually has a nonqualifying assumable is like finding the proverbial needle in a haystack.

Qualifying Assumptions Are Limited.   Today's FHA and VA mortgages do permit assumptions, but only by credit-qualifying owner-occupants. If your credit or income is shaky, or if you plan to "flip" the property or put tenants in it, neither FHA nor VA will approve the assumption.

Multiple Creditors, Multiple Title Problems.   Many homeowners who face foreclosure must also contend with the claims of other creditors. Check to see if any of these creditors has filed a *lis pendens* or a tax lien (Internal Revenue Service or other taxing authority) or have secured a judgment against the homeowners.[1] To gain clear title, you may have to clean up and settle with a variety of creditors—not just one mortgage lender.

---

1. A *lis pendens* is a recorded legal document giving notice that an action affecting a property has been filed in court.

Workout with Credit Counselors.   Most lenders today (especially FHA, VA, Fannie Mae) encourage financially troubled homeowners to seek credit counseling and loan workout with nonprofit agencies such as CCCA (Credit Counseling Centers of America). Neither the homeowners nor the lenders may need a profit-minded workout specialist.

Save Equity through Bankruptcy.   In many states, homeowners can file bankruptcy and save all or part of their home equity. True, 15 or 20 years ago, only the most shameless or financially ruined Americans would consider bankruptcy. Now, bankruptcy serves as just another tool of financial planning, and around 1.5 million couples and individuals elect to file for bankruptcy each year. When someone can get rid of all those credit card balances and unpaid medical bills—and at the same time save their most valuable asset (their home)—why do a workout with a foreclosure specialist?

Bankruptcy Doesn't Ruin Credit.   As a related issue, the threat of "ruined" credit doesn't instill the same fear in Americans today that it did a decade ago. Today it's not easy to actually *ruin* your credit. After a bankruptcy discharge, people with steady jobs can immediately obtain credit cards (albeit secured), car loans, and home loans (e.g., seller financing, subprime lenders). After a bankruptcy, with two years of clean credit, FHA, VA, and sometimes even Fannie Mae/Freddie Mac lenders will approve reestablished borrowers. Again, this fact reduces the probability that you can persuade homeowners to transfer a large chunk of their home equity to you so that they can "save their credit."

Estimating Repair and Renovation Costs.   Before you finalize a preforeclosure purchase with a property owner, you must also thoroughly inspect the property and accurately estimate the costs of necessary repairs, renovations, and perhaps environmental cleanup. Too often, in their eagerness to do a foreclosure deal, unsuspecting buyers gloss over the inspection and make only an eyeball guesstimate of expected costs. Much to their dismay, they soon learn that slick foreclosure sellers can put one over on naive buyers, just as slick foreclosure sharks may at times take advantage of distressed property owners.

Prequalify Homeowners and Properties

By detailing various negatives in the preceding discussion, I don't mean to say that you can't make money working with property owners facing foreclosure. You can. But only if you strictly prequalify the homeowners and the property. Before moving forward toward a workout, check its potential by answering the following eight questions:

1. Do the homeowners enjoy substantial equity in their property?
2. If necessary, is the lender likely to cooperate in a short sale?
3. Will the lender permit you to assume the mortgage? As an investor? As an owner-occupant? At what interest rate? If no assumption, will the lender waive the prepayment penalty (if any)?
4. Can you satisfy yourself through a title check or title insurance that the sellers can convey a marketable title, that is, a title free of consequential clouds (actual and potential)?
5. Do the homeowners rule out bankruptcy as a solution to their financial distress?
6. Would the property owners lose more economically in a bankruptcy than they would stand to gain? (As noted previously, bankrupts may emerge from bankruptcy with their unsecured debts extinguished and their most valuable assets [IRA, 401(k), home equity, life insurance cash value, furniture, clothing, car] preserved.)[2]
7. Can you *firmly* establish how much you must spend to repair, redecorate, and renovate the property?
8. Is the potential profit margin large enough to justify your investment of time, money, effort, and opportunity cost (i.e., the profits of other deals you pass up to invest in this one)? Use the following tally to help you answer this question:

Market value after improvements	$_____
less	
Acquisition price (cash, notes, assumed mortgages)	$_____
Mortgage assumption fee	$_____
Legal fees	$_____
Back property taxes and assessments	$_____
Back payments and late fees	$_____
Closing costs	$_____
Cost of improvements	$_____
Holding costs until sold or rented	$_____

---

2. Congress (at the request of bankers and credit card companies) is now moving toward tighter bankruptcy laws. If enacted, such tightening may abolish or dilute the preferential treatment of home equity. As proposed, the new bankruptcy law would also force most petitioners to pay back part of their debts. Unlike today, most people would not emerge from bankruptcy debt free (except for their mortgage, if any).

Miscellaneous $_____
Time and effort (imputed value) $_____
Opportunity costs (imputed value) $_____
equals
Profit potential $_____

Do your answers to these eight questions reveal any deal killers? Does the amount of profit potential look high enough to offset your risks? Yes? Then you've discovered what could prove to be a profitable transaction.

Finding Homeowners in Default (Prefiling)

Ideally, you would like to learn the names of homeowners who are heading into foreclosure before their lender files a formal legal notice. Although this is difficult, you might try the following techniques:

Networking.   Choose an area of town that offers good potential.[3] Then develop strong networking relationships with some of the people who know the neighborhood such as mail carriers, delivery truck drivers, school personnel (teachers, principals), social service workers, busybody residents, real estate agents, local merchants, church leaders, and credit counseling personnel.

Through this network of contacts, you want to learn who's thinking about selling her home, who's been recently laid off, who's spending above his means, who's having trouble paying the bills. Obviously, much of this information falls into the category of gossip. It may not be easy for an outsider to ferret it out, and the information you receive may not prove reliable.

Nevertheless, routinely talking with people, making subtle inquiries, and staying attuned to what's happening in the community (and especially your "farm" area) can at times turn up a great find of valuable insider knowledge. Many people who succeed in real estate do keep their ears to the ground.

Mortgage Collections Personnel.   Some foreclosure specialists develop personal relationships with the lending personnel responsible for collecting delinquent accounts. Of course, nearly all lenders prohibit their employees from revealing private information about customers. But we all know that what is prohibited and what is practiced can deviate substantially.

---

3. For example, an area where many people live who have been affected by a major local employer's downsizing.

Perhaps an even greater obstacle than privacy now thwarts this approach. That obstacle is distance. In the good old days, local lending personnel handled the great majority of mortgage lending and collections. Today, a mortgage loan in Peoria, Illinois, may be owned by a bank headquartered in San Francisco and serviced by a company located in Boston. To the extent that out-of-town personnel deal with the early stages of homeowner default, your chances of getting special information diminishes.

Driving Neighborhoods.   When you really get to know the territory, you can keep your eye out for homes that begin to appear unkempt, or perhaps suffer a sudden or mysterious vacancy. Often these indicators signal a property owner in financial distress. Asking a neighbor or two may confirm your suspicions. You may discover a prime prospect with whom you can negotiate—before the rush of foreclosure vultures wing in to compete for the pickings.

Finding Homeowners (Postfiling)

Once a lender moves its collection efforts into the legal arena, you can learn the names and addresses of distressed property owners in at least four possible ways:

1. Personally visit the clerk of civil court's office and ask to see the list(s) of foreclosure filings.[4]
2. Subscribe to a specialized legal newspaper that reports court filings.
3. Read the "legal notices" section of your local daily (or weekly) newspaper.
4. Go on-line. Although currently many counties throughout the United States are lagging behind in the Internet revolution, within a few years even the most backward (or obstinate) will post foreclosure filings in cyberspace.

Remember, as soon as the foreclosure (default) filing hits the public records, competition for quality deals may get heated. Success at this point will depend on how well you present yourself and your offer to the distressed property owners.

---

4. In many counties (such as my own), the clerk of court provides only legal descriptions, not street addresses. This limited information means more work to translate clerk data into usable data. It's also further evidence that the foreclosure process seems designed to *minimize* the selling price of a property.

Meeting the Property Owners

When you visit with the property owners, you must not only try to make a good investment but also develop an approach that will aid the troubled owners and end their distress. If everything goes according to plan, the owners will receive cash for some of their equity, their credit will be salvaged, and you will acquire title to the property.

To avoid a quick brush-off, do not phone the owners until after you have personally met with them. A personal visit not only is more professional but also allows you to closely inspect the property.

Begin with an introduction of who you are and why you're there. Suggest assistance. Mention that you have discovered through your sources that the property might be for sale. If, in fact, the property is for sale, you can begin to discuss the outlines of a transaction. If the owner has not put the property up for sale, a different approach is required.

Time is on your side when you are negotiating to purchase property in foreclosure. Pressure is on the owner to remedy the situation so as not to lose the property. It is to your advantage to explain that while you're interested in making a good investment, it will also be a good decision for the owners, who can realize some cash and prevent a serious blemish on their credit record.

During periods of stress, property owners often hide the truth about their personal matters. Understandably, the loss of home or property stirs the emotions. Therefore don't rely on owner statements. Verify all details about the property and its liens.

Here are several suggested approaches to open negotiations with an owner in foreclosure:

> "If you'll allow me to make a complete financial analysis of the property, I can be back within twenty-four hours with a firm offer that might solve your current dilemma."
>
> "My purpose in being here is to pay you cash for your equity, which you would probably lose in a foreclosure sale. Therefore, by working with me, you can save your credit, move away much better off, and start over."
>
> "May I review the documents on your home? Do you have a copy of the mortgage, the title policy, and the loan payment record?"

As a professional investor, you should be able to act faster and offer better results to a troubled owner than anyone else. Do not be put off by cosmetic damage to the house as long as the house is structurally sound.

A run-down house usually presents more opportunity for the investor. In fact, the more cosmetically run-down, the better. Every easily curable defect offers profitable opportunity to the shrewd distressed-property investor and renovator.

Each defect must be noted; then an accurate cost estimate to correct such defects must be made. Your deal with the owner will then be made on the basis of the estimated repair cost, plus a reasonable profit. Once you acquire the property, make every effort to renovate it within the budget arrived at under your repair-cost estimate.

You need not be a jack-of-all-trades and repair everything yourself. But it's essential to discover problems and know how much it will cost to repair each one. You must know what homes typically sell for in that neighborhood. It is obviously poor judgment to invest in a property if the total cost of renovation plus purchase price is greater than its fixed-up market value.

By thoroughly checking out the entire property, carefully analyzing it, then honestly evaluating the sales price once renovation is complete, you can feel confident that your risk has been minimized and you will realize a worthwhile gain.

When you've analyzed the numbers carefully, and the total costs of renovation and acquisition exceed the resale value, don't necessarily abandon the project. Go back to the troubled owner (or mortgage lender) and reopen negotiations. Point out that you must make a reasonable profit. If you're still unable to arrive at a good deal, look elsewhere.

Two More Potential Problems

Up to this point, I have assumed that you were able to (1) meet directly with the property owners; (2) explore the exact nature of their situation; (3) evaluate the property; and (4) work through potential win-win-win (owners-lender-you) possibilities. But you may not be able to meet directly with the owners if they are represented by a realty firm or if they have abandoned the property and moved from the community.

Realty Firms.   I have found it difficult to work with property owners in foreclosure when they have listed their home for sale with a realty firm. Most run-of-the-mill real estate agents know next to nothing about foreclosure workouts. Rather than help, they hinder the creative, cooperative process that workouts require.

Second, real estate agents want to be paid in cash at closing. When a sales agent expects to pull $5,000 or $10,000 out of the owner's equity, it squeezes your negotiating range. The amount of that commission comes straight from monies that would otherwise be available to you, the lenders, and the property owners.

On occasion, though, I have dealt with savvy agents who understand that if they insist on a full commission, they will kill the deal. In one such transaction, the agent agreed to accept just $1,000 in lieu of $4,500. (As this agent realized, he wasn't giving up a fee of $4,500 for a fee of $1,000. Instead he was earning a fee of $1,000 in lieu of earning nothing at all.)

Realty Agents Can Hurt Property Owners.   Sometimes realty agents actually hurt the property owners' efforts to sell their home by accepting an overpriced listing. Say the distressed owners owe $180,000 on a home with a market value of $200,000. To get the listing, an agent may lead the owners into falsely believing that they can get the property sold at a price of $210,000. "Great!" the owners think, "We will be able to net $15,000 to $18,000."

Sadly, 60 to 90 days pass, and the overpriced property doesn't sell. The owners are panicked. The lawyers are closing in for the kill. But now the listing is stale. To really grab buyer attention requires a severe price cut to maybe $190,000. By this time, though, the unpaid mortgage balance along with missed payments and late fees may total around $200,000. There's no way a sale will clear out the mortgage debt and the sales commission. More often than not, foreclosure becomes imminent.

Quick FSBO Beats Realty Listing.   When you talk with low-equity distressed sellers, try to persuade them not to list with a realty firm in hopes of getting some pie-in-the-sky sales price. Property owners almost always stand a better chance of minimizing loss by going for a quick, discounted FSBO (for-sale-by-owner) sale. In some cases, they should even *pay* someone (cash, note, barter) to take over their loan—or to buy the property and arrange new financing.

Property owners in foreclosure must forget the idea of maximizing gain. They must focus on eliminating the possibility of severe loss. Most distressed property owners must be forced to see that time is not their friend. Time is their enemy. The frequently heard homeowner refrain, "We're going to try this for a while and see what happens," does not make sense.

Sometimes you fish; sometimes you cut bait. Foreclosure means it's time to cut bait. It's not prudent for property owners to keep throwing the line into new waters. To work successfully with these distressed property owners, you must repeatedly encourage them to act immediately.

Sidestepping the Sales Agent.   To avoid working with noncreative, uncooperative sales agents who currently represent homeowners in foreclosure, recall a technique first mentioned in Chapter 5. First, a reminder: Do not contact listed property owners in person. Do not discuss the property or its owners with a sales agent. If you violate these warnings, the sellers may end up owing a sales commission—even if you wait to buy the property until after the real estate agency listing has expired.

Rather, write the sellers a letter. Tell them you wish them well in trying to sell their house through a realty agent. However, should these efforts not prove fruitful, ask the owners to contact you immediately after the listing expires. Tell them that without the obstacle of a sales commission, you believe that a mutually satisfactory price and terms can be arranged.

Date of Expiration.   You might ask a friend (or acquaintance) who works as a realty agent to find out when the owners' current listing contract ends. About two weeks before that date, write the owners and again express your genuine interest in buying their property. You might tell them that even if they wish to relist their property, they can write your name into the listing agreement as an exception. In that way, the owners remain free to negotiate directly with you without becoming liable for payment of a sales commission.

By operating in this manner, you are not behaving unethically. Nor are you cheating the sales agent. Realty agents earn their commissions only when they "procure" a sale. You are not in any way relying on the services of the listing realty firm. Therefore that firm is not legally or morally entitled to a commission.

Vacant Houses.   To discover a vacant house in foreclosure means to discover both a problem and an opportunity. It's a problem because you may have to do some detective work to locate the owners. Unless the owners have purposely tried to disappear, though, you can probably locate them in one of the following five ways:

1.   Contact nearby neighbors to learn the owners' whereabouts, or the names of friends or family who would know.
2.   Call the owners' telephone number and see if you get a "number changed" message.
3.   Ask the post office to provide the owners' forwarding address.
4.   Find out where the owners were employed and ask coworkers.
5.   Contact the school that the owners' children attended and ask where their school records were sent.

After you locate the owners comes opportunity. Because they have abandoned the property, they probably aren't entertaining any pie-in-the-sky hopes for a sale at an inflated price. At this point, they may view any offer you make them as "found money."

In some cases, you will learn that the owners have split up and gone their separate ways. This type of situation raises another problem: Especially in hostile separations, working out an agreement with one owner in the belief that you can convince the other(s) to go along often proves futile. To avoid this difficulty, negotiate with all owners simultaneously.

◆ ◆ ◆

Property owners who default and face foreclosure need help. Sadly, few act quickly to cut their losses. Rather, they believe the illusion that "something will turn up." They suffer through denial, depression, and indecision, which further block productive solutions. All in all, for you to successfully address the emotional and financial distress of such owners requires (1) an empathetic demeanor, (2) perseverance, (3) extensive fact gathering, and (4) creative, outside-the-box thinking.

When you become the type of person who can bring these skills together, you're on your way to a profitable career as a foreclosure specialist. But before you can truly succeed, you have one more skill to develop: You must learn to negotiate with the mortgage lenders and lien holders who hold claims against the owners' property.

Satisfying Lenders and Lien Holders

Before you talk specific numbers in your preforeclosure negotiations, always identify who holds legal claims against the property and in what amounts. As a starting point, ask the property owners for this information. However, before you irrevocably commit yourself to a deal, verify the owners' figures through a title report issued by a lawyer or title insurer. Also verify claims through direct contact with claimants. Your investigation may turn up claimants in the following categories:

- ◆ Mortgage holders (first, second, third . . .)
- ◆ Taxing authorities (federal, state, local)
- ◆ County or city special assessments
- ◆ Homeowners' association fees and assessments
- ◆ Unpaid sewage or water bills
- ◆ Special assessment or bonding districts
- ◆ Judgment creditors
- ◆ Mechanics liens for labor or materials provided to the property
- ◆ Spousal (or ex-spousal) rights, including dower and curtesy
- ◆ Lost heirs

One way or another, you will have to decide how you want to satisfy the claimants you find. You can use some combination of the following four techniques:

1. Pay off immediately any or all claimants for the full amount of their claims.
2. Pay off over time any or all claimants for the full amount of their claims.
3. Pay off immediately any or all claimants at a mutually agreed discount.
4. Pay off over time any or all claims at a mutually agreed discount.

To illustrate by example, consider a house that would sell in a market value transaction for around $110,000. The owner agrees to deed the property to you if you will agree to take care of all the outstanding liens, which total $105,000:

First mortgage	$78,000
Second mortgage	$18,000
Roofing contractor	$3,000
Credit card judgment	$6,000
Total	$105,000

Obviously, in this situation, the deal is not workable. The potential profit margin of $5,000 is much too low. But what if you could persuade the first mortgage lender to extinguish its old $78,000 balance and write you a new loan on the property in the amount of $88,000 (80 percent loan-to-value ratio) and waive all closing costs? You then work out discount deals with the other creditors. After negotiations, your total payoff looks like this:

First mortgage	$78,000
Second mortgage	$10,000
Roofing contractor	$2,000
Credit card judgment	$2,500
Total	$92,500

By combining $88,000 in proceeds from the new loan and $4,500 in out-of-pocket cash, you have just bought a $110,000 property for $92,500.

All Parties Are Better Off. If this property had completed its trip through foreclosure, only the first-mortgage lender stood a chance of emerging whole. But more than likely, after adding up continuing lost interest payments, late fees, attorney fees, foreclosure expenses, and REO risks and carrying charges, the first-mortgage lender, too, may have ended up worse off. As for the other parties, here's how they would gain from this workout proposal:

◆ *The property owners.* Theoretically they lost $5,000 in equity, but as a practical matter, that was $5,000 they were never going to see. Far more important, the workout not only kept a foreclosure entry off their credit record but also rescued them from a possible deficiency judgment.

◆ *The second-mortgage holder.* Again, theoretically the property held enough value to liquidate the full $18,000. As a practical matter, this second mortgagee was better off to take a quick and sure $10,000 and cut its potential losses. Owing to the low prices bid at foreclosure sales, in all likelihood, this lender would have ended up empty-handed.[5]

◆ *Roofing contractor.* Not a chance of collecting any money from a foreclosure sale. (Accepting $2,000 beats nothing.)

◆ *Credit card judgment.* Not a chance of collecting any money from a foreclosure sale. (Again, $2,500 beats nothing.)

In any given situation, the specific numbers could come out better or worse for the respective parties—including you. It all depends on the parties' relative negotiating power and skills, their need for cash, their need to avoid risk, and their capacity for understanding. To succeed in the face of this ambiguity, entrepreneurial workout specialists typically develop a strong ability to size up people and situations. You have to figure out fast whether a deal looks doable.

Answer the following questions: Who is willing to settle for how much? Who stands to lose the most? Who needs cash now? Who is willing to wait? What concessions will the first-mortgage lender make, if any? Do the parties truly understand the likely adverse outcome of a foreclosure sale?

Sometimes Losing Less Is Winning. In a foreclosure sale, only the lawyers win. More often than not, all other parties lose. But think what happens when all parties agree to work with each other—rather than against each other. You can create an outcome where everyone walks away better off. Maybe they receive less than they hoped for, certainly less than they were theoretically entitled to, but far more than they could expect from a bidder at a foreclosure auction.

---

5. Alternatively, of course, a second mortgage lender might bid at the foreclosure auction or step in and remedy the owners' default(s). Usually, lenders who hold second mortgages will elect this option only when the market value of the property greatly exceeds the amount of all liens superior to that of the second (or third) mortgagee.

PROFIT FROM THE FORECLOSURE AUCTION

Although foreclosure sales typically lose money for lenders, lien holders, and property owners, savvy bidders can turn these sales into big profits. But it's not easy. Bidding blind doesn't work. You have to do your homework.

Why Foreclosures Sell for Less than Market Value

A typical foreclosed property sells at a price much lower than its market value. Why? Because foreclosure auctions don't come close to meeting the criteria of a market value transaction:

Sale Characteristics

Market Value Sale	Foreclosure Auction
No seller or buyer duress	Forced sale
Buyer and seller well informed	Scarce information
60- to 120-day marketing period	5 minutes or less selling time
Financing on typical terms	Spot cash (or within 24 hours)
Marketable title	No title guarantees
Warranty deed	Sheriff's (or trustee) deed
Seller disclosures	No seller disclosures
Close inspection of physical condition	No physical inspection
Yard sign	Rarely a yard sign
"Homes for sale" ads	Legal notice listing

As you can see, foreclosure auctions seem purposely designed to yield the *lowest possible sales price.* They take place under conditions that violate all principles of effective marketing.

Adverse Sales Conditions.   The auction sellers (sheriff's office, clerk of court, trustee) provide potential buyers no information about a property other than its legal description. They insist on cash. They offer no "contingency" contracts to allow buyers time to arrange financing. The seller rarely holds an open house or sets up appointments to show the property. Buyers must take the property "as is" with absolutely no guarantees or assurances about title quality, physical condition, or environmental hazards.

No Guarantee of Vacancy.   The foreclosure authorities don't even agree to convey the property free of occupants (owners, tenants, squatters). You may buy a property at a foreclosure auction and spend several months (or longer) trying to evict the people staying there. Clever occupants can use many delay tactics. Here are several:

- ◆ File bankruptcy.
- ◆ Claim that the foreclosure sale violated due process.
- ◆ Organize a "people's protest" of some sort.
- ◆ Continuously make idle promises, "We'll be out by the end of next week."
- ◆ Seek intervention from some type of child welfare office or other social service agency.
- ◆ Claim a female in the household is pregnant.
- ◆ Seek protection under a lease agreement (even though foreclosure sales nullify leases if made after the mortgage on the property was recorded in the public records).
- ◆ Threaten you or the property with physical harm unless you permit the occupants to stay on for "just a little while."

Although it's rarely a question of *if* you can get the people out—certainly you can—it's commonly a question of *when*, and at what amount of cost and effort.

◆ ◆ ◆

For most would-be buyers, the risk, expense, and aggravation of foreclosure sales deter them from even showing up to bid. When you consider the lame marketing efforts, the adverse conditions of sale, and the potential occupancy problem, is it any wonder that foreclosed properties deserve to sell at a fraction of their market value?

Make the Adverse Sales Efforts Work for You

You might look at the foreclosure sales process and say, "Too many potential problems. No way do I want to take those kinds of risks. Besides, how could I ever come up with so much cash on short notice?" Clearly, that's the attitude of the great majority of real estate investors. It explains why at most sales the foreclosing lender "wins" the bid at a price equal to (or slightly above) its outstanding balance.

Overcome the Risks of Bidding.   Risk looms large to block your path to foreclosure profits. So the key to savvy bidding lies in knowing as much about the property as due diligence demands.

How can you get this information? First, meet with the property owners to talk over preforeclosure workout possibilities. Even when those discussions end without agreement, you'll still have been able to learn about the property (market value, fix-up needs, improvement opportunities), the neighborhood, and the owner's intentions. This step alone puts you way ahead of the game. Second, research the title records yourself. If you find no obvious problems, get the quality of title verified by a lawyer or title insurer.

Time and Money.   Meeting with owners and checking the title will cost you time, legwork, and perhaps several hundred dollars. But if you buy only one property out of every ten you investigate, you can still turn a handsome profit. Just make sure the market value of the fixed-up property will exceed the total amount of your bid price and fix-up costs by a healthy profit margin. (When buying as an investor, seek *at least* a 20 to 30 percent profit margin depending on the quality and marketability of the property.)

Inferior Liens Wiped Out.   When you buy a property in foreclosure, all liens inferior to the one being foreclosed will usually get wiped out. Assume that the first mortgagee is prosecuting the foreclosure. You win the auction by outbidding this lender by $1,000. The first mortgagee takes what it's owed. The next claim in line takes whatever money is left.

Judgment creditors, mechanics liens, second mortgagees, tenant leases, and any other claims disappear. Only existing tax liens, special assessments, and perhaps past-due homeowners' association fees may survive.

For any specific property, discuss the "priority" and "wipeout" issues with legal counsel. But realize that many (if not all) of those preforeclosure liens that clouded the title will vanish. This fact torques up your preforeclosure negotiating leverage. Creditors who don't settle before foreclosure will likely end up with nothing after foreclosure—unless, of course, they too plan to show up at the foreclosure auction and bid a price that exceeds all claims superior to the lien holder who is forcing the foreclosure.

How to Arrange Financing

After you put together enough information to adequately manage the risks of buying at foreclosure, you still face the problem of financing. How are you going to get the cash to close the sale? If you lack wealth or credit, you're probably out of luck. Unless you bring in a money partner, you really can't play the foreclosure game.

However, if you can even temporarily raise cash—for example, take out a home equity loan, get a cash advance on a credit card, sell (or borrow against) stocks, or maybe take out a signature loan—you can bid at a foreclosure auction. Then, after the foreclosure paperwork clears, you can place an interim or longer-term mortgage loan against the property and pay off your short-term creditors.

Investors who routinely buy foreclosed properties generally establish a line of personal credit at a bank. Then they can draw on the money whenever they need it. Or they maintain cash balances (money market funds) in amounts sufficient to cover their usual buying patterns.

The Foreclosure Sale: Summing Up

Few real estate investors choose to bid regularly at foreclosure sales. The great majority prefer to avoid the time, expense, risks, and financing difficulties that foreclosure buying entails. You, too, may agree with this view.

But if you are willing to learn the foreclosure game (as it's played in your locale), do your homework, and manage your risks, you can build profits quickly. You can often buy properties at foreclosure auctions for a fraction of their market value. Your challenge is to learn which of these properties meet the test of a true bargain—and which ones to avoid because they carry severe risks, expensive problems, or excessive (upside-down) financing.

Naturally, too, foreclosure opportunities expand and diminish as real estate markets weaken or strengthen. In strong real estate markets, foreclosure bargains become ever more difficult to locate. In contrast, economic downturns provide manna for foreclosure specialists.

7

PROFITING FROM REOS
AND OTHER SPECIAL SALES

When a mortgage lender "wins" the bid at a foreclosure auction, the foreclosed property ends up as a "real estate owned" (REO). The lender may hold on to the property and try to resell it. More typical today, though, the lender cashes out its interest and turns the property over to either the U.S. Department of Housing and Urban Development (HUD), the U.S. Department of Veterans Affairs (VA), the Federal National Mortgage Association (Fannie Mae), or the Federal Home Loan Mortgage Corporation (Freddie Mac). In any of these situations, you may find an opportunity to buy at a bargain price, bargain terms, or possibly both.

THE BENEFITS OF BUYING DIRECT
FROM A MORTGAGE LENDER

In nearly every instance, you can say one thing for certain about an REO: The lender (or guarantor) wants to sell the property as quickly as possible. Mortgage lenders like to make loans and collect monthly payments. They do not like to own and manage vacant or rental houses. As a result, they will often grant buyers of their REOs favorable terms such as low or no closing costs, below-market interest rates, and low down payments.

If the property needs fix-up work (that the lender would prefer not to remedy), the lender may accept offers at deep discounts from market value. Just as important, before closing the sale of their REOs, lenders normally clean up title problems, evict unauthorized occupants, and bring all past-due property tax payments and assessments up to date. Some lenders, too, permit buyers to write contingency offers subject to appraisal and professional inspection.

Safer than Buying at the Foreclosure Sale

Buying an REO directly from a lender typically presents no more risk than buying directly from any other property owner.[1] Normally, you can buy an REO much more safely than you could have bought the same property at its foreclosure sale. Depending on the lender's motivation, its internal policies and procedures, and the property loan-to-value ratio (LTV) at the time of the foreclosure sale, you might even be able to buy at a price lower than market value.

Why a Lower Price?

Let's say the market value of a property at the time of its foreclosure sale was $165,000. The lender's claims against the property totaled $160,000. To win the property away from the lender, you would have had to bid more than $160,000—a price that's too high to yield a profit.

However, once the lender owns the property and tallies its expected holding costs, Realtor's commission, and the risks of seeing the (probably) vacant property vandalized, it may decide to cut its losses. It may accept an offer from you within the range of $140,000 to $150,000 (especially if you offer cash, which you may borrow from some other mortgage lender).

FINDING LENDER REOS

In desperate times, REO lenders often turn to mass marketing and highly advertised public auctions to unload their REOs. In stable and strong markets, they generally (but not always) play it low key. No lender wants to publicize the fact that it's "throwing down-on-their-luck families out of their homes." Absent tough times and mass advertising, you can find

---

1. Several exceptions might include (1) states where the foreclosed owners may have a right of redemption; (2) cases where the foreclosed owners still retain some legal right to challenge the validity of the foreclosure sale; or (3) instances where a bankruptcy trustee or the Internal Revenue Service (tax lien) is entitled to bring the property within their powers. Rarely would any of these potential claims be worth losing sleep over. But before closing an REO purchase, you might want to run these issues by legal counsel.

REOs in three different ways: (1) Follow up after a foreclosure sale; (2) cold call lender REO personnel; and (3) locate Realtors who typically get REO listings.

Follow Up after Foreclosure

You can learn of lender REOs by attending foreclosure auctions. When a lender casts a top bid for a property in which you're interested, button-hole the bidder and start talking business. Or try to schedule an appointment to see the officer who takes charge of the management and disposition of REOs. When you show the lender how your bargain offer will actually save (make?) the bank money, you'll be on your way to closing a deal.

Beware of the stall. Nearly every financial institution is run by standard operating procedures, management committees, and other precautionary rules that frequently work against sensible decisions. If you run into a bureaucratic stone wall, you must persevere. The reward of following through doesn't just lie in getting a good deal on a property now. More important, you will build personal relationships that will open the bank's doors for you in future transactions.

Cold Call REO Personnel

All mortgage lenders experience at least a few borrower defaults. No one has yet designed a foolproof system for predicting which loan applicants will fail to pay. It follows, then, that at one time or another, all mortgage lenders must end up with REOs—even if they eventually pass them along to HUD, VA, or some other guarantor.

Sometimes, too, lenders pick up REOs without going through foreclosure. During the last real estate downturn, many lenders would open their morning mail to find the keys to a house, a deed, and a note from the distressed owners, "We're out of here. It's your problem now."

To find REOs that lenders have acquired through foreclosure or "deed-in-lieu" transfers, you can cold call mortgage lenders. You might ask for a list of their REOs. This technique, though, seldom turns up much. For various reasons, lenders may keep a tight hold on this information. Nevertheless, it doesn't cost to ask.

Until you establish relationships with REO personnel, you may find that the following approach works better: Rather than ask for a complete list of REOs, narrow your focus. Tell lenders what you're specifically looking for in terms of location, size, price range, floor plan, condition, or other features. In that way, a lender can answer your request without disclosing the full number of REOs within its inventory.

Locate Specialty Realtors

Many mortgage lenders *avoid* (though they do make exceptions) selling directly to REO investors for two reasons: (1) As mentioned, they don't like the unfavorable publicity, and (2) they want to promote good relations with Realtors.[2] Because most mortgage lenders expect Realtors to bring them new loan business, the lenders can't then turn around and become FSBO (for sale by owner) dealers. "You scratch my back and I'll scratch yours" sets the rules in business.

As one part of your efforts to find REOs, cultivate relationships with Realtors who specialize in this market. (In fact, HUD, VA, Fannie Mae, and Freddie Mac almost always sell their REOs through Realtors.) In most cities, you can easily find REO specialists by looking through newspaper classified real estate ads.

Once you have identified several advertised foreclosure specialists, give each one a call. Learn their backgrounds. Do they only dabble in the field of REOs and foreclosures? Or do they make this field their full-time business? For example, when I recently telephoned REO specialist John Huguenard in Orlando, Florida, he talked with me for an hour and a half about property availability, detailed financing and purchase procedures, hot areas of town, rehab potential, estimating repair costs, portfolio lenders, strategies for buying and managing properties as well as selecting tenants, and a dozen other related topics.

At one point during our conversation, he asked, "I'll bet you haven't talked to any other agents who know as much as I do about REOs and foreclosures, have you? I've been doing this for twenty-three years. Last year, I sold ninety houses and rehabbed sixteen others for my own account." John was right. I hadn't.

Hire a Professional.   John is the kind of real estate professional you want to find. Although many realty agents claim expertise in REOs and foreclosures ("Sure, I can do that for you"), only a few make it their prime activity, day in and day out, year after year. When you work with an agent who's really in the know, you won't have to do your own legwork and door knocking. Your agent will screen properties as soon as—if not before—they come onto the market. You will then be notified immediately.

Plus, specialty agents with in-depth knowledge will also stay on top of the finance plans that portfolio, government, and conventional lenders

---

2. Also, most lenders don't want to waste time with all of those investor wanna-bes who have just read a "nothing-down" book or "graduated" from a foreclosure guru's seminar.

are offering to homebuyers and investors. (Again, for example, John Huguenard knew of portfolio lenders doing 100 percent LTV investor loans for investor acquisition and rehab.)

HUD, VA, Fannie, and Freddie Won't Sell Direct to Buyers.   No matter what approach to acquiring REOs and foreclosures you choose to follow, you will benefit by talking with realty pros who make the business a career. As noted earlier, though, if you buy an REO from HUD, VA, Fannie Mae, or Freddie Mac, you *must* process your offer through a licensed real estate agent. Only in certain exceptional circumstances would any of these organizations deal directly with a potential buyer.

To guide your discussions (remember, credibility counts) with these pros, you'll need to learn the general procedures and practices that each of these respective organizations follows.

HUD HOMES AND OTHER HUD PROPERTIES

Each year the FHA (Federal Housing Administration), a division of HUD, insures hundreds of thousands of new mortgage loans. (Nationwide, the total number of outstanding FHA mortgages runs into the millions.) FHA loans are originated by banks, savings institutions, mortgage bankers, mortgage brokers, credit unions, and other types of mortgage lenders.

If borrowers fail to repay these lenders as scheduled, the owner of the mortgage may force the property into a foreclosure sale. Rather than keep the property in its own REO portfolio, however, the lender turns in a claim to HUD (FHA's parent). HUD then pays the lender the amount due under its mortgage insurance coverage and acquires the foreclosed property. Next, HUD puts the property (along with all the others it has acquired in similar fashion) up for sale to the general public.

In some cities such as Atlanta, Georgia, HUD may sell as many as 1,000 properties a year. In the San Francisco Bay Area, HUD's annual sales may total fewer than 150 homes. Depending on the strength of the housing market and the geographic area, the number and selection of HUD properties will vary widely. Still, every area can be counted on to have at least some HUD homes.

Like all sources of bargain properties, HUD homes do offer profit opportunities to investors. But you cannot bid blindly and expect to snag a great buy. Investors and homebuyers must first do their homework (through neighborhood and property value analysis). Only then can you confidently buy properties for substantially less than their market value (after fix-up work).

Although HUD is best known for selling houses, you may actually be able to buy any of the following types of HUD properties:

- Vacant lots
- Single-family detached residences
- Duplex or two units on one lot
- Triplex (three units)
- Fourplex (a four-unit building)
- A planned unit development (PUD)
- Condominiums

Now let's look at several of HUD's most important practices and procedures.[3]

Homeowners versus Investors

In the contest for HUD homes, HUD definitely favors owner-occupants over investors in two ways: (1) Owner-occupants get first choice, and (2) HUD offers FHA low- or nothing-down insured mortgages only to homebuyers, not to investors.

Homebuyers Get First Choice. During the first five days after a HUD home hits the market, HUD will accept bids only from homebuyers. If the property doesn't sell, for the next five days, HUD opens the bid process to both investors and homebuyers. But the competition isn't equal. The investor can win the bid only if no qualified homebuyer submits an offer. In other words, even when an investor offers a higher price (net to HUD), the homebuyer gets the property. It's only during the third sales period (provided, of course, that the property hasn't sold during either of the two previous periods) that HUD evaluates bids without regard to buyer status.

You might think that homebuyers would snap up all of the great buys and investors would be stuck with the dregs. On the one hand, that may be true. If as an investor you're looking for "red ribbon deals" at a bargain price, your pickings will be slim. That type of HUD home typically sells fast. On the other hand, if you're looking to buy a "fixer," you can often find some good buys because first-time homebuyers (HUD's primary market) scare easily.

---

3. Remember, HUD may change its policies and procedures at any time. Depending on the local balance of foreclosure supply and demand, HUD may ease up or tighten any of its rules. It may also add buyer incentives or withdraw them. Be sure to consult a local realty professional to learn what HUD is doing in your area right now.

As one HUD investor told me, "I always look for properties with the highest fear factor. Most homebuyers are afraid of homes that need work. They don't want the risk of cost overruns. They think they lack the knowledge and time to handle the fix-up. And they're right. But I do know how to deal with these things—and that knowledge gives me the advantage to earn good profits through rehab for rental or resale."

No Investor Financing. In recent years, HUD has refused to offer investors FHA insurance to help them buy HUD homes. However, HUD does offer homebuyers a variety of "relaxed" qualifying, low- or nothing-down FHA loan programs that they can use to acquire (and rehab) owner-occupied residences. Although HUD has said that it plans to reopen the FHA 203K (acquisition and rehab) mortgage program to investors, insiders tell me they have their doubts. Stay tuned on this one.

Nevertheless, the lack of FHA-insured loans hasn't in itself discouraged many investors from bidding for HUD homes. For now (at least), HUD property investors can choose their financing from a good selection of portfolio and Fannie Mae loan products that often carry both lower closing costs and a lower interest rate than FHA loans. (Talk with your local foreclosure pro.)

Owner-Occupant Certification

To deter investors from falsely claiming the favored homebuyer status, HUD sets stiff procedures and penalties. All intended owner-occupants must sign a purchase contract addendum that reads as follows:

> I/We certify that I/we have not purchased a HUD-owned property within the past 24 months as an owner-occupant. This offer is being submitted with the representation that I/we will occupy the property as my/our primary residence for at least 12 months.

In addition, the sales agent who submits the homebuyer's offer must also sign a statement that he or she is not knowingly representing an investor. The penalties for false certification of owner-occupancy range up to a $250,000 fine and two years in federal prison. Investors should never falsely claim that they intend to make a HUD home their personal residence.

"As-Is" Condition

HUD does not warrant the condition of any of the homes it sells. Even when HUD/FHA offers insured financing, HUD inspects the home for its own benefit only, *not* for the benefit of the home's buyer.

HUD Recommends Professional Inspections.   Because HUD homes are sold "as is," HUD encourages prospective bidders to obtain professional independent home inspections *before* they submit a bid. Unlike most sellers in the private market, HUD does not accept offers with an inspection contingency. What you see (or don't see) is what you get.

However, HUD's refusal to accept inspection contingencies does make buying more difficult. Because professional inspections cost $150 to $300, hopeful buyers are expected to incur this fee up front without any certainty as to whether they will actually submit the winning bid. Naturally, most people don't want to spend hundreds of dollars inspecting properties that they may not be able to buy.

This fact explains why most first-time buyers avoid HUD "fixers." There's too much chance the inspection fees will turn out to be a wasted expense. On the other hand, HUD's policy of "as is—no contingencies" favors experienced investors who not only can better estimate repair expenses but are better situated financially to accept the risks.

Lead-Paint Exception.   HUD does make one inspection contingency exception. For homes built before 1978, HUD mandates a lead-paint disclosure to buyers. HUD also allows winning bidders the option to obtain a lead-paint risk assessment prior to closing. If hazards are found, HUD has the right to (1) remedy the hazards at HUD's expense and then proceed to settlement, (2) refuse to remedy and attempt to renegotiate the contract to come up with an agreement that's acceptable to the buyer, or (3) simply reoffer the property to the buyers on an "as-is" basis.

In addition, HUD strongly encourages owner-occupants who have children under age seven to have their kids tested for "elevated blood level" (EBL). A positive reading permits the buyers to either cancel the contract or have the property tested for the presence of lead-based paint on all chewable surfaces and, where lead-based paint on chewable surfaces is identified, have such surfaces abated.

Although HUD seems most concerned with owner-occupants, as an investor, you too want to clearly identify any lead-based paint hazards. Absent proper treatment and resulting injury of tenants, you may be subject to large civil (and possibly criminal) penalties. Follow HUD's warnings. Don't gloss over the lead-paint hazard.

Disclosures and Repair Escrows.   In addition to the lead-paint warning, HUD may disclose to buyers various property defects that it knows about. Also, in some instances, HUD will agree to insure a mortgage for a property only if the buyers agree to make certain listed repairs. Neither of these actions by HUD, however, pushes aside the "as is—no warranties" feature of all HUD sales. Partial disclosure doesn't mean full disclosure. Caveat emptor still rules at HUD.

Discovering HUD Homes for Sale

As noted, to learn about HUD homes, first establish a relationship with a foreclosure pro. Together you might review the general availability, price ranges, and types of HUD properties that tend to come up for sale in your area. Then ask the pro to mail you (snail mail or e-mail) HUD listings as soon as HUD releases them. Alternatively, ask your sales pro to screen the listings and notify you only when a home that fits your criteria hits the market.

If you prefer to search on your own, you can drive neighborhoods looking for HUD For Sale signs; consult your local newspaper for HUD's weekly advertisement; or go to one of the many Web sites that post HUD listings and buying information such as www.hud.gov/buy home; www.towerauction.com; or www.loans4rehab.com.

Potential Conflict of Interest

Although most foreclosure professionals will work hard to find you a good deal, potential conflict of interest does arise in the sale of HUD homes. First, if you do not submit a winning bid, your sales agent does not earn a commission. An unethical agent could pressure you to raise your bid even if the value of the property doesn't justify a higher price. Second, sales agents may submit bids from competing buyers who are bidding on the same property. If you bid $80,000, an agent could tell another more favored buyer to bid $80,100 to knock your bid out of consideration. Third, HUD typically pays brokers who submit a winning bid a 5 percent sales commission plus, on occasion, a $500 (or more) selling bonus for designated properties. Again, this reward may create a financial incentive for the agent to push you into bidding high.

Naturally, you don't want to unjustly insinuate that your agent is likely to engage in underhanded sales tactics. But it's certainly reasonable for you to inquire about the specific ways your agent handles these potential conflicts of interest.

Buyer Incentives

During market downturns, HUD may ease up on its terms of sale in areas where unsold inventories of HUD homes are accumulating to unmanageable levels.

Lower Down Payments. Ordinarily, with FHA-insured financing, owner-occupant buyers pay from 3 to 5 percent down. Although these down payments are typical, HUD sometimes runs "specials" offering low or no down payment. For example, several years ago, all HUD-owned, FHA-insurable properties throughout the state of Georgia were being financed under either FHA 203(b) or FHA 203(k) with just $300 down. Usually, down payment specials apply only to owner-occupants. Check with HUD-approved sales agents in your area to see what deals HUD may be offering.

Other Incentives.   In addition to specials with low or no down payment, HUD local offices may run other types of incentive programs for buyers of HUD properties. For example, to encourage quick closings during a market surplus in Indianapolis, HUD offered a $2,000 early closing bonus (less than 30 days) to investors and owner-occupants. In Chicago, HUD has offered a rebate of up to $1,000 to renters who buy a HUD home for owner occupancy. In Boston, HUD offered a 5 percent purchase price credit on certain designated properties, a $250 bonus to buyers who had arranged a lender's preapproval, and a $675 early closing bonus (less than 45 days). In Baltimore, the early closing bonus was $900, but settlement had to take place within 15 days of contract acceptance. On occasion, to reduce its inventory of unsold homes, HUD offers "clearance sales" at deep discounts. Some years back in Houston, HUD ran a huge "turkey day" sale on Thanksgiving.

As you can see, HUD can authorize its regional and local offices to modify (loosen) HUD's overall financial requirements. If HUD properties are not selling fast enough in Chicago, for instance, you can bet that HUD will increase buyer incentives for its Chicago-area properties. Similarly, when sales are booming in a given city and HUD has relatively few properties available, HUD not only refuses to offer incentives but may refuse to accept bids at less than a property's list price. Generally, you can score the best deal on HUD properties in down markets. But regardless of the market, it's worth your time to investigate the HUD opportunities that may be available in your area.

Insured with Repair Escrow

Sometimes when an as-is HUD property doesn't meet the standards of an FHA 203(b)–insured loan, it will be listed as "insured with repair escrow." In these cases, HUD will approve the use of the FHA 203(b) program, if the buyer brings the property up to FHA standards shortly after closing. To pay for these repairs, HUD typically places part of the purchase price (usually less than $5,000) into a repair escrow account the buyers may draw on. If the buyers perform much of the work themselves to save on labor costs, then those savings can be credited toward reducing the buyer's outstanding mortgage.

Say you buy a HUD home that's been approved for an $80,000 FHA 203(b) mortgage that includes a $5,000 repair escrow. You pay $2,500 for materials and supplies and provide $2,500 of your own labor. If the house passes HUD's inspection, your loan balance with drop to $77,500. You will have earned "sweat equity" of $2,500 plus any other instant equity that has resulted because your improvements have boosted the market value of the property above your purchase price. Here's how the numbers might look:

Date of Closing

Purchase price	$82,500
Loan balance	$80,000
Equity	$ 2,500

After Value-Boosting Renovation and Sweat-Equity Credit

Market value	$87,500
Loan balance	$77,500
Equity	$10,000

As you can see, bought right and strategically improved, a HUD home insured with escrow can help you quickly build home equity wealth.

The Bid Package

As might be expected of a government agency, HUD doesn't make the buying process easy. Unlike a private purchase, where you simply write out your offer on any valid contract form, HUD requires a specific contract submission package. You must use only HUD-approved forms and documentation. You must complete all of the required forms, addenda, and enclosures fully and accurately. In addition, your contract package submission must arrive in HUD's regional office according to HUD's posted schedule.

HUD may (and does) refuse to accept bid packages that do not conform to its specifications. Given HUD's well-known inflexibility, work only with conscientious foreclosure professionals who know in detail the ins and outs of HUD's requirements.

Bid Rules

Space doesn't permit me to go through all of HUD's bidding rules and procedures, but here are several of the most important ones:

Net Return to HUD. HUD does not necessarily accept the bid that offers the highest price. Instead HUD accepts the offer that yields the largest amount of net proceeds.

For example, assume that a property is listed for $80,000 on an insured-sale basis. HUD receives two bids on this property. The following illustrates how HUD calculates which offer it will accept:

Bid 1: Selling broker investing for himself

Bid price	$80,000
Deduction (credit report)	− 50
Net to HUD	$79,050

Bid 2: Owner-occupant buyer

Bid price	$83,500
Deduction (commission, loan fees, and closing costs)	− 7,300
Net to HUD	$76,200

In this example, the largest net proceeds to HUD came from bid 1, although bid 2 offered a higher price for the property. Bid 2 requests HUD to pay a 5 percent sales commission and various loan fees and closing costs, for a total deduction of $7,300. Bid 1 requests HUD to pay $50 for a credit report; however, it does not request HUD to pay for any other expenses. Also, Bid 1 comes from a real estate broker, who in this case elects to waive the commission and thus improves the competitiveness of the bid. (Of course, for an investor-broker to have his or her bid considered, HUD's owner-occupant preferential period must have ended.)

To help prospective buyers increase the net to HUD, some real estate agents voluntarily reduce their sales commissions or, when legal, offer to rebate part of their commission to their buyers. Even if an agent doesn't volunteer this fee reduction, ask for it. Especially where your bid price is low, a reduced commission may give your bid the winning edge.

Earnest Money Deposits. Generally, HUD refunds the earnest money deposit to bid-winning owner-occupants if they are subsequently turned down for their mortgage loan when attempting to buy an "insured" or "insured with escrow" HUD home. To avoid (or at least reduce) this problem, many HUD offices require buyers to submit a lender preapproval letter with their contract offer.

For cash as-is properties, owner-occupant buyers who fail to close because they can't arrange financing (or for any other reason) generally lose their deposits. Similarly, investors who, after winning a bid, fail to close their intended purchase on *any* property forfeit their deposit. The only exceptions to this policy are instances of "great hardship" that must be petitioned and are reviewed by HUD on a case-by-case basis. To play it safe, get your credit approval lined up *before* you submit an offer to buy a HUD property.

Settlement Period.   Usually, HUD purchase contracts require buyers to close their purchase within 45 days after being notified that HUD has accepted their bid. However, at HUD's discretion, HUD may grant buyers one or more 15-day extensions to close, if the buyers agree to pay an extension fee of either $10, $15, or $25 per diem—depending on the price of the home.

Multiple Bids.   HUD allows brokers to submit offers from different buyers on the same property:

> *Owner-occupant buyers:* In some HUD regions, brokers may submit bids by the same owner-occupant buyer on several properties even within the same bid period. If all of the offers submitted by a single buyer apply to properties on which others have also bid, the first bid from that buyer that is accepted eliminates the remainder of that person's bids from consideration.

> *Investors:* Brokers may also submit offers by the same investor on more than one property within the same bid period. Should one of the offers submitted by the investor win the bid, it does not eliminate his or her other offers from consideration.

No Occupancy before Closing.   Buyers are prohibited from occupying or working on a HUD property before a sale is closed.

HUD May Reject an Offer.   HUD reserves the right to reject any bid, offer, or contract that is incorrectly drawn or that is submitted as a result of an incorrect listing or other error.

Contract Revision.   Should a sales agent want to revise a contract offer already submitted, that agent must deliver a letter of request to HUD. The letter must be signed by the buyer, stating the reasons for the revision together with a revised contract complete with attachments and addenda. After review by HUD, the broker will then be advised on whether such revisions will be allowed.

Bid Cancellation.   Buyers may cancel their bid by submitting a written request, which includes the reasons for their cancellation, through their selling broker. The broker will forward the request to HUD along with other pertinent information. HUD then determines on a case-by-case basis whether to refund the earnest money deposit.

If a buyer cancels an all-cash, as-is contract at any time, or cancels an insured sale after bid acceptance, HUD will typically keep the earnest money deposit. HUD deviates from this policy only in hardship cases and always requires full documentation before refunding.

Procedures after Closing.   After closing, all boarding-up material (all wood and hardware) used at the home becomes the property of the buyer. HUD does not remove boarding-up material, regardless of the type of sale. The padlock or lockbox is to be returned to the HUD Area Management Broker by the seller broker as a condition of receiving his or her commission check.

VA HOMES

The U.S. Department of Veterans Affairs (VA) guarantees the payment of home loans for eligible veterans. This guarantee permits veterans to finance their home with 100 percent (zero down payment) loans. However, just as FHA-insured mortgages are subject to foreclosure, lenders foreclose when VA borrowers fail to make their payments as scheduled. In return for a loan payoff, lenders give the foreclosed homes back to the VA, which then tries to sell them as quickly as possible.

VA's Similarities to HUD

To sell its foreclosed properties, the VA follows many rules that are similar to those of HUD. For example, here are 12 major ways the programs resemble each other:

1. The VA sells through a sealed bid process. Likewise, as either a potential homeowner or an investor, you may submit multiple bids during the same bid period.
2. You cannot *directly* negotiate with, or submit a bid to, the VA. You must submit your bid through a VA-approved broker (your foreclosure professional).

3. The VA sells its homes on an as-is basis. Even though it may partially disclose a home's defects, it offers no warranties. Caveat emptor.
4. The VA does guarantee title and permits buyers to obtain a title policy.
5. The VA accepts bids that yield it the highest net proceeds (not the highest price). If your bid obligates the VA with fewer closing expenses or sales commissions, you can win the bid over others who offer higher prices, but also higher costs (a lower net) to the VA.
6. Just as HUD/FHA charges FHA buyers an insurance fee, the VA charges buyers who choose its financing a 2.25 percent guarantee fee.
7. The VA accepts bids only on VA forms. Errors in completing the forms may invalidate the bid.
8. The VA publicizes its homes through a combination of newspaper ads, broker lists, and Internet postings (http://homeloans.va.gov/homes).
9. Local VA offices report to regional directors, who may issue policies and procedures that differ from those in other regions throughout the country.
10. The VA may choose to keep your earnest money deposit if you fail to close a winning bid for any reason other than inability to obtain financing.
11. As with HUD home contracts, VA purchase offers do not include a contingency for postpurchase property inspections. You may, though, inspect a property before you bid.
12. When necessary, the VA evicts holdover tenants or homeowners before placing a VA home on the market. At closing, you will receive a vacant property.

Big Advantages for Investors

Although in many ways the VA follows rules similar to HUD, it differs in two important ways that work to the advantage of investors:

1. The VA does not give owner-occupant buyers preferential treatment. The VA looks for the highest net offered by any credible buyer—homeowner or investor.
2. The VA offers financing to investors on quite favorable terms. At present in my area, for example, investors can close financing on a VA home with total cash out-of-pocket of less than 6 percent of a property's purchase price. In addition, the VA typically applies "relaxed" qualifying standards. VA buyers (who need not be

veterans) must show *acceptable*, not perfect, credit records. (For specifics in your area, talk with your foreclosure pro.)

With such favorable terms of financing, VA homes in good (and even not so good) repair frequently sell at top-of-the-market prices. However, many investors still find the program attractive for these three reasons:

1. High leverage permits you to accelerate your wealth-building returns.
2. Even at top-of-the-market prices, many VA homes pull in rents high enough to provide a positive cash flow from day one of ownership.
3. The VA allows future buyers to assume your VA financing. For investors who want to "fix and flip," an assumable loan makes a great benefit. Plus, in periods of high interest rates, a lower assumable VA rate gives your sales efforts a big advantage.

Overall, VA homes provide an excellent source of properties and financing for beginning and experienced investors alike. Make sure you investigate this opportunity in your area.

FANNIE MAE AND FREDDIE MAC PROPERTIES

Fannie Mae and Freddie Mac are the two largest players in the nation's secondary mortgage market. These mortgage companies don't make loans directly to homebuyers, but they do buy more than 50 percent of the home mortgages that are made by other mortgage lenders. Sometimes when these loans go bad, Fannie (or Freddie) may force the lender to buy back its loan. Then the lender ends up with a foreclosed house in its REO portfolio. However, lenders who have followed all of Fannie's (or Freddie's) underwriting guidelines when originally making these mortgages can require Fannie (or Freddie) to take ownership of their foreclosed houses.

Agent Listings

As a general rule, Fannie and Freddie do not use the sealed-bid sales procedure that's common to HUD and VA. Instead both companies choose a realty firm and give that firm an exclusive listing. Typically, the realty firm then places the REO property into MLS. The realty agent who takes on responsibility for a foreclosed property first inspects it and then recommends the best way to fix it up to maximize its sales price.

Seldom a Bargain.   Because Fannie and Freddie frequently spend thousands of dollars to put a property in top condition, and then price that property aggressively, you won't find many bargain buys among their REOs. In fact, only in out-of-the-ordinary circumstances will Fannie and Freddie consider lowball or wheeling-and-dealing types of offers. They even try to price their "as is—no repairs" properties as high as the market will bear.

First-Time Homebuyers—Special Financing.   Fannie and Freddie primarily direct their marketing efforts toward highly credit-qualified homebuyers (especially first-time homebuyers). Rather than use the bargain price appeal, these companies attract buyers with well-presented homes and special financing.

Freddie even permits homebuyers to "customize your Homesteps home." Under this option, Freddie invites buyers (for a price, of course) to upgrade their home's carpeting, padding, vinyl, appliances, and window blinds. Freddie also sells most of its homes for 5 percent down, no private mortgage insurance (which typically saves buyers $50 or $80 per month), lower closing costs, and an attractive interest rate.

All Properties Sold "As Is."   Even though Fannie and Freddie fix up most of their properties, neither offers any type of warranty that guarantees the condition of a property. However, unlike buying from HUD or the VA, as a Fannie/Freddie buyer, you may submit a contract that includes an inspection contingency. If the home qualifies, you can purchase your own home warranty plan just as you (or the sellers) can with most other home sales.

Investors Accepted

Both Fannie and Freddie will accept offers from investors with no priority listing period that applies only to owner-occupants. Both companies also offer special financing for credit-qualified investors that requires a 15 percent down payment (in contrast to the conventional down payment of 20 percent to 30 percent for investor-owned properties). Closing costs may come in a little lower, too. Investor interest rates usually sit on the low side of market. You can locate Freddie and Fannie properties, respectively, at www.homesteps.com and www.fanniemae.com/homes.

FEDERAL GOVERNMENT AUCTIONS

Each year the federal government (in addition to HUD/VA) sells all types of seized and surplus real estate including homes, apartment complexes, office buildings, ranches, and vacant and developed land. Among the most active sellers are the Internal Revenue Service (IRS), Government Service Administration (GSA), and the Federal Deposit Insurance Corporation (FDIC). On occasion, you can also find properties offered by the Small Business Administration (SBA). Although space here doesn't permit full discussion of each of these agencies, you can locate their properties and sales procedures at the following Web sites:

Internal Revenue Service at www.treas.gov/auctions/irs

Government Services Administration at http://propertydisposal.gsa.gov/propforsale

Federal Deposit Insurance Corporation at www.fdic.gov/buying/owned/real/index

Small Business Administration at http://app1.sba.gov/pfsales/dsp

SHERIFF SALES

In addition to foreclosures, you might want to follow sheriff sales or other legally mandated involuntary property sales. These sales may result from property tax liens, civil lawsuit judgments, and bankruptcy creditors.

Because of the local nature of these types of forced sales, we can't go into the details that relate to specific sales procedures or the relative possibilities for finding bargain prices. We can only say, "It all depends." Yet if your goal is to leave no stone unturned in your attempt to locate good deals, talk to lawyers, courthouse officials, foreclosure speculators, and others who are in the know about these types of sales. Because these sales take place under less-than-ideal marketing conditions, it's only natural to expect selling prices that fall substantially below a property's market value.

BUY FROM FORECLOSURE SPECULATORS

Another way to profit from foreclosure and forced sale auctions without actually bidding is to buy from a winning bidder shortly after the foreclosure sale.

Say a foreclosure speculator puts in a winning bid of $145,000 on a property that would appear to have a market value of $195,000 if it were fixed up and marketed effectively. After the auction, you offer the speculator $170,000 (or whatever). To minimize risk, you attach several contingencies to your offer that permit you to get the property thoroughly inspected, evict any holdover owners or tenants, clear up title problems, seek title insurance, and arrange financing. If the property checks out satisfactorily, the sale closes, and the speculator makes a quick $25,000 (more or less). You get the property at a discount without the costly surprises that can turn a superficially promising foreclosure buy into a loss.

PROBATE AND ESTATE SALES

Probate and estate sales present another potential source of bargain properties. When owners of properties die, their property may be sold to satisfy the deceased's mortgagee and other creditors. Even when the deceased leaves sufficient wealth in cash to satisfy all claims against the estate, heirs still normally prefer to sell the property rather than retain ownership.

Probate

To buy a property through probate, you submit a bid through the estate's administrator (usually a lawyer) or executor. Then all bids are reviewed by the probate judge assigned to the case. Depending on local and state laws, the judge may then select a bid for approval or reopen the bidding. Because of legal procedures and delays, bidding on probate properties can require perseverance. Judges wield substantial discretion in deciding when and whether to accept a probate bid. You can never tell for sure where you stand.

An acquaintance of mine tells of a probate property that came up for sale in an area of $150,000 homes. The probate administrator listed the house for sale at $115,000. A flurry of bids came in that ranged from a low of $105,000 up to a high of $118,000. Several months later the judge looked at the bids, announced the high bid at $118,000, and then solicited additional offers. Eventually, the judge approved the sale at a price of $129,850 to someone who had not even been involved in the first round of bidding.

After all was said and done, the successful buyer did achieve a bargain price—provided that the property held no unpleasant surprises. (Unlike forced sales "on the courthouse steps," buyers in probate sales can generally enter and inspect the properties before submitting a bid.) To learn about probate sales in your area, talk with a probate lawyer or the clerk of county court. Also look at local newspapers that announce upcoming sales.

Estate Sales

In some situations, an estate's assets need not be dragged through the probate process. You may be able to buy directly from the heirs or the executor of the estate. In fact, some buyers of estate properties follow the obituary notices, contact heirs, and try to buy before the property is listed with a real estate agent. To succeed in this approach, you would naturally need to develop an empathetic demeanor.

Estate sales frequently produce bargains because heirs eagerly want cash. They may also need the money to pay off a mortgage, other creditors, or estate taxes. Out-of-town heirs (especially) may not want to hold a vacant property for an extended period until a top-dollar buyer is found. Once again, pressures of time or money can lead to sales prices that fall below a property's market value.

PRIVATE AUCTIONS

Increasingly, many sellers who want to liquidate their properties turn to private auctions. During the last economic downturn in California, banks and thrifts were pooling their REOs and jointly auctioning off dozens (sometimes hundreds) of properties at a time. New home builders, too, have increased their use of auctions. Sometimes home builder auctions involve closeout sales where a builder wants to get out of a current project so that he can devote time and energy to his next new development. On other occasions, a home builder's auction may represent a last desperate attempt to raise cash to head off project foreclosure or company bankruptcy. In Dallas, a wealthy homeowner tired of trying to sell his $1.6 million home (listed price) through a brokerage firm and was eager to move into his newly built $4.4 million home. So he hired an auctioneer. On a pleasant Saturday morning, hundreds of people showed up, and within minutes of the opening bid, the home had a new owner. The winning price: $890,000.

Prepare for an Auction

Attend a major real estate auction. You'll have fun. Often a band is playing, food and drinks are served, and a festive mood prevails. The auction company wants to make potential bidders feel good. But beyond this display of cheer, the auction company is promoting one goal: Sell every property at the highest possible price. Auctioneers are paid a percentage of the day's take, plus, perhaps, a bonus for exceeding a certain level of sales.

To find a bargain, don't get caught up in the festive frenzy and abandon good sense (as the auction company wants you to). Instead, attend the auction armed with information. Prepare to walk out a winner—not simply a buyer. Here's how you can make that happen:

◆ *Always thoroughly inspect a property.* During the weeks before most private auctions, the auction company will schedule open houses at the properties to be sold. If you can't visit an open house, contact a real estate agent and ask for a personal showing. (Most auction companies cooperate with Realtors. If an agent brings a winning bidder to the auction, that agent will be paid a 1 percent or 2 percent sales commission.) Sometimes auction properties sell cheap because they are nothing more than teardowns waiting for a bulldozer. Or they may suffer any of a number of other problems. Even new properties aren't necessarily defect free. Check them out before you bid.

◆ *Appraise the property carefully.* Even if the property is free of defects, you can't assume value. You must figure it out by studying recent selling prices of comparable properties. Don't count on list price to guide you. Just because you buy a property 25 percent below its previous listing price doesn't mean you have bought at 25 percent below the property's market value.

◆ *Set a maximum bid price.* Remember, you're looking for a bargain. Market value tells you what a property might sell for if fixed up and marketed by a competent and aggressive real estate agent. Market value does not tell you the price you should bid. Before the auction, set your maximum bid price. Don't let the auctioneer's "boosters" cajole, excite, romance, bamboozle, or intimidate you into going higher.

◆ *Review the paperwork that will accompany a successful bid.* Before the auction begins, review the property tax statements, environmental reports, lot survey, legal description, and the sales contract you'll be asked to sign.

◆ *Learn what type of deed the seller will use to convey the property.* With a general warranty deed, the seller guarantees clear title subject only to certain named exceptions. Other types of deeds convey fewer title warranties. Don't accept a deed without understanding its limitations (liens, easements, encroachments, exceptions, missing heirs, etc.). All in all, title insurance is your best guarantee. If a property's title is uninsurable, consult a real estate attorney to obtain an opinion of title.

◆ *Be prepared to pay the deposit.* To become eligible to bid, register with the auction company before the auction begins and show proof of deposit funds (amount varies by auction). You will then be issued a bid card that will tell the auctioneer that you are an approved bidder. Without a bid card, the auctioneer won't recognize your bid.

- *Find out if financing is available.* Often auction companies pre-arrange financing on some or all of their properties. If so, find out the terms and qualifying standards. If not, determine how much time the auction company gives you to arrange your own financing. Unlike most government agency property auctions, private auction companies typically do not expect their successful bidders to pay cash for their properties.
- *Learn whether the sale is absolute or subject to a reserve price.* Usually auction properties are either offered absolute or with reserve. If absolute, a property is sold no matter how low the top bidder's price. With a reserve price, the top bid must exceed a prearranged minimum amount, or the property is pulled out of the auction. On occasion, though, the owner of a property may "nod" to the auctioneer and approve a bid that does not meet the reserve price.

How to Find Auctions

Most auction companies advertise their upcoming auctions in local and sometimes national newspapers (e.g., the *Wall Street Journal*). Auction companies not only want to attract as many bidders as possible; they want to draw large crowds so that they can create a sense of anticipation and excitement. In addition to advertising, most auction companies will place your name on their mailing lists.

Local auction companies are listed in the Yellow Pages. Large-scale local auctions, though, are frequently handled by auction companies that operate nationwide. These include Fisher Auction Company, Hudson and Marshall, J. P. King, Kennedy-Wilson, Larry Latham, NRC Auctions, Ross Dove and Company, and Sheldon Good and Company. Even if you decide not to bid, large auctions are fun to attend. Try one. You'll learn the tricks of the trade as you watch the professional auctioneers and investors vie with one another.

8

QUICK PROFITS
THROUGH FIX AND FLIP

Would you like to build wealth quickly? Are you willing to thoroughly research properties? Do you enjoy creative work? Then fix, flip, and profit may provide your best route to real estate success. For a glimpse of your potential opportunities, consider the experiences of Pat Williams and the Browns (Ray and Annie B.)

FIX, FLIP, PROFIT!

Several years back, just as California was heading into a deep recession, Pat Williams and her husband split up. Out of work and with two children to support, Pat needed to make some money quickly. She decided to invest in real estate. Given the deteriorating economy of the Golden State at the time, you might think that Pat was off her rocker. Not at all: Pat knew how to capitalize on adversity.

During the next five years, as many California home prices fell by 20 to 30 percent, Pat bought and resold six homes. After each sale, she banked between $20,000 and $40,000. Her total profits exceeded $150,000. What was her secret? A keen eye for a bargain, hard work, and perseverance. "The deals are not marked with a big red flag," Pat says. "I had to weed through a lot of properties and get up to speed on the market."

When Pat says she had to "weed through" a lot of properties, she means that literally as well as figuratively. Relying on seller financing, Pat's home-buying strategy was to ferret out and buy run-down, bargain-priced houses known as fixer-uppers. Applying the knowledge she had gained about the market, Pat would renovate and revitalize these proper-ties to enhance their value. Then she would sell at a higher price. With her quickly learned savvy, Pat didn't wait for the California real estate market to turn around. She created her own housing appreciation.

Would you like to earn an extra $20,000 to $40,000 over the next year or two? Or would you prefer to create instant equity and boost your potential rental income? Then buy a bargain- priced fixer-upper. Locate a property that offers great promise for improvement. Don't worry about your personal likes and dislikes concerning the property's features. Just find a house or small apartment building that you can buy low, create value, boost rents, and sell high.

LOOKING FOR "FIXERS"

As you compare neighborhoods and properties, keep your eye out for ideas you can use to improve the houses and apartments you evaluate. Although most books and articles on real estate investing tell you to buy fixer-uppers, keep in mind that a fixer-upper is *any* home that you can redecorate, redesign, remodel, expand, or romance. The name of the home improvement game is profitable creativity. You can make nearly any home or apartment live better, look better, and feel better.

Throw away the notion that only run-down houses and apartments fit the definition of a fixer-upper. Sure, poorly maintained properties may offer good potential for value-enhancing improvements. But to keen observers, even meticulously kept properties aren't immune to profitable change. When you stay alert to opportunity, you can always find ways to make a property more desirable to potential tenants. Consider the experi-ence of Raymond and Annie Brown.

The Browns Create Value in a Down Market

When Raymond Brown and his wife, Annie B., bought a vacation retreat home they call Woodpecker Haven, Raymond says, "I thought it was a done property. It was only five years old."

Annie B., though, viewed the home from a different perspective. As an interior designer with a forward-looking imagination, Annie B. simply said the home "had great potential." As Raymond tells the story, "Here are some of the improvements my enterprising wife accomplished to transform a livable property into an exquisite home":

- ◆ Landscaped the front and rear yards.
- ◆ Installed a drip irrigation system.

- Built a stone fence around the pool.
- Added decks around the rear of the house.
- Installed in both bedrooms French doors that led out to the decks.
- Remodeled the guest bedroom and bath to create a master bedroom for visitors.
- Built a fireplace, bookshelves, and cabinets and installed track lighting in the living room.
- Trimmed overgrown trees and shrubs to enhance a picture-perfect view from the front porch.

Although Raymond and Annie B. invested $75,000 in these and other improvements, they added around $175,000 in value—throughout a falling market. "We bought our Sonoma retreat," says Raymond, "just as home prices were peaking, and sold several years later, two months before prices bottomed out . . . . Yet we made a $100,000 profit. Our secret? Woodpecker Haven was a fixer-upper we renovated inside and out."

As the experience of the Browns demonstrates, a fixer is any home that could look better, live better, and feel better than it does. (Remember, at the time they bought, Woodpecker Haven was only five years old. Recall, too, both the Browns and Pat Williams made their big gains in a *falling* market.) To fix up a home or apartment building may require you to scrape encrusted bubble gum off floors and counters, patch holes in the roof, fight a gnarled mass of weeds and debris in the backyard, or pull out and replace rusted and obsolete kitchen and bathroom plumbing fixtures. But fixing up a property can also mean visualizing ways to redecorate, redesign, remodel, expand, or bring romance into the property.

In fact, to profit from fix-up work, you don't necessarily have to get your hands dirty. Yes, your sweat equity can pay big dividends, but creativity, imagination, and market research pay much better. To create value, you can (1) look for houses that obviously need work; (2) focus on properties whose creative possibilities would be overlooked by most buyers; or (3) find a property where you can improve both its physical condition and its overall appeal and liability. The better you can envision opportunities that other potential buyers are likely to pass up, the greater your potential for profits.

Research, Research, Research

When you buy a property to create value, no rules or suggestions apply to all cities, all types of homes, or all kinds of tenants or buyers. Features that one person loves, another may hate. What's popular in California may look out of place in Kansas. Today's most faddish options may become outdated tomorrow. What suits you may not appeal to the tastes and lifestyles of most people. Money spent for a remodeled bath in Atlanta may pay back $3.00 for each $1.00 invested. In Milwaukee, returns for the same improvements may fall to 50 cents per dollar spent.

With so many variables entering the value equation, planning for profits requires that you learn what features your future tenants or buyers will pay for. To create value, refuse to let your personal tastes or preconceived notions stand unchallenged. Instead, like smart home builders who want their homes to sell, you have to research your market. You need to develop a market-based improvement strategy.

Ask local Realtors and property managers to tell you the turn-ons and turnoffs for tenants, homebuyers, and property investors. Identify unique niches for uncommon yet highly desired features. Tour new home developments and popular apartment complexes. Notice colors, decorating themes, floor coverings, and floor plans. Discover the models, features, and amenities that are selling best. Which ones are rarely chosen? Which features are functional, rather than merely glitzy? What types of apartment units command the highest rents and display the lowest vacancies?

Visit open houses to excite your creative impulses. Look for ways other property owners have remodeled, redecorated, or redesigned their properties to make them more livable or more appealing. Talk to friends, relatives, and acquaintances who have remodeling experience. Buy a box full of those supermarket and bookstore guides with titles like *1,001 Ideas to Improve Your Home or Apartment Living*. The more creative ideas you can come up with, the better you can design a profit-generating improvement strategy.

IMPROVEMENTS TO CONSIDER

When shopping properties with an eye toward creating value, corral your enthusiasms as well as your negative reactions. Don't dwell on whether you like or dislike a property. Instead, answer this question: Based on what you've learned from market research, can you spend $5,000 to reap a return of $15,000? Or maybe $50,000 to reap a return of $150,000. In other words, don't judge a home personally. Judge its potential profitability. Would any of the following action possibilities materially boost the value of the property?

- Clean thoroughly.
- Add pizzazz.

- Create more usable space.
- Create a view.
- Capitalize on owner (builder) nearsightedness.
- Eliminate a negative view.
- Bring in more natural light.
- Reduce noise.

Thoroughly Clean the Property

Whether you plan to hold or flip a property, before you place it onto the market, clean it thoroughly. Many owners of small rental properties don't realize the necessity of spotlessly clean apartments or houses. Many owners seem to take the view "Why clean the place thoroughly? The tenants will leave it like a pigsty anyway." But actually, such low expectations often bring about the unwanted result. When rental units aren't meticulously maintained, top-quality renters are turned off. They go elsewhere. It is precisely those tenants who accept units with dirt-encrusted windows and light fixtures, stained carpets, grease-layered stoves, and dust-laden windows blinds who are likely to treat your property as a pigpen.

If you display a pride-of-ownership cleanliness, you will not only attract better-quality tenants but demonstrate to your tenants the degree of cleanliness you expect. When I first became a landlord, I confess that I operated with the "why clean thoroughly" attitude. After seeing how badly tenants can wreck a property, it's easy to reduce standards. But I soon learned that such an attitude is a self-defeating downward cycle. Once I began to offer units that were head and shoulders above the competition, I was always able to choose the best tenants from a long list of applicants.

Again, let me emphasize: The cleanliness rule applies not just to investors who buy, fix, and rent. It's also critical for fix-and-flip investors. No matter that you plan to flip (sell) the property to another investor or to a homebuyer, a spotless unit will sell (rent) quicker and at a higher price. Tenants and buyers alike discount heavily for dirt and debris. It works like this: Cleaner units attract higher-quality tenants, and investors pay more for properties with better tenants because better tenants mean lower risk, less trouble, and near-certain rent collections.

Add Pizzazz with Color Schemes, Decorating Patterns, and Fixtures

Before you paint or redecorate your properties, get out and tour several new home developments and new upscale apartment projects. Look through a variety of home decorator magazines. Can you enhance the appeal of your units with more modern color schemes, wallpaper patterns, or special touches like chair moldings, mirrors, fancy plumbing, light fixtures, or patterned tile floors? Don't go wild with creativity or personal flair, but adding just the right amount of pizzazz (or romance) can make your units stand out from the crowd.

Create More Usable Space

Have you seen the ads of the California Closet Company or any of its imitators? This company took the simple idea that closet space could be used more effectively and turned it into a $50-million-a-year business. Now the company applies the same principle to garages, workshops, and home offices. You can do the same thing. Figure out how to create more usable space, and you've increased the value of your property.

But don't just mull over using existing space more effectively. Maybe you should convert an attic, garage, or basement to additional living area. Or you might enclose a porch or patio, add a second story, or build an accessory apartment. Keep asking yourself, "How can I use or create space to create more sales appeal or generate more income from these units?"

Also think about "rightsizing" the living area within the units. "Rightsizing" the living area means reducing the size of large rooms by adding walls or separate areas, or perhaps combining small rooms to make larger areas. In other words, every storage and living area within a house or apartment should be proportionate to market tastes and preferences. When floor areas are perceived as "too large" or "too small," you can't get top rents or a top price. By rightsizing, you better fit the space to buyer or tenant needs.

In another sense, rightsizing can pertain to making units themselves larger or smaller. Several years ago a Manhattan investor noticed that two-bedroom apartments were a glut on the market and rent levels were severely depressed. On the other hand, those few buildings that offered four-bedroom apartments had long waiting lists. So he bought a building of two-bedroom apartments at a steep discount, combined the apartments into four-bedroom units, rented all of them immediately at premium rent levels, and then sold the property for twice the price that he had paid 18 months earlier.

Create a View

When I was looking for a lakefront home in Winter Park, Florida, I discovered a depressing fact. Most older houses were built with ordinary building plans even when they were built on view lots. As a result, a large majority of the lakefront houses I looked at failed to fully capture the view potential of their sites. Similarly, not long ago I was touring a new home development in northwest Albuquerque and came across a home situated such that it could have offered spectacular views of the Sandia Mountain Range. But it didn't.

Although I entered the house full of anticipation, disappointment soon set in. None of the rooms downstairs even had windows facing the mountains. Surely, though, the upstairs would be different. I imagined a master bedroom suite with large windows and perhaps a deck facing out to the mountains. But, again, no. The master bedroom was situated to look straight at the house next door. And on the mountain side of the house was a small child's bedroom with no view window.

If you can find older (or even newer) homes or apartments that fail to fully capture a potential view of a lake, ocean, mountain range, park, woods, or other pleasant surroundings, you may have discovered a great way to add value to a property.

Capitalize on Owner Nearsightedness

Quite often the current owners of ill-designed properties have become so accustomed to the property as it exists, that they don't even realize its possibilities. After remodeling my lakefront home in Winter Park to achieve views from eight of the nine rooms in the house, the previous owners stopped by and exclaimed, "Wow! If we could have imagined these changes, we might never have sold the house."

This example emphasizes my overall theme that profitable improvements begin with creative imagination. Don't rush into fixing up a property without first considering all types of possibilities. Too many fix-and-flip owners think property improvement means slapping on a fresh coat of white paint and laying new beige wall-to-wall carpeting. Such improvements may help, but don't limit yourself to such commonplace ideas. Don't focus on what your open eyes see. Instead focus on what you can imagine with your eyes closed and a range of creative possibilities.

Eliminate a Negative View

Some buildings suffer diminished value because their windows look out directly onto an alley, another building, or perhaps a tangle of power lines. For such properties, your goal is to eliminate a negative view and convert it into a positive whenever possible. Can you change the location of a window? Can you plant shrubbery, bamboo, or leafy trees? Can you add decorative fencing?

At the Black Oak Bookstore in Berkeley, California, the owners transformed an area that had looked out directly into a plain concrete block wall. To remedy this negative, the owners planted ivy to run by the concrete wall, added hanging plants, a rock garden, and wooden lattice work. The results are quite stunning and a 200 percent improvement over the old, plain concrete wall.

You can even turn a plan backyard into a beautiful view. The owner of a house I almost bought in La Jolla, California, did just that. In her back-yard, this seller had created a large, spectacular flower, shrub, and plant arrangement built up and designed within 8" x 8" lawn timbers. To create a view from inside the home, she replaced the back walls and small windows with sliding glass doors. (Unfortunately, this feeble description in no way conveys the buyer impact this improvement actually achieved.)

This owner had spent around $15,000 to create this stunning effect, but in doing so, she added between $35,000 and $50,000 in price. The house clearly displayed a competitive advantage over other "similar" houses in the neighborhood.

Enhance the Unit's Natural Light

Today, most homebuyers, investors, and tenants prefer properties with loads of natural light. You can achieve this effect by adding or enlarging windows, changing solid doors to those with glass, or installing skylights. In addition to the positive influence of the sunshine itself, brighter rooms seem more spacious. To enhance this effect, determine if you can add volume to interior rooms by tearing out a false ceiling; at times it can even pay to eliminate an attic area. When you create a brighter, more spacious look, you dramatically improve the way a home lives and feels.

Consider the experience of home seller Joan Phelps: "The previous owners had brick all across the inside wall, so it was very dark and dreary," says Joan. To solve this problem Joan and her husband spent $2,620 to tear out much of the brick and add windows on each side of the fireplace. The result was terrific. When the couple put their home up for sale, "We had two offers and a backup buyer the first weekend. First impressions really sell," Joan advises.

Not only did the Phelpses get the price they wanted, but another nearby house with the same old design sat on the market unsold for months. People (tenants and buyers) will pay a premium for a bright, cheery property. Can you add windows, skylights, lighter window treatments (get rid of those heavy dark drapes)? Can you rip out those low ceilings? With more height, you can bring in more light as well as elimi-nate that closed-in feeling created by low ceilings.

Reduce Noise

Homebuyers, investors, and tenants also will pay for quiet and discount heavily for noise. More home insulation, caulking, earth berms, trees and shrubs, and soundproof windows are all possible solutions. I recently attended a home improvements fair where one exhibitor had a boom box blasting hard rock music. But this offensive noise machine sat behind the exhibitor's product: sound-insulating windows. As shoppers approached, the man at the exhibit closed the window. The noise disappeared. Quite an effective demonstration of how soundproof windows can muffle or eliminate outside noise.

If you're thinking of buying a multiunit building, make sure you test the soundproofing between units. If you can hear a television, people walking or talking, or toilets flushing, beware. Unless you can figure out a solution to the noise problem, you will face repeated problems in retaining tenants and keeping them satisfied. Similarly, smart investors won't show an interest in buying the property unless you remedy this problem. Noise generates high tenant turnover, and no smart investor wants turnover.

REQUIRED REPAIRS AND IMPROVEMENTS

Always bring your properties to market in tip-top physical condition. Certainly, creative, appealing improvements add the most value. But to realize those potential profits, the property should not show signs of wear or abuse; all systems must operate; and the property must not display any hazards to health or life. When thinking about how to improve your property, look carefully at the following areas. The more problems you overcome, the fewer criticisms buyers (renters) will raise during property showings and negotiations.

Plumbing

All faucets should be checked for leaks and drips. Where washers are needed, replace them. Avoid tightening the handle down to the extent that the seat is damaged. Buyers will frequently turn all the faucets on and off to see if there is any damage in the internal workings. All the drains should drain quickly. Check the toilets to determine whether the water shuts off automatically as it is supposed to. Replace toilet seats that are discolored or cracked. Check the perimeters of all bathroom fixtures, showers, and bathtubs. Repair cracks with caulking compound, especially where leaks are present. If it is cold outside, protect pipes exposed to the weather. Remove stains of previous leaks. A stain is a dead give-away to a buyer that you have a plumbing problem.

Electrical System

All electrical outlets should work properly, and their locations should be known. A negative feature of many older properties is an insufficient number of outlets to handle today's many electrical appliances. The fuse or circuit breaker box should be in good working order. Any fluorescent bulbs that are weak or slow in coming on should be replaced or the starters should be replaced if necessary. Burned outlets should be replaced. An outlet should never have a large number of cords plugged in with adapters and extension cords. This situation suggests insufficient outlets and is also a fire hazard.

Heating and Air-Conditioning

The heating and air-conditioning system should perform effectively. Nothing would be more negative to a buyer than to walk into a property in the middle of summer and find that the air-conditioning is inadequate to cool the property (or that the heating system is inadequate to heat it properly in the winter). Filters on the furnace and air-conditioning equipment should be changed before showing the property. Some buyers will inspect the filters. If a very dirty one is found, the person may assume that the filters have not been changed regularly and that the system itself may have received some damage. Clean filters indicate to many buyers that you have taken proper care of the equipment. Also heating and air-conditioning duct outlets should be cleaned. If the property has gas heat or a gas water heater, throw away old matches from previous manual pilot lightings. Failure to do so will indicate trouble in keeping the pilot lit.

Windows

Replace all cracked or broken windows. Broken pulleys and damaged frames and sills should be repaired. All windows that open should lift up and down easily. Never show a property where the windows have been painted shut. Extreme turnoff to buyers. Fix broken or malfunctioning screens.

Appliances

Appliances such as built-in oven, range, garbage disposal, dishwasher, or refrigerator that are to be included in the sale (or rental) should function properly. Refrigerators should be kept defrosted, and ovens should remain clean while the property is on the market (if tenants occupy the property, get them to cooperate with you in keeping their appliances and their living units in neat and clean shape during the sales effort).

Walls and Ceilings

Walls and ceilings should be attractive. Repair all cracks in plaster. Faded or dark-colored walls should be painted or papered. Strive for a bright, cheerful look in the property. To reduce your work, buy prepasted wallpaper and good-quality paint that will cover with just one coat. Paint and wallpaper are probably the two items that will return the most gain relative to their cost. Use color schemes that will enhance the overall effect that you are trying to achieve for the property.

Doors and Locks

Screen or storm doors should be checked for screens that are in need of replacement and springs that are too weak. All doors should open and close easily without being too tight or too loose. Consider replacing cheap, flat-panel hollow-core doors with ones more substantive in strength and decor. Doors that are too tight can be planed relatively easily to stop their dragging. Because security is a major factor in many buyers' (or tenants') minds, replacement of worn locks or locks that are easily picked or broken with a sturdier variety can add to the property's desirability. However, don't go overboard in installing too many locks, chains, and bolts. Lock overload can make the buyer (tenant) question the safety of the neighborhood.

Landscaping

Property owners who spend thousands of dollars on landscaping may not see their money returned for this expenditure. A well-kept yard, though, will enhance resale potential. So get the yard in shape. The grass should be cut and leaves raked. Dead or unattractive shrubbery should be removed and perhaps replaced with new shrubbery. If time and season permit, planting flowers or installing flower boxes can significantly increase the attractiveness of the property.

Storage Areas

All storage areas should be cleaned and items of no value thrown away. This job will need to be done anyway before you hand over possession to a buyer and will materially add to the appearance of spaciousness within the storage areas. It is difficult to imagine how roomy a closet, attic, or basement is when that area is crammed to the brim. Spaciousness in closets is a very important factor. Again, here's another area of property preparation where you may need to enlist the cooperation of your tenants.

General Cleaning

Again, I emphasize that the property should be cleaned from top to bottom. Most buyers want a property that that looks like it has been well taken care of. Bathrooms and kitchens are especially important. Special efforts to remove stains on sinks, toilet bowls, and bathtubs as well as countertops and cabinet areas can add wonders to the appeal of a property. Potted flowers in bathrooms and kitchens also add to the appeal. Floors should be scrubbed and carpets vacuumed regularly during the selling period. Clean windows and mirrors are also very important. (One more time, if tenants occupy the property, get them to keep the property in top condition. Investors will make conclusions about the quality of your tenants from how neat and clean they maintain their units. If your tenants won't practice tidy housekeeping, replace them with tenants who will honor your requests.)

Safety and Health Factors

While cleaning and repairing your property, take special note of anything that might cause someone to stumble, fall, or otherwise suffer injury. Loose carpeting, torn linoleum, loose handrails, and scattered wires and cords can be dangerous. You are responsible for the safety of all the people coming in and out of your property. Also, safety factors help sell a property because investor buyers want their own tenants to be safe.

Likewise for environmental concerns such as asbestos, lead paint, radon, or underground oil tanks. Check with state and federal EPAs to get their booklets that tell property owners how to safely and legally remedy environmental hazards. Of course, you should make environmental issues a critical part of your own prepurchase property inspection.

Roofs

Closely inspect the roof for both aesthetics and function. If the roof leaks, adequately repair it. Don't do a quick fix to hid a serious problem for just long enough to get the property sold. Clear the roof of all debris or plant growth. If the roof is discolored, check with a home improvement store to see if you can use some type of roof "paint" to enhance its appearance.

Buyers hate old roofs. Buyers love new roofs. If the roof is near the end of its life, replace it. Again, though, as with repairs, don't go the cheapest route. Search out the most cost-effective solution, not merely the lowest cost per se. Smart buyers will recognize shoddy work.

Major Improvements and Alterations

If you consider adding a room, modernizing a bath or kitchen, converting a garage to a recreation room or some similar change, keep the amenities and characteristics comparable with others in the neighborhood. Avoid "improvements" that look weird or create clearly substandard space or space usage and livability. You want to create harmonious improvements that easily integrate (blend in) with the total property.

CAN YOU IMPROVE A LOCATION?

"What should you look for when buying a house?" asks the *Dallas Morning News* in one of its feature articles: "Location, location, location." Why? Because, as the article reports through interviews with experts, "You can change nearly anything about a house—anything except its location. That's why location is so important."

What do you think? Are these so-called experts right? Is it true that "you can't change the location of a property"? If you answered no, it's not true, you're right. Contrary to conventional wisdom, you can improve a home's location. Location does not merely refer to a fixed position on the face of the earth. Rather, it includes a complex set of attributes such as neighborhood demographics, appearance, prestige (reputation), school quality, crime rates, convenience to shopping, accessibility to employment, zoning laws, deed restrictions, property tax rates, government services, and a dozen other influences. Acting together, you and neighboring property owners (and tenants) can favorably impact any or all of these neighborhood features. Indeed, one of my favorite examples is South Beach, Florida.

The South Beach Example: From Derelicts to Fashion Models

In the mid-1980s, the South Beach area (SoBe, as locals call it) of Miami Beach had deteriorated to the point where crack dealers and prostitutes openly sold drugs and sex. Derelicts and criminals filled SoBe streets and flophouse hotels. Tourists visited the area at their own peril. Most locals simply wrote the neighborhood off as another loss to urban decay. But visiting New Yorker Tony Goldman saw things differently. "I took a ride around the area, and it was love at first sight. I was smitten," recalls Tony.

Instead of problems, Tony focused on potential. In his mind's eye, he imagined rehabbing the neighborhood buildings to highlight their art deco architecture. He envisioned sidewalk cafés and restaurants. He saw a tree-lined, beautiful Ocean Drive, the main thoroughfare of South Beach. He saw streets free of criminals. And he imagined new residents exhibiting pride of ownership.

To bring this dream to life, Tony, along with friends, investors, and civic leaders, formed a community action group. The group brought pressure on the police to rid the neighborhood of crime. They began a cleanup and rehab campaign. They convinced the city to float a $3 million bond issue to fund public improvements. They generated a new enthusiasm and community spirit.

How successful were they? As one resident remarked, "Tony put the chic back into SoBe." Within just a few years, SoBe became one of the hottest (no pun intended) neighborhoods in the Miami area. Condo sales, rent levels, and home prices jumped. Restaurants, cafés, and clubs filled the neighborhood. Because of these improvements, SoBe has become one of the foremost locations in the country for fashion photography shoots. Hundreds of former New York models now call South Beach home.

Community Action and Community Spirit Make a Difference

In his review of the book *Safe Homes, Safe Neighborhoods*, real estate columnist Robert Bruss says, "This is an action book . . . . This is a welcome and a long-overdue book for activists who want to learn how to improve a neighborhood." This book illustrates perfectly how community action and community spirit can improve the quality of neighborhoods and lives. Without a doubt, many city and suburban neighborhoods must tackle problems of one sort or another. Besides crime, these problems may range from barking dogs to speeding high schoolers to a lack of parks, sidewalks, or storm sewers. But regardless of the specific problems to be solved (or prevented), as Tony Goldman proved with South Beach, people acting together can make a difference.

"While it may seem that everywhere crime is on the rise," observe Stephanie Mann and M. C. Blakeman, authors of *Safe Homes, Safe Neighborhoods* (Nolo Press, 1993, p. 143), "in many neighborhoods the opposite is true. In cities and towns across the country, local crime prevention groups have reduced burglaries and car break-ins; helped catch muggers, rapists, and kidnappers; established Block Parents and other child-safety projects; driven out drug dealers; eliminated graffiti; and, in general, made their homes and streets safer. All it takes is a few people to get things started. By identifying and focusing on a neighborhood's main concerns—and working with police and each other—neighbors can make a difference."

For more on this topic, also see the previously mentioned *Fixing Broken Windows* (George Kelling and Catherine Coles, Free Press, 1996).

Many Neighborhoods Offer Potential

When you search and compare neighborhoods, look beyond the present. Imagine potential. "Fixing" neighborhoods can create far more value than merely fixing properties.

List all of a neighborhood's good points. How can you and other property owners, tenants, police, concerned citizens, and community leaders join together to highlight and take advantage of these features? List the neighborhood's weak points. How can you and others eliminate negative influences? Who can you enlist to promote your cause? Can you mobilize mortgage lenders, private investors, Realtors, not-for-profit housing groups, church leaders, builders, contractors, preservationists, police, local employers, retail businesses, schoolteachers, principals, community redevelopment agencies, elected officials, civic groups, and perhaps students, professors, and administrators of a nearby college or university?

Throughout the United States, people of all sorts have joined together to revitalize and reinvigorate hundreds of neighborhoods. From South of Market in San Francisco, to the Madison Valley in Seattle, Lakeview in Chicago, Boston's North End, Manhattan's SoHo, Miami's SoBe, and the "M Street" neighborhood in Dallas, neighbors, merchants, real estate investors, homeowners, and tenants have organized campaigns to make living, working, and shopping in these areas more desirable. "We liked the community," says real estate investor Rob Rowland of Cumberland (Atlanta), "but the community association was too passive. It needed some oomph, so we incorporated and worked hard to get to know people and inspire them to upgrade their yards and properties."

In speaking of a San Diego neighborhood that's poised for turnaround and redevelopment, Lori Weisberg says, "To the outsider, there's very little here that seems inviting . . . . Yet, where most people see a shabby area . . . visionaries see an exciting new downtown neighborhood adorned with a grand, tree-lined boulevard, a central plaza, artisans' studios, loft housing, and crowned with a sports and entertainment center . . . . [Already] there are pockets of gentrification—a budding arts district, scattered loft conversions, and . . . structures well-suited for preservation . . . . But [the total revitalization and redevelopment] does have to be imagined."

"There's no doubt," says Pam Hamilton, an executive with San Diego's Centre City Development Corporation, "this project will happen—it's just a question of when." What's true of San Diego is true in cities throughout the United States. By locating a neighborhood that's poised for turnaround or gentrification, your property fix-ups can pay double (or even quadruple) dividends.

WHAT TYPES OF IMPROVEMENTS PAY THE GREATEST RETURNS?

Newspaper and home improvement magazines frequently run articles that tell you a remodeled kitchen will pay back, say, 75 percent of its cost; a remodeled bath, 110 percent of its cost; or a swimming pool, 40 percent of its costs. Never rely on any of these specific figures. They're chiefly nonsense. Instead you must evaluate every property and every project on its own merits.

Before you estimate potential returns, research competing properties and tenant (buyer) preferences. You need to achieve a competitive advantage over other properties. In addition, budgets for projects can vary enormously depending on who does the work, what materials are selected, and the skill and creativity with which the job is undertaken.

How Much Should You Budget for Improvements?

As you plan your improvements for income properties, develop a cost/income estimate. Study market housing prices and rent levels. Figure out how much you can increase the sales price or rents for each project you undertake. As a rule of thumb, every $1,000 you invest in improvements should increase your net operating income at least $200 a year. You can see the logic of this rule by applying the value formula discussed in Chapter 3:

$$V = \frac{NOI}{R} \quad \text{or} \quad \frac{NOI}{V} = R$$

(Recall that V is the value to be estimated, NOI is net operating income, and R is the overall rate of return on capital.)

If your improvements of $1,000 yield $200 more a year in net income, you're earning 20 percent on your investment. Of course, you can choose whatever rate of return figure you think appropriate. Some investors use 10 percent; others may go as high as 40 percent. The exact rate you use is not so important. What matters is that before you jump into renovating an income property, temper your enthusiasm with a realistic look at the amount of increased rents your investments of time, effort, and money are likely to produce.

Beware of Overimprovement

The improvement budgeting process keeps you from overimproving your property relative to its neighborhood and relative to the prices (rent levels) your buyers (tenants) are willing and able to pay. To avoid these problems, survey the top rental rates in the neighborhood for the size and quality of units you intend to rent. If $850 a month is tops and your present inferior units rent for $700 a month, using the 20 percent rule, you should spend no more than, say, $6,000 to $9,000 per unit for improvement. These figures assume that after renovations you could raise your rents to $800 or $850 a month and pocket another $100 to $150 a month in income:

$$\frac{\$1,200 \ (12 \times \$100)}{.20} = \$6,000 \text{ cost of improvments}$$

$$\frac{\$1,800 \ (12 \times \$150)}{.20} = \$9,000 \text{ cost of improvments}$$

Again, these numbers won't necessarily apply in your market, but it's the method that counts. You want to run through the numbers so that you satisfy yourself the market actually supports the selling price or rent level you intend to ask. Moreover, these calculations reveal whether your hoped-for rent level (if realized) will give you an adequate payback on your investment.

Other Benefits

On some occasions, you may want to invest more in your improvements than rent increases would seem to justify. Besides higher rents, your renovated units should attract a better quality of tenant, reduce tenant turnover, and cut losses from bad debts and vacancies. More attractive units also give you greater pride in ownership. Notwithstanding these points, however, you still must work the numbers. Good tenants and pride of ownership are a worthwhile blessing only if you're collecting enough rents to pay your property expenses and mortgage payments.

No-No Improvements

Nearly all real estate investors have developed their no-no list of improvements. Robert Bruss, for example, says, "Smart fixer-upper homebuyers and investors look for properties with 'the right things wrong.' " To Bruss, the "right things wrong" include cosmetic improvements such as painting, landscaping, carpets, and light fixtures. On his list of no-nos are roofs, foundations, wiring, and plumbing.

Although Bruss is clearly right, in general, remember that you're dealing in specifics. Whether you can profitably improve any specific property depends on the price you pay for the property, the amounts you spend to improve it, and its value (or rent levels) after you've completed the work. By this standard, cosmetic fixers can be overpriced, and serious fixers may be underpriced. No universal rule applies. You must always analyze the financial details.

I know of a house that sat on the market for nearly a year because of serious foundation problems. No one wanted it. Eventually, though, an investor bought the property at a steep discount. He then jacked the house up 12 feet, repaired the foundation, built a new first story, set the old house (renovated) back on top, and resold the completed two-story house for a $42,000 profit. Not bad pay for three months of work.

BUDGETING FOR QUICK RESALE PROFITS

To budget formally for fix-and-flip profits, you must accurately estimate (1) the eventual sales price of the property, and (2) the total costs that you will incur from acquisition to closing.

Estimate the Sales Price First

Never forget: The market determines the price at which you can sell (or rent) your rehabbed property. Never estimate a future sales price by simply adding your costs to your purchase price and building in a profit margin. Cost-plus pricing doesn't work. Yet how many times have I heard sellers say, "We have to get $225,000. We have at least that much invested. We put $18,000 just into the kitchen"?

Folks, no one will care how much you put into the property. Buyers only care whether you're offering the most competitively priced property. When you plan for profits, you start with the price that a reasonably well informed buyer will pay for your creation.

Also beware of pricing your beautifully rehabbed property as if it were located in a more upscale neighborhood. To stay on the safe side, aim for a sales price that sits at least 20 percent below the highest-valued property on the block. The closer you push toward (or above) the top price limit of the neighborhood, the more difficulty you will face in trying to get your price (or rents)—even when your property shows clear superiority over the others.

Estimating Costs

After you've established a realistic sales price for the upgraded property, you begin to develop your cost estimates. Sales price comes first for two reasons: First, by focusing on a realistic price, you will intuitively recognize that certain extravagant expenses will blow the budget and vanquish any possibility of profits. Second, a realistic sales price will help you figure out the most you could pay for a property and still earn a profit.

Sales Price Less Costs and Profit Equals Acquisition Price

Consider this example: You find a property that after your improvements would quickly sell for $280,000. You further figure that your costs and profit will total as follows:

Acquisition expenses and closing costs	$3,750
Cost of borrowed funds (interest)	4,000
Selling expenses @ 6%	16,800
Materials for fix-up	22,000
Labor	12,000
Closing costs at sale	2,500
Profit	25,000
Total	$86,050

Because $280,000 equals your realistic selling price, you calculate that you can pay no more than $193, 950 for the property.

Your sales price	$280,000
Costs	61,050
Profit	25,000
Maximum acquisition price	$193,950

When you back your costs and required profit out of your expected (realistic) sales price, you set a top limit for your acquisition price. Using this technique will guarantee you a profit—as long as you accurately estimate and comprehensively include all of the costs necessary to buy, hold, fix up, and dispose of the property.

Accurate and Comprehensive Cost Estimates. At this point, you're probably thinking, "Okay, so how do I learn how much my rehab will cost?" Good question. Although you will develop this skill through experience, as a starting point, draw from the following six suggestions.

1. Shop till you drop. Learn the typical costs of materials by visiting a variety of home improvement suppliers, lumber yards, and hardware stores. Talk with knowledgeable store personnel. Compare price/quality tradeoffs. Learn alternative solutions to various types of common problems.
2. Take classes. Many community colleges and home improvement centers offer classes and seminars for beginning remodelers, renovators, and rehabbers.
3. Read books and magazines. Property improvements now total more than $150 billion a year. An entire industry of publishers caters to this need for knowledge.
4. Consult property inspectors. Accompany your property inspector as he performs your prepurchase inspections. Ask for advice about potential costs and remedies.
5. Secure multiple estimates. Contractors and tradespersons typically provide free cost estimates. Use this opportunity not only to solicit bids but also to discuss alternative ways of curing a property's deficiencies.
6. Talk to other property owners. You probably already know people who have improved their properties. Talk with them. Learn from their experiences.

Estimating costs and following through with improvements requires effort and knowledge. To enjoy the sweet-tasting fruit, you must suffer a few thorns. And that explains why buying fixers can prove so lucrative. Most people don't want the bother.

COMPLY WITH LAWS AND REGULATIONS

A word to the wise: Verify the legality of your planned improvements before you commit to buying a property. Your plans may fall within a variety of rules and regulations mandated by homeowner associations, zoning boards, health officials, fire marshals, and environmental agencies. Should your work require permitting, don't try to illegally evade this requirement. Repairs or improvements that fail to comply with regulatory and permitting requirements put you at great risk.

How will they find out? Complaining neighbors, drive-by patrol, your buyer's prepurchase property inspector, property tax assessment appraisers, and other tradespeople who may at some later date visit the property to give repair estimates—to name just a few. Build the cost of regulations and permits into your cost estimates. Noncompliance risks big dollars to save pennies.

SHOULD YOU BUY A "FIXER"?

As I travel throughout the country and talk to realty agents, investors, and homebuyers, I'm amazed at the number of people I meet who have bought homes that had sat on the market for months, if not years. Yet after buying these homes that had been rejected by dozens of other home shoppers, these buyers were able to turn the sow's ear into a silk purse and earn profits of tens (sometimes hundreds) of thousands of dollars.

I'm not saying that just because a property sits unsold for months or years it offers undiscovered promise. Many properties remain unsold because they're overpriced money traps. And certainly, most of the best bargains sell within days of being listed (which is one strong reason why you may want a market-savvy Realtor working for you to identify these gems before they're picked up by someone else).

Nevertheless, it's true that many buyers reject properties too quickly. They walk in, do a quick-take with a pass-through tour, and then say something like, "Let's get out of here. It's way too dark, the rooms are too small, and did you notice that awful burnt-orange shag carpeting in the bedroom?"

"Yes," the spouse replies, "and how about those ugly kitchen appliances and that green linoleum floor—not to mention the garbled floor plan and water stains on the ceiling? This house needs too much work. Anybody would be crazy to buy this nightmare."

Well, yes, anybody would be crazy to buy that house—unless, of course, they could buy it at a steep discount, rehab, redecorate, and resell it for a quick profit of $10,000 to $50,000 (or more). Or perhaps, if in finding a discounted fixer they were able to buy property in a higher-priced neighborhood they could otherwise not have afforded. Then these buyers wouldn't be called crazy. They'd be called smart.

Too Little Time?

If you are busy with kids, jobs, church, clubs, charities, social engagements, or school activities, investing in properties that need work may seem like a chore to avoid. But it's for this very reason that buying a fixer—remember, a fixer is any house you can improve, not just those that are run-down—can yield good profits. Owing to lack of time, most investors (and homebuyers) want red-ribbon deals. Move the tenants (or furniture) in and start collecting rents (or living in and enjoying the home). On top of that desire for immediate benefit, most buyers lack creativity, imagination, and knowledge. They can see things they don't like, but they can't envision value-enhancing solutions. With relatively few buyers who are willing and able to imaginatively renovate and redesign houses, fixers can get discounted steeply.

You can't expect to easily find a $200,000 house discounted by $50,000 merely because it needs paint, new carpets, and a thorough cleaning. Properties with readily solved problems tend to sell with smaller discounts. Still, you can't tell for sure. So look for those properties where other buyers say, "Forget it, let's move on" within moments of driving up to the curb or walking through the front door. Maybe with persistence, you can locate a real bargain that needs only TLC.

Put Your Creativity to Work

In most cases, your best opportunities for big profits lie with ideas and designs that most people would never think of. Educate and discipline yourself to think through questions such as "How can I overcome these shortcomings?" and "What opportunities for improvements can I create?"

Now, returning to the question—"Should you buy a fixer?"—listen to the wisdom of career fix-and-flip investor Suzanne Brangham.[1] In her book *Housewise* (HarperCollins, 1987, p. 185), Brangham tells beginning investors:

> Your buying power does not depend on the amount you can pay today with the funds sitting in your bank account . . . . As you learn more about real estate . . . you will understand that a little money can buy a lot—if you know how to pick the right house, bargain properly, and roll over your profits [possibly tax free, I might add] from one sale to another . . . . So get started now in property improving so you can eventually get all of the homes and properties you want, but can't afford right now. By starting small and repeatedly stepping up from one [lower-priced] property into another [higher-priced] property, you can quickly build a magnificent net worth.

---

1. Suzanne began her fix-and-flip career with a $40,000 condo in the early 1970s. Less than 10 years later, she was fixing and flipping million-dollar-plus houses. Although now somewhat dated, *Housewise* still makes for a great read.

9

MORE TECHNIQUES FOR HIGH YIELDS AND FAST PROFITS

long with fix and flip, you can employ a variety of other techniques to boost your real estate returns and build profits faster. Tune your possibility thinking to these multiple channels:

1. Lease options
2. Lease purchase
3. Conversions
4. Master leases
5. Assignments: flipping purchase contracts

LEASE OPTIONS

Many tenants would like to own their own homes. Yet for reasons of blemished credit, self-employment (especially those with off-the-books income or tax-minimized income), unstable income (commissions, tips), or lack of cash, they believe that they can't currently qualify for a mortgage from a lending institution. For these renters, the lease option (a lease with an option to purchase) solves their dilemma. Properly structured, the lease option permits renters to begin to acquire ownership rights in a property. Simultaneously, it also gives them time to improve their financial profile (at least from the perspective of a mortgage lender).

Here's How It Works

As the name implies, the lease option essentially rolls two different types of contracts into a combination contract. Under the lease agreement, the tenants sign a rental contract that covers the usual terms and conditions (see Chapter 3), such as the following:

- Monthly rental rate
- Term of lease
- Responsibilities for repair, maintenance, and upkeep
- Sublet and assignment
- Pets, smoking, cleanliness
- Permissible property uses
- House rules (noise, parking, number of occupants)

The option part of the contract gives tenants the right to buy the home at some future date. As a minimum, it will include (1) the amount of the option payment, (2) the option purchase price for the house, (3) the date on which the purchase option expires, (4) right of assignment, and (5) the amount of the rent credits that will count toward the purchase price of the house.

Benefits to Tenant-Buyers (An Eager Market)

In recent years, the benefits of lease options to tenant-buyers have been extolled by the respected, nationally syndicated real estate columnist Robert Bruss as well as most books written for first-time homebuyers. For example, in my book *Yes! You Can Own the Home You Want* (Wiley, 1995, p. 59), I tell hopeful homebuyers:

There's simply no question that lease options can bring home ownership closer to reality for many renters in at least six ways:

1. *Easier qualifying.* Qualifying for a lease option may be no more difficult than qualifying for a lease (sometimes easier). Generally, your credit and employment record need meet only minimum standards. Most property owners will not place your financial life under a magnifying glass as would a mortgage lender.
2. *Low initial investment.* Your initial investment to get into a lease option agreement can be as little as one month's rent and a security deposit of a similar amount. At the outside, move-in cash rarely exceeds $5,000 to $10,000, although I did see a home lease optioned at a price of $1.5 million that asked for $50,000 up front.
3. *Forced savings.* The lease option contract typically forces you to save for the down payment required when you

exercise your option to buy. Often, lease options charge above-market rental rates and then credit perhaps 50 percent of your rent toward the down payment. The exact amount is negotiable. And once you have committed yourself to buying, you should find it easier to cut other spending and place more money toward your "house account."

4. *Firm selling price.* Your option should set a firm selling price for the home, or it should include a formula (perhaps a slight inflation-adjustment factor) that can be used to calculate a firm price. Shop carefully, negotiate wisely, and when you exercise your option in one to three years (or whenever), your home's market value could exceed its option price. If your home has appreciated (or you've created value through improvements), you may be able to borrow nearly all the money you need to close the sale.

5. *100 percent financing possible.* You also can reduce the amount of cash investment you will need to close your purchase in another way: Lease-option a property that can be profitably improved through repairs, renovation, or cosmetics. By increasing the home's value, you may be able to borrow nearly all the money you need to exercise your option to buy.

   For example, assume your lease option purchase price is $75,000. Say by the end of one year, your rent credits equal $2,500. You now owe the sellers $72,500. Through repairs, fix-up work, and redecorating, you have increased the home's value by $10,000. Your home should now be worth around $85,000. If you have paid your bills on time during the previous year, you should be able to locate a lender who will finance your purchase with the full $72,500 you need to pay off the sellers. Or, as another possibility, you could sell the home, pay the sellers $72,500, and use your remaining cash from the sale to buy another home.

6. *Reestablish credit.* A lease option can also help renters buy who need time to build or reestablish a solid credit record. Judy and Paul Davis wanted to buy a home before prices or interest rates in their area once again rose above their reach. But the Davises needed time to clear up credit problems created by too much borrowing and Judy's layoff. The lease option could be the possibility that helps the Davises achieve their goal of home ownership.

When prospective tenants and homebuyers think through the preceding list of benefits, they become a ready market for lease options. You just need to offer them the right property and terms.

Benefits to Investors

Although you can structure lease options in many different ways, they nearly always provide these benefits to *investors:* (1) lower risk, (2) higher rents, and (3) guaranteed profits.

Lower Risk.   As a rule, tenants who shop for a lease option will take better care of your property than would average renters. Because they intend one day to own the house, they will treat it more like homeowners than tenants. Also, they know that to qualify for a mortgage, they will need a perfect record of rent payments. (If your tenant-buyers don't know that fact, make sure you impress it into their consciousness.) As a minimum, lease option tenants expect to pay up front first and last month's rent, a security deposit, and, more than likely, an option fee of $1,000 to $5,000 (possibly more). Taken together, all of these factors spell lower risk for you the property owner.

Higher Rents.   Lease option tenants will agree to pay higher-than-market rents because they know you will apply a part of that monthly rent to the home's purchase price. The tenants view these "rent credits"—actually they should be called purchase price credits—as forced savings that will contribute toward a lender's required down payment.

From your immediate standpoint, the higher rent payments increase your monthly cash flow and boost your cash-on-cash return. In high-priced areas where newly bought rental properties awaken a hungry alligator, the increased rent of a lease option may turn a negative cash flow into a positive.

Guaranteed Profits.   Experienced investors know that (on average) fewer than 50 percent of lease option tenants take advantage of their right to buy their leased home. Sometimes they change their mind. Sometimes their finances fail to improve as much as they hoped. Sometimes their personal circumstances shift (separation, divorce, job relocation, additional children).

Whatever the reason, the tenants (at least in part) forfeit their rent credits, option fee, and any fix-up work they have performed around the house. As a person you may feel badly for the tenants. But as an investor, their loss means your gain. When they do not go through with their purchase, you end up with more profit than you would have earned under a traditional rental agreement.

Even if the tenants do buy, you still win, because in setting your option price, you built in a good profit margin over the price you originally paid for the house. This technique works especially well in transactions where you have bought at a bargain price. In addition, you gain more than you would have from a straight sale of the property because you didn't have to pay high marketing costs or Realtor commissions.

For investors, the lease option makes for truly a win-win agreement. You win when your tenants buy, and you win when the tenants don't buy and relinquish their right.

The Lease Option Sandwich

The lease option sandwich truly magnifies your profit potential. Instead of buying a property, you find motivated sellers who are willing to lease-option their property to you at both a bargain rental rate and a bargain price. Typically, these sellers were not advertising their property as a lease option. In fact, they may not even have thought of the idea until you put a proposal in front of them.

Ideally, through this lease option, you gain control of the property for two to five years. Your cash out of pocket totals less than you would probably have paid in closing costs had you immediately bought the property.

Next, you spend some money on spruce-up expenses (if desirable) and readvertise the property specifically as a lease option. You find tenant-buyers and sign them up on a lease option with you as the lessor. Your tenant-buyers agree to pay you a higher monthly rental and a higher option price than you've negotiated for yourself in your role as lessee with the property owners. You profit from the difference.

Your rate of return skyrockets because you gain control of a property with almost no cash investment. The up-front money you've collected from your tenant-buyers exceeds the amount you paid to the property owners. Essentially, you're buying wholesale and selling retail—without actually having to pay for your inventory.

Does the Lease Option Sandwich Really Work? Theoretically, it can work. (Just make sure you protect yourself fully in the lease option contracts you sign.) Robert Allen and James Lumley, for example, two well-known real estate investors and book authors, claim to have used this technique successfully to generate big profits with little or no cash.

Personally, I have never tried it. For my taste, giving someone an option to buy a property that I don't yet own seems fraught with dangers. Nevertheless, *in theory* it can yield high returns. If you're interested in biting into a lease option sandwich, read James Lumley's *Five Magic Paths to Making a Fortune in Real Estate* (Wiley, 2000).

How to Find Lease Option Buyers and Sellers

To get the best bargain on a lease option, don't look exclusively to sellers who advertise lease option. These sellers are trying to retail their properties. It will be tougher for you to find a bargain here. Instead look to motivated for-sale-by-owner (FSBO) sellers in the "Homes for Sale" classified ads. Or you might also try property owners who are running "House for Rent" ads. As previously mentioned, often the best lease option sellers will not have considered the idea until you suggest it.

In your search for tenant-buyers, you will often see three classified newspaper ad categories from which to choose: (1) homes for sale, (2) homes for rent, and (3) the specific category "lease option" that some newspapers include. Unfortunately, no one can say which ad category will work best in your market. Experiment with each of these choices. To learn which one is pulling the best responses, ask your callers to tell you in which category they saw the ad. Don't assume that any single category listing will draw the largest number of qualified callers.

A Creative Beginning with Lease Options (for Investors)

To start building wealth fast without investing much money up front, try the lease option approach of Suzanne Brangham. Although Brangham stumbled into her investment career quite fortuitously, you can follow her path more purposefully. From her book *Housewise* (p. 39), here's her story:

> While searching for the ideal career, I was also looking for a place to live. I located a lovely but dilapidated apartment house. The building was making a painful transition from rentals to condominiums. Units were for sale or rent. But sales were practically nonexistent.
>
> With my head held high, preliminary plans and a budget tucked under my arm, I decided to make the manager an offer he couldn't refuse.
>
> I told him that in lieu of paying the $800-a-month rent that was being asked for a 2-bedroom, 2-bath unit, I would renovate the entire apartment. I would agree to spend $9,600 for labor and materials, the equivalent of a full year of rent pay-

ments. Along with a 12-month lease, I also requested an option to buy the unit at its $45,000 asking price.

Three months later, Brangham was on her way. She then bought her renovated condo unit at her lease option price of $40,000. Then, simultaneously, she sold the unit to a buyer for $85,000. After accounting for renovation expenses, closing costs, and Realtor's commission, she netted $23,000. Brangham no longer had a home, but she had found a career.

Twenty years, 23 homes, and 71 properties later, Brangham had become not just independently wealthy, but a nationally recognized author, speaker, and entrepreneur. In *Housewise*, she tells about her renovation experiences and the career she found by chance. As I've said, it's a great book for anyone who would like to learn hundreds of profit-making ideas that can be applied to buying and renovating fixers.

LEASE PURCHASE AGREEMENTS

As a practical matter, the lease purchase agreement works about the same as a lease option. However, instead of gaining the right to either accept or reject a property, the lease purchaser *commits to buying*. As an investor, you can often persuade reluctant sellers to accept your lease purchase offer, even though they may shy away from a lease option. The lease purchase offer seems much more definite because you are saying that you will buy the property—but you would like to defer closing until some future date (six months to five years, more or less) that works for you and the sellers.

"Seems" More Definite

I say "seems" more definite because there is a loophole. You can (and should) write an escape clause into your purchase contract called "liquidated damages." With a liquidated-damages clause, the sellers could not sue you to go through with your purchase if you choose to back out. Nor could they sue you for any actual monetary damages that they may have suffered owing to your failure to buy. Instead, the liquidated-damage clause permits your sellers to pocket your earnest money deposit.

In effect, your earnest money acts like an option payment. No matter what the purchase contract appears to say, in reality you have not firmly committed to buy.

Amount of the Earnest Money Deposit

The real firmness of either a lease option or a lease purchase contract lies in the amount of the up-front money the seller receives—regardless of whether it's called an "option" fee or an "earnest money" deposit. If you want to convince a seller that you intend to complete a lease option or a lease purchase transaction, put a larger amount of cash on the table. By the same token, if you truly do want to keep your options open, negotiate the smallest walk-away fee that you can, even if it means yielding more concessions in the other terms of your agreement.

Contingency Clauses

You can also escape from your obligation to buy a property through the use of contingency clauses. If the contingency (property condition, ability to obtain financing, lawyer approval, sale of another property, etc.) isn't met, you can walk away from a purchase and at the same time rightfully demand the return of your earnest money or option fee. Because contingencies, option fees, and earnest money deposits form such an integral part of most private market transactions (as opposed to foreclosures and government sales), this topic is discussed more fully in Chapter 10.

CONVERSIONS

Apartments with new life as condominiums. . . . Gas stations now operating as retail outlets (Seven-Elevens). . . . Old homes converted to office space. . . . What was once farm acreage is now a sprawling urban shopping center. These properties are examples of adaptive use of both land and buildings brought about by a locale's growth and change.

An oversupply of gas stations throughout the city serves as an example. Because of stiff competition among these service stations, the unprofitable ones shut down and become vacant. A new use becomes imminent.

Conversions provide boundless opportunities for the creative investor. Converting an old house located in the downtown area can be very profitable. Office space sometimes rents at twice the rental rate of housing. Of course, the opposite also can occur. Recently, in London, housing prices have climbed so high that all types of retail, warehouse, and offices were being converted to apartments.

Several years ago, when Andrew McLean worked for Wolverine Development in Lansing, Michigan, the company was involved with investing in strategic corner locations in the path of the city's outward growth. The company would purchase single-family homes on a potentially good corner location, with the long-term intention of converting these homes to a more profitable rental use. This method had a great advantage over investing in similarly located vacant land because the houses would generate rental income until growth made conversion profitable.

Converting land use and its buildings is like turning straw into gold. But how can you take advantage of these changes in land use? Begin by obtaining an overall zoning map from your city's planning department. Each area of the city has a particular zoning (residential, multiunit, agricultural, commercial, and industrial) limiting its land use. A good conversion prospect would be a residential home already located within a commercial zone. If the property you wish to convert is located in a residential zone, it would require a change in zoning for you to accomplish your objective. Applying for a variance or zoning change may require money, time, and effort. The easiest properties to convert are those that are adjacent to the zoning you wish to convert to. If you're interested in pursuing this matter, check with your local planning department and inquire about the necessary procedure.

Condominium Conversion

To convert an apartment building into individual condominium units, purchase the apartments inexpensively enough so that each unit will easily convert to a salable condo. Because of legal procedures and incidental costs to convert, not to mention the time and effort, as much as a 1.5 to 2.0 rule of thumb is sometimes required. In other words, to earn a good profit, a $50,000 apartment rental unit might have to sell for $75,000 to $100,000 as a condo. A large markup is necessary to cover the marketing, renovation, and attorney costs, plus the risk and talent necessary to make such a conversion.

Consider the legal procedures necessary to accomplish condominium conversion: First, the city may have to approve the change in use. You will be required to submit plans explaining exactly how you intend to make the conversion. Should the city consider your plans adequate, it will approve the conversion. If not, certain changes, such as additional parking or bathrooms, may be needed before you get permission from the city. Planners may also raise the "affordable housing" objection. In the San Francisco Bay Area, apartment building owners could make huge profits by converting their units to condos. But alas, the city severely limits such conversions in its efforts to maintain a large number of rentals. Few other cities restrict conversions with such tight controls.

Before going ahead with plans for a condo conversion, study the local area to learn what comparable condo units are selling for. If you can purchase an apartment building at a low enough price, and renovate and sell the converted units and earn a profit while absorbing time and costs to convert, then by all means go ahead with your plans.

To illustrate how you might calculate the potential profits of converting rental apartments into individually owned condominium units, here's an example for a 16-unit building:

Acquisition price	$480,000
Rehab at $7,500 per unit	120,000
Attorney fees (condo document preparation, government permitting process, sales contract preparation, closing document review)	40,000
Marketing costs (advertising, sales commissions)	45,000
Mortgage interest (12-month renovation and sellout)	50,000
Incidentals (architect, interior design, landscaping, government permits)	35,000
Total costs	$770,000
Cost per unit	$48,125

In this example, the investor paid $480,000 ($30,000 per unit) to acquire this 16-unit rental property. After all costs of conversion, her total investment increased to $770,000 ($48,125 per unit). But these figures haven't yet considered profits. If the investor wants to net around $10,000 per unit, she will need to sell the units at a price approaching $60,000 each (twice the amount of her original per unit purchase price).

The figures in this example merely illustrate this conversion technique. Yet every item from acquisition cost to incidentals is subject to wide variance depending on the local market, the specific property to be acquired, the amount of planned renovation, the degree of complexity of the condo conversion laws and procedures, and the marketing strategy to be adopted. To decide whether such a project is feasible in your area, research rental properties, condo prices, and conversion laws. Do some scratch-pad feasibility calculations. If preliminary estimates look promising, talk with an investor, contractor, attorney, or real estate consultant experienced in the conversion process. With the knowledge gained from these talks (and perhaps some follow-up research), you can decide whether this investment approach offers you enough profit potential to compensate for risks such as cost overruns, slow sales, and permitting delays.

Tenants in Common

In some parts of the country, oppressive rent control and tight condo conversion laws make it almost impossible to convert rental apartments into condominiums even though such conversions would prove profitable. However, innovative real estate investors and entrepreneurs have found several ways to circumvent these restrictive regulations. In Berkeley, California (also commonly known as the People's Republic of Berkeley), and other left-wing-dominated cities in the San Francisco Bay Area, innovative investors pioneered a conversion concept called TIC.

The term "TIC" (pronounced T-I-C) stands for tenant in common and is a popular form of joint ownership that's been given a unique twist to create a hybrid property—something between, say, a co-op and a condominium.

As the plan typically works in the Bay Area, an investor (or group of investors) locates, say, an older four-unit rental house that because of rent controls has a depressed market value of $600,000 ($150,000 per unit). As individual condo units, the apartments would sell for $250,000 each, for a total building value of $1,000,000; however, restrictive conversion laws eliminate this possibility.

But here's where creativity counts. Investors buy the property. They then advertise for four households (individuals, married couples, partners, friends, families) who would like to own one of the individual units. Once found, they sell them pro rata shares of ownership in the total building at a price of, say, $200,000 each (if the units are of unequal quality, the pro rata division would charge some owners more and others less). Next, the respective joint owners enter into long-term leases for "their" units with all the other owners.

Although in a legal sense, all of the households jointly own the entire building, in a practical sense, each becomes the proprietor of a specific unit. Later, if one of the co-owners wishes to sell his or her share of the building, he or she can do so. The buyer pays the seller the value of his or her ownership interest in the total property and obtains leasehold rights to the unit.

Besides circumventing restrictive condo conversion laws, TICs have another advantage: Organizing a TIC is much simpler and less costly than the legal documentation and government permitting that is typically required when condo conversions are allowed. In fact, since with a TIC all you are doing is selling a building to a group of co-owners, typically no special laws apply.

Although the TIC concept in rental properties has been implemented primarily as a response to excessive government, it need not be limited to that use. Even if you don't live in a "People's Republic," you might explore this investment technique in your area. Because a TIC is far easier to structure than a condo conversion, it might be a good way to gain experience in "buying wholesale" and "selling retail." Your greatest obstacles will be finding a lawyer who can give you competent legal counsel and explaining the concept to potential buyers and building co-owners.

To learn more about the TIC concept, consider taking a tax-deductible trip to the San Francisco Bay Area and talk to investors, unit owners, and attorneys who have firsthand experience with these types of properties. Maybe you can pioneer the concept in your area.

Converting Apartments to Office Space

Office space may rent for twice the rental rate of comparable apartment rental space. Just from this observation, it would appear profitable to convert apartments to office space. But before going forward with such a conversion, at least consider four important questions:

1. Is the property you wish to convert within a commercial zone? If not, can it be easily changed to the proper zoning?
2. What is the current vacancy rate for office space in the area of the subject property? If too much space is already available, conversion would be unwise.
3. Do you have adequate parking for office space? The city may require one parking space for every 250 to 500 square feet of rentable office space.
4. How much will it cost to convert? Could you borrow the money to finance such a conversion? And finally, will the cost, legal procedures, and time and effort be worth the eventual profit you will realize?

Study the property and the market carefully. Thoroughly figure the finances of the projected conversion. Keep in tune with the requirements. If you can convert at a reasonable cost and earn a good profit, take a chance. While pursuing ample rewards, you'll gain valuable experience.

MASTER LEASES

To make money in real estate, you need to control a property. The most common way to obtain this control is through ownership. Some investors, though, don't buy their properties—at least not right away. Instead, they master lease them.

Say you locate a 12-unit apartment building that is poorly managed and needs upgrading. You could offer to buy the property. But you don't have the financial power to arrange new financing, and the owner doesn't want to sell the property using a land contract or purchase money mortgage. At present, the property barely produces enough cash flow to pay expenses, property taxes, and mortgage payments. The owner wants to turn this money pit into a moneymaker but lacks the will to invest time, effort, money, and talent.

The solution: Master lease the entire building and guarantee the owner a steady, no-hassle monthly income. In return, you obtain the right to upgrade the building and property management to increase its net operating income (NOI).

Generally, a master lease gives you possession of the property for a period of 5 to 15 years and an option to buy at a prearranged price. During the period of your lease, you would pocket the difference between what you pay to operate the property, including lease payments to the owner and the amounts you collect from the individual tenants who live in each of the apartments. This technique resembles the "lease sandwich" discussed earlier, only it applies to multiple-unit buildings as opposed to single-family houses. Here's how the before-and-after numbers might look:

Before (Owner Management)

Gross potential income at $500 per unit	$72,000
Vacancy losses at 15%	10,800
Effective gross income	$61,200
Expenses	
Utilities	14,400
Maintenance	8,360
Advertising	2,770
Insurance	3,110
Property taxes	6,888
Miscellaneous (evictions, attorney fees, bad debts, vandalism, pest control, bookkeeping, etc.)	5,000
Total expenses	40,528
Net operating income	20,672
Mortgage payments	19,791
Before-tax cash flow (cash throw-off)	$881

After (New Management)

Gross potential income at $575 per unit	$82,800
Vacancy losses at 4%	3,312
Effective gross income	$79,488
Expenses	
Utilities	2,230
Maintenance and upkeep	13,200
Advertising	670
Insurance	2,630
Property taxes	7,300
Miscellaneous (evictions, attorney fees, bad debts, vandalism, pest control, bookkeeping, etc.)	2,500
Total expenses	28,530
Net operating income	50,958
Leasehold payments to owner (master lessor)	25,000
Before-tax cash flow (master lessee)	$25,958

How might someone achieve such a spectacular turnaround? (1) Upgrade the property and implement a thorough maintenance program; (2) with a more attractive property and a more attentive management, attract and retain high-quality tenants; (3) meter the apartment units individually to reduce utilities; (4) raise rents to reflect the more appealing condition of the property and the more pleasant ambiance created by higher-quality, neighbor-considerate, rule-abiding tenants; (5) shop for lower-cost property and liability insurance coverage; and (6) reduce turnover and encourage word-of-mouth tenant referrals to eliminate most advertising expenses.

Not only did this property turnaround increase the NOI, but correspondingly, the higher NOI, lower risk, and more attractive apartments led to a much higher building value. This meant that when the investors exercised their option to buy, they were able to arrange 100 percent financing to pay off the owner, yet still give the lender a 70 to 80 percent loan-to-value ratio as measured against the property's new higher value.

In lieu of buying the master-leased property, you might sell your leasehold and option rights to another investor. Given the much better NOI that you've created, these rights will command a substantial price. In effect, an investor would pay for the right to earn $25,958 per year (plus future increases) for the remaining term of the master lease, and the right to buy the property at a now bargain price.

As you can see from this example, a master lease with option to buy can create significant profit opportunities for investor-entrepreneurs who are willing to tackle turning a poorly managed, run-down property into an attractive, effectively operated apartment building.

ASSIGNMENTS: FLIPPING PURCHASE CONTRACTS

Generally, when you sign a contract to buy or option a property, you may later assign that contract to another investor. This technique, which is called contract flipping, offers significant profit opportunities with relatively little up-front cash investment.

A developer announces plans to build a luxury high-rise condominium project with units priced from $225,000 to as much as $775,000. However, the units won't be ready for occupancy for 18 months. In the meantime, buyers can contract for a unit with an earnest money deposit of $5,000. You pick a choice-view unit priced at $500,000 and give the developer $5,000 of earnest money. During the construction period, this project receives rave reviews and wonderful publicity. Buyers are now signing up on waiting lists. The value of your reserved unit jumps up to $550,000. Yet your purchase contract gives you the right to buy it at a mere $500,000. What do you do? If you want a quick $45,000 profit, "flip" your contract. Assign your right to buy this unit for a payment of $50,000. You've just made a ninefold return on your original investment.

If this new project receives bad reviews, if mortgage interest rates skyrocket, or if the local economy goes into the tank, the market prices of these units could fall, and you may have to forfeit your $5,000 deposit. Contract flipping, then, is more like speculating than investing.

You need not limit use of this technique to projects under construction. Some savvy investors scout the market for bargain-priced existing properties, place the seller under contract with a small deposit, and then locate another investor who will pay them a fee (premium) for the right to step in and buy the property on the favorable terms previously negotiated. Although any type of contract flipping has its risks, for investors who are skilled in spotting underpriced properties, this technique can yield high returns in short time periods.

SUMMARY

Buy, manage, and hold for increased rents and property appreciation remains a time-tested, effective way to build wealth in real estate. As an alternative strategy, however, you can buy, fix up, and resell your properties using a lease option purchase contract. Under the right market conditions, this technique can increase your returns two ways: (1) The option price you offer your tenants should exceed the price you paid for the property plus the amounts you paid for improvements, and (2) during the rental period, your rent collections and option fee monies will exceed the monthly income you would receive from a straight rental. Once you develop a system that will work in your market, the lease option investment technique can prove to be a real moneymaker.

In addition to lease option, other alternative investment strategies include the fix and flip, property conversions, TICs, master leases, and contract assignment. Although each of these techniques involves risk, specialized expertise, and market knowledge, in the right circumstances, any one of them can pay off with high profits.

The overall point: You need not wait for market forces to generate your real estate returns. Through creativity, knowledge, and alertness to opportunity, you can achieve returns that substantially outperform the market. As pointed out at the beginning of this book, most entrepreneurial investors can earn far more in real estate than in the stock market. In the stock market, you buy and *hope* prices go up. But you exercise no control over the results. In contrast, with real estate, you can use your mind, your knowledge, and your talents to create a strategy that will produce good returns in any type of market.

10

NEGOTIATE A
WIN-WIN AGREEMENT

Negotiators typically adopt one of three negotiating styles: (1) adversarial, (2) accommodating, and (3) win-win. Most lawyers rely on the adversarial style. They make outrageous demands. Then they push, pull, or threaten to move you as close as possible to their position. Adversarial negotiators don't care whether their "opponents" end up satisfied. All they care about is winning for themselves.

In contrast to the adversarial approach, the accommodating negotiator easily gives in to every request. Accommodators feel powerless to create the outcome they really want. They often feel helpless because of the lack of money, time, information, knowledge, or experience. Accommodators detest conflict. They would rather lose than stand their ground. When negotiating through a real estate agent (or other third party), accommodators typically delegate too much responsibility. "Oh, just do what you think is best" or "Let's just agree and get the whole thing over with" are two common responses of accommodators.

In pursuing a win-win method, negotiators adopt a little of the adversarial style and a little of the accommodating style. Most important, though, they adopt a more complex perspective. Win-win negotiators recognize that every negotiation brings forth multiple issues, priorities, and possibilities. They also recognize and respect the other party's (not opponent's) concerns, feelings, and needs. Win-win negotiators don't think along a single line of contention—especially that of price.

Win-win negotiators primarily work to secure a strong, mutually beneficial agreement that everyone is committed to seeing through to completion. By reading through this chapter, you can learn how to shape a win-win agreement. In addition, you can learn to avoid falling prey to the win-lose transactions of the adversarial "hard-ballers," or becoming one of those "passive-accommodators" whose eagerness to do a deal traps them into unwise concessions.

WIN-WIN PRINCIPLES

To set the stage for effective negotiations, here are 15 principles that should guide you to a win-win agreement:

1. Find common interests that can precede the negotiation. Don't just jump into talk about price and terms. Use some chitchat to warm up the relationship before you get down to business. Don't provoke a competitive spirit or a win-the-game attitude about the negotiation. You win the game when you buy a property at a good price, not when you drive off a potential seller because you failed to yield on a relatively minor point.
2. Recognize that negotiation is a cooperative enterprise. It provokes an emotional experience with both parties having needs, wants, and feelings that have to be considered. Learn as much as you can about the sellers. Engage in empathetic conversation.
3. Recognize the proper time to stop. Successful negotiators can feel tension building. Pushing the negotiations for that last dollar in purchase price or that last concession has killed many sales. Beware, too, of pushing so hard that you destroy the trust of the relationship. If parties lose trust in each other, negotiations become much more difficult to maintain on a win-win basis.
4. Listen carefully to the objections and arguments of the seller. Try to determine what the seller really wants. Often people seek results indirectly. If what a person actually wants is brought forth, the negotiations will yield a better outcome. Many times, disagreements arise simply because two parties are not communicating what they think they are communicating. Listen far more than you talk.
5. Use questions in negotiations as a means to identify needs. Carefully notice that phrasing questions can be just as important as knowing what questions to ask. An old story goes that a clergyman asked his superiors, "May I smoke while praying?" Permission was denied. Another clergyman, though, used a different approach. He asked, "May I pray while I am smok-

ing?" Of course, you know the answer. A skilled negotiator should be adept at phrasing questions to identify a seller's needs without causing offense.

6. Give logical and practical reasons to support your viewpoints. Likewise, seek explanations for what the seller wants.

7. Never quickly say no to a proposition suggested by a seller even when you think the offer ridiculous. Take time to reflect so that the seller's input seems important. Always try to return the negotiations to the goals you hold in common with the seller.

8. Remind the seller of the property's negative features. But do so in a way that doesn't arouse retaliation—especially if you are negotiating with a homeowner. Speak in terms of the market, the features, or the decorating schemes that tenants prefer. Don't insult the seller's tastes or handiwork. Say, "Tenants usually prefer neutral carpet colors such as beige or earth tones." Don't say, "How could I possibly get this place rented with that tasteless marbled purple carpet and that pink foil wallpaper?"

9. Because many sellers expect to negotiate (as opposed to agreeing flat out with your requests), leave room in your offer for bargaining. Even though price and terms may rank most critical to the negotiations, possession date, closing date, personal property, repair escrow, and other issues can also present trade-off points.

10. Stay realistic. You may face a seller's market or a buyer's market. You may face a timid seller or an assertive one. You may meet sellers where the wife is eager to sell the house, but the husband couldn't care less. Each negotiating situation differs from all others. Don't lose sight of the realities of the transaction in which you are participating. This recommendation brings up another important point: Only the seller benefits when two or more buyers compete for the same property. Avoid getting involved in a bidding war. The heated competition makes it difficult to obtain a good buy. Besides, why compete head-to-head when other potential bargains are available down the street?

11. Don't concede easily. If you do, a sophisticated seller will press on for more easy victories. Always hesitate before acting. Suggest tit for tat. Give only when you ask for something in return.

12. Beware of oral concessions. Oral concessions tip your hand to a higher price or other unfavorable terms that you are willing to accept. Or they may be used as a ploy by sellers to get you to orally commit to a price. Once the seller feels you are committed that far, he or she will write up the offer for an even higher

amount. Each time you offer or counteroffer, make sure the terms are written. Use a contract-of-sale form and change the relevant terms that are subject to the negotiation with each party initialing those changes.

13. Recognize the risks of negotiating. When you reject a counteroffer from a seller, that counteroffer is dead unless the seller chooses to revive it. Likewise, when you counter a seller's offer, your counter kills the seller's proposal. Also, the seller is free to withdraw an offer (counteroffer) at any time before you accept it. A seller or buyer may withdraw an offer without obligation even if the withdrawing party has promised to keep the offer open for a stated period.

14. Stockpile information early. The more you learn about a seller's financial capabilities, family situation, likes and dislikes, priorities, time constraints, available options, previous offers (accepted or rejected), past real estate experiences, perceptions about the property's condition and value, and any other factors that might bear on the transaction, the better you can adapt your offer and negotiating strategy to the seller's situation and personality. You not only need to secure this information; you need to secure it as early as possible while you are in the relationship-building stage of your negotiations.

    If you jump into a hot and heavy debate over price and terms before you've built an information stockpile, you will generally find that the sellers clam up. They guard their disclosures much more closely. As another point, most sellers aren't stupid or naive. They put forth their own information agenda in terms of what they would like you to believe. Don't accept the information you obtain as unvarnished fact. Look for nuggets of truth, but keep your bunkum detector finely tuned.

15. Control the reference points of the negotiation. All sellers base their asking price and terms on certain reference points. The seller may believe that comparable properties have sold with a monthly gross rent multiplier of 125, or maybe a capitalization rate of 9.5 percent, and will therefore apply those norms to figure a fair price for his or her property.

    To negotiate effectively with this seller, learn the reference points the seller is using, and why. Once you gain this information, attempt to explain why those norms aren't applicable and why the reference points you've selected are fairer or more appropriate. You might point out that the comp properties with cap rates of 9.5 percent are newer (better location, more stable tenants, better condition, etc.) than the seller's property. In fact, true comps to the seller's property have typically sold with cap rates in the range of 11 to 11.5 percent.

The seller may know the house down the street just sold for $180,000, but doesn't realize that its owners carried back financing at 6.0 percent and included in the transaction $15,000 worth of personal property. You can try a curt approach ("I'll give you $155,000. That's my top offer. Take it or leave it"). But you win more negotiations when you first persuade the seller to accept a reference point that's favorable to your offer. Then edge the seller toward the agreement you want.

THE PURCHASE CONTRACT

Although no "standard" purchase contract actually exists, the following discussion explains the most important issues buyers and sellers should address when they structure their written agreement.

Names of the Parties

Your agreement should include the names of all parties to the transaction. It is especially important that all owners (sellers) are named and are immediately available to sign your offer as soon as you reach an agreement. Be wary of negotiating with a seller whose spouse or partners do not actively join the negotiations. If they don't agree to sign, you have no deal.

Some sellers will claim that their co-owners will go along with whatever they say. Yet after you commit, the seller will come back and say, "Gee, I'm terribly sorry. My partner refuses to sign. He thinks I'm giving the property away. He wants another $25,000, but I've told him I can't renege and change the terms. But he insists. So I'll tell you what, if you can agree to another $10,000, I'll go back to my partner and do my best to convince him to go along. I'm really sorry, but sometimes this guy's a jerk, and there's little I can do to reason with him."

This "good-guy-bad-guy" ploy is one of the oldest tricks in the book. But it often works. Sellers (and buyers) continue to use it. Just don't be surprised when you have it pulled on you—if you've proceeded to negotiate with someone who lacks the legal authority to carry out the agreement. (Substitute the word "client" for "spouse" or "partner," and you'll encounter this same tactic from lawyers.)

Site Description

Identify the subject property by street address *and* legal description. As a safeguard, walk the boundaries of the property as you refer to a survey or a plat. When walking the boundaries, note encroachments. Make sure the size of the lot you think you're buying is actually the size you're getting. Especially where a subject site borders a vacant lot, field, creek, or other unclear delineation, don't assume the lot lines run where they appear to run. Visually verify where surveyed boundaries actually lie.

Building Description

Often, your real estate agreement needs to identify only the lot, not the building. That's because the legal definition of real estate (the surface of the earth) automatically includes all structures permanently attached to the land.

If the seller, however, has represented to you that the buildings are of a specific size or are built of certain materials, or of a certain historic date or design, then write those features (whatever they are) into the property description. In Berkeley, California, buyers sued the sellers of a gracious old home because the sellers had (mistakenly) told the buyers that the home had been designed by Julia Morgan, a famous Bay Area architect of the early 1900s. The buyers claimed that they had not just agreed to buy a house on a specific site. Rather, they had contracted to buy a Julia Morgan house. Because the house lacked the Julia Morgan prestige, the buyers believed they were entitled to damages. (The court agreed and awarded damages to the buyers.)

If you think you're buying a prewar brownstone, or maybe the house where Grover Cleveland was raised, write it into your agreement. Let the sellers know exactly what you expect to receive in all its critical details. Should your expectations (the seller's material representations) prove false, you may have legal recourse for contract recision, damages, or both.

Personal Property

Although the legal definition of real estate applies to land and buildings, it does not necessarily include the personal property that may form part of your agreement with the sellers. (Generally, the term "personal property" refers to items that are not "permanently" attached to a building or the land.) Say the sellers of a fourplex provide their tenants window air conditioners, miniblinds, ranges, refrigerators, and ceiling fans. If you offer to buy that property, expressly list these items in your written purchase contract.

While it's true that some courts have broadened the concept of real estate to include personal property that is "adapted for use" with a specific property, you definitely do not want to depend on litigation to force the sellers to convey the personal property that you believed to be included in the sale. Leave no doubt—write it out. Go through every room of the property and list every item that the sellers might plausibly maintain was not a part of your agreement because it was their "personal property" and therefore not included with the sale of the real estate.

This listing of personal property serves another purpose, as well. It requires the sellers to clearly point out what personal property belongs to them and what belongs to their tenants. Property investors who do not obtain an accurate list of the seller's personal property may later find themselves in dispute with tenants when the tenants claim, "That refrigerator is ours. That junk icebox the landlord provided was carted off to the dump two years ago. We bought this refrigerator from Betty's parents." To be doubly safe, at the time you buy, ask the tenants to sign off on any list of personal property that the sellers prepare.

Price and Financing

When you prepare your offer, spell out precisely the purchase price of the property and the terms of the financing. List the amounts payable, how payable, when payable, and the interest rate(s). Make it easy for a disinterested third party to interpret your meaning. Leave nothing to decide at some later date. "Seller agrees to carry back $20,000 on mutually agreeable terms" does not meet the contractual requirements of specificity.

If you are planning to arrange new financing, or even if you are assuming the seller's mortgage, the same advice holds: Don't leave the amount and terms of financing open to question. Several years ago, I agreed to purchase a property and assume the seller's below-market rate mortgage. However, just before closing, the lender pointed out that it intended to increase the interest rate to the market level. Fortunately, my contract with the sellers specified that the mortgage assumption would go forward at the same below-market interest rate that the sellers were paying. Rather than lose the sale and risk a lawsuit, the sellers had to buy down the mortgage interest rate from the rate the lender would otherwise have charged.

If you agree to arrange new financing, spell out the maximum terms (e.g., 7 percent, 25 years, 20 percent down). Then, if it turns out that (in good faith) the best loan you can find is at 7.75 percent, 20 years, 25 percent down, you need not complete the purchase. You can walk away and obtain a return of your earnest money deposit.

Earnest Money Deposit

Contrary to popular belief, the validity of your purchase offer does not depend on the amount of your earnest money deposit or, for that matter, whether you've even paid a deposit. Earnest money is nothing more than a good-faith showing that you intend to complete your purchase. More than anything else, choose your deposit amount as part of your negotiation strategy.

Large deposits signal to the sellers that you are a serious buyer. Some investors use large deposits to offset their lowball offers. A large earnest money deposit tells the sellers, "You can count on me to buy your property. This large deposit proves that I mean what I say. Wouldn't you rather go for a sure thing now rather than wait for a better offer that may never come along?"

In contrast, a small deposit may signal that you're financially weak, or that you're trying to tie up the property cheaply while you mull over other options. But here's the rub: Smart sellers won't accept contracts that don't establish commitment.

To some degree, whether your deposit will be seen as large or small, serious or trifling, depends on local custom. Therefore, gauge the impression you will make with the size of your deposit by the amounts local sellers and realty agents think reasonable for the type of transaction you're entering.

Just keep in mind that a seemingly low deposit diminishes your credibility. A relatively high deposit bolsters your credibility. Perhaps the best of both worlds is to employ a low deposit strategy and rely on other factors to support your credibility as a buyer, such as current ownership of multiple properties, strong FICO credit score (see www.myfico.com), high net worth, and personal integrity. But this trick is difficult to pull off. As a rule, few things speak louder than ready cash.

Quality of Title

For assurance of title, you need a real estate attorney or, much better, a title insurer. Your purchase agreement will specify the title guarantees and exceptions that govern your transaction. Make sure you know what these are before you sign. This precaution is especially necessary when you buy properties through foreclosure, tax sales, auctions, probate, or other sales where the previous owner (title holder) of the property does not sign the deed.

Probate judges, clerks of court, sheriffs, and bank officials do not warrant a title in the same way that the previous owners could. You can partially overcome this potential problem by purchasing title insurance.

But like all types of insurance, title policies list a variety of limits, exceptions, and conditions. They don't cover everything. Although a title policy offers good protection, you (or your attorney) must still identify any important title risks that remain for you to assume.

Property Condition

Your offer to purchase should address the issue of property condition in two ways. First, ask the sellers to complete a property disclosure statement that lists every conceivable problem or defect that has now or ever affected the property or the neighborhood. In addition, ask what efforts the sellers, previous property owners, or neighbors have implemented to solve the problem. ("Oh yes, we kept blowing fuses, so we just rewired around the fuse box. Now we never have any problems." Or maybe, "Well, there was a crack cocaine house down the street, but the Neighborhood Watch group got the police to close it down.") The more you can get the sellers to tell you about the property and the neighborhood, the more accurately you can judge the property's market value.

Second, while you can learn a great deal from the sellers, you can't learn everything. Sellers can disclose only what they know. As added protection, include a property inspection contingency in your offer that permits you to check out the property with one or more specialists who can verify the condition of the plumbing, heating and air-conditioning, electrical system, roofing, and foundation.

Your contingency clause can state that repair costs should not exceed some designated amount (say $1,000). Ideally, the sellers should pay these costs. But if you've negotiated a bargain price, then you might accept responsibility. If repair costs exceed your specified amount, your contingency clause should give you the right to void the purchase agreement and obtain a refund of your earnest money deposit.

Preclosing Property Damage (Casualty Clause)

Most purchase agreements require the sellers to deliver a property to the buyer on the date of closing (or the date of possession) in essentially the same condition as it stood on the date the purchase agreement was signed. If the property suffers damage (fire, earthquake, vandalism, hurricane, flood) after the purchase contract has been signed, but prior to closing, the sellers must repair the property at their expense. Alternatively, in the event of damage, the sellers may be allowed to terminate your purchase agreement and return the earnest money deposit to you.

Two points are in order here: First, don't assume the sellers retain responsibility for the property. The form purchase contracts used by

HUD, VA, and Fannie Mae, for example, shift this responsibility to their buyers. Always read your contract language and know what you are agreeing to. If you do accept the risk of preclosing property damage, check with your insurance agent. See if you can secure coverage to protect against property losses during this interim period.

Second, be careful about accepting contract language that gives sellers the right to return your earnest money and terminate the purchase agreement should they find themselves unwilling or unable to repair any property damage. Say you bargain hard and get the sellers down to a price of $335,000. After accepting your offer, they begin to harbor second thoughts. Then along comes another offer at $355,000. Mysteriously, the property suffers a $5,000 fire. Now what will the sellers do?

They may drag their feet on repairs and claim problems settling with their insurer. Then, because they "can't" restore the property to its previous condition in time to meet the scheduled closing date, they void your contract and return your deposit. The sellers effectively used the casualty clause to shut you out of your bargain price.

To eliminate this potential difficulty, cancellation of the contract should be at your option, not the option of the sellers. In addition, the contract could impose either financial penalties on the sellers for failure to repair or it could set up an escrow repair credit to compensate for the amount of the damage.

If you're using bank financing, the bank may refuse to close your loan until the damage has been satisfactorily repaired. That puts you in a catch-22. You can't repair the property until you close your loan, but the lender won't close your loan until after you've made the repairs. This type of problem doesn't occur often, but if you prepare for this risk ahead of time, you and your attorney can draft a casualty clause that adequately protects your interests.

Closing (Settlement) Costs

Many real estate transactions involve thousands of dollars in closing costs. Title insurance, appraisal, mortgage points, buy-down fees, application fees, lender-mandated repairs, lawyers' fees, assumption fees, recording fees, transfer taxes, document stamps, survey, property inspections, escrow fees, real estate brokerage fees, and other expenses can quickly add up to a fair-sized chunk of money. Who pays each of these costs—you or the sellers? Local custom frequently dictates, but negotiation can override custom. If the sellers won't drop their price as low as you'd like, shift your emphasis to settlement costs.

Sometimes, sellers who won't budge $2,500 off their quoted price will agree to pay that much or more for settlement costs that are traditionally borne by buyers. (Indeed, a 3–2–1 interest rate buy-down that costs the sellers $5,500 can prove more advantageous to you than will a $5,500 reduction in price. A reduced interest rate will improve your cash flow and allow you to qualify for a larger mortgage.) When it can work to your benefit, give the sellers their price. As a trade-off, insist that they pay all (or most) of the closing costs. Recall, though, the price/terms caveat.

Closing and Possession Dates

Your purchase agreement should set dates for settlement and possession. When sellers (or buyers) place great importance on either a quick (or delayed) closing date, that date can play a valuable role in the negotiations. Because of a need for ready cash, the sellers might trade a lower price for a fast settlement. Or for tax reasons, the sellers may prefer to delay settlement for six months or more.

The same goes for the date of possession. The sellers might want a fast closing, but they may also want to keep possession of the property (especially if it's their home) for some period that extends beyond the settlement date. Maybe their new home isn't yet completed. Maybe they would like to postpone moving until after their children finish the school term. Their reasons vary, but as a smart negotiator, you should feel out the sellers on their preferred closing and possession dates. Then use this information to shape your offer. If you're willing to meet the sellers' needs on this issue, they may meet your requests on price or terms.

Leases

When you buy a property that is occupied by tenants, examine each of their leases before you write up your offer. Especially investigate the following issues:

- *Rent levels.* How much do the tenants pay in rents? Are any tenants in arrears? Have any tenants prepaid? How long have the current rent levels been in effect?
- *Concessions.* Did the tenants receive any concession for signing their leases such as one month's free rent, a new 18-speed bicycle, or any other incentives that lower the effective amount of rents the tenants are paying? Conversely, do any tenants seem to pay high rents only because of an under-the-table agreement with the sellers to help improve the income statement that the sellers show prospective buyers?
- *Utilities.* Do the leases require the tenants to pay all of their own utilities? If not, which utilities are the owners obligated to provide?

♦ *Yard care, snow removal, and other services.* Who provides yard care, snow removal, or other necessary services such as small repairs within the rental units? Who pays for garbage and trash pickup? Do the leases obligate the sellers to provide laundry facilities, off-street parking, a clubhouse, exercise room, child care center, or commuter transportation?

♦ *Furniture and appliances.* Check the leases to determine whether the owners are required to provide tenants with furniture or appliances. If so, which ones, what quality, and who is responsible for maintenance, repairs, and replacement?

♦ *Duration.* What term is remaining on each of the leases? Do the tenants enjoy the option to renew? If renewed, does the lease (or rent control laws) limit the amount of rent increase that you can impose?

♦ *Security deposits.* How much money has the owner collected from the tenants in security deposits? Have any tenants prepaid their last month's rent? Do the sellers retain an inspection sheet that shows the condition of each of the units at the time the tenants moved in? Have the tenants signed those inspection sheets?

♦ *Tenant confirmation.* Whenever feasible, ask the tenants to confirm the terms of the lease as the sellers have represented them. Make sure the sellers (or their property manager) have not entered into any side agreements with tenants that would modify or override the terms of the lease. Learn whether the sellers have orally promised any of the tenants special services, rent relief, or other dispensations.

When you buy a rental property, you must honor valid leases. These obligations not only affect the amounts of your future rental income and operating expenses but also restrict your plans for tenant eviction, property renovation, or conversion (e.g., converting rentals into condominiums). Although you own the property, the tenants were there first. Their valid leasehold rights trump your rights of ownership.

Contingency Clauses

Most investors hedge their purchase offers with a financing contingency and a variety of inspection contingencies. If the investor can't get financing on the terms specified, or if the condition of the property doesn't meet the investor's standards (as written into the purchase contract), the deal may be called off, and the investor would receive a return of his or her earnest money.

Other Contingencies.   In addition to financing and inspection contingencies, you can condition your purchase offer on one or more other issues. If you plan to renovate the property, you can include a government permit contingency. If government doesn't approve your plans, you may pull out of the purchase without penalty. You can include contingencies for government approval in any area where your plans are subject to regulatory review (e.g., converting apartments to condominiums, rehab with rent increases, increasing or decreasing the number of rental units, eliminating on-site parking, asbestos removal, etc.).

Other types of contingencies may pertain to attorney review, the sale of another property, raising funds from coinvestors, professional market value appraisal, or even some type of market study (feasibility analysis). Indeed, as a buyer, you can condition your purchase on anything you want ranging from the approval of Uncle Harry to an eclipse of the sun.

Contingencies and Negotiation Strategy.   Even though you *can* condition your offer on anything you want, that doesn't mean the sellers will accept it. They may tell you, "No way are we going to take our property off the market for several months while you try to put together a syndication deal. Come back and talk to us after you've raised the money." The more you hedge your offer with deal-threatening contingencies, the less likely the sellers will sign it. On the other hand, a clean "no-strings-attached" offer may gain the sellers' approval even when your price or terms don't meet their expectation.

Sellers prefer firm offers. Choose your contingencies carefully. Consider them as part of your overall negotiating strategy. Write an offer that looks certain to close, and you may find that your sellers will relax demands on other important contract issues.

Assignment and Inspection

In many states, buyers may freely assign their real estate purchase contracts. However, assume nothing. Talk this issue over with qualified counsel. As a buyer who (at least on some occasions) may want to flip a contract, make sure that the sellers cannot raise any legally valid objections. As a safeguard to avoid conflict, you could insert an assignment clause similar to the following: "Buyers may assign this Contract and all rights and obligations hereunder to any other person, corporation, or trustee."

In contrast, the sellers may oppose such broad language and try to negotiate language such as: "Buyer may assign this Contract only with the written approval of the sellers. Consent by the sellers shall not be arbitrarily withheld."

The sellers may want the right to approve your assignees just to satisfy themselves that the assignees possess the credit and financial capacity to complete the purchase. In addition, the sellers may want you to remain liable for damages (or specific performance) should your assignees default. Obviously, you would like to avoid (or limit) this liability.

As another point, when you obtain the right of assignment, you also need to insert a clause that permits you reasonable access and entry so that your potential assignees can inspect and evaluate the property. Without the right to show the property, the right to assign loses much of its effectiveness.

Recording in the Public Records

If you are writing up a lease option, lease purchase, contract for deed, or some other type of purchase offer that delays closing of title for, say, more than six months, consider a clause that permits you to record the signed contract in the public records. This recording serves notice to the world of your rights in the property.

Without this notice, the sellers may place mortgages or other liens against the property that could jeopardize your interests. Also, without a recording, the sellers' judgment creditors, or perhaps the Internal Revenue Service, may be able to gain a priority claim to the property. Again, you need to discuss these issues with competent local legal counsel. You certainly do not want to make payments to the sellers over a period of years, only to find later that the sellers cannot deliver good title.

Systems and Appliances

Regardless of whether your closing will take place within 30 days or three years, your contract should clearly lay out who is responsible in the interim for maintenance, repair, and replacement of any malfunctioning systems (heating, air-conditioning, electrical, waste disposal, well water) or appliances. Also, to the extent possible, spell out how to resolve the "repair or replace" dilemma.

For example, if the air-conditioning (AC) goes out, the sellers may want to repair it at a cost of $450 in lieu of a system replacement that would cost $2,200. Yet if the repairs will only keep the existing AC clanking and clunking for, at best, 6 to 12 months, you may insist on the replacement—especially if during those coming 6 to 12 months you will be taking full ownership responsibilities.

Environmental Hazards

Today, with both heightened costs for environmental cleanups and extensive regulatory controls, your contract needs to address any environmental hazards that may affect the property. Lead paint, asbestos, urethane formaldehyde, underground heating oil tanks, radon—and who knows what other dangers the Environmental Protection Agency may discover—can cost property owners thousands in remedial or replacement expenses. Ideally, you might like to include a contract clause as follows: "Sellers warrant that the property complies with all current federal, state, or local environmental laws, rules, or regulations. Sellers agree to indemnify buyers for all required cleanup costs that shall be necessary to remedy environmental hazards that existed during the sellers' period of ownership."

This language is only suggestive, but it covers two main questions that you should address: (1) Is the property free of hazards? (2) If hazards are discovered, who is going to pay for the cleanup? Under federal (and many state) laws, any owner of a property may be personally required to pay for its environmental cleanup—even when that owner is completely innocent of creating the hazard.

No Representations

Up to this point, we've looked at contract clauses from the buyer's perspective. However, when you sell a property, always include a clause something like the following: "All oral or written representations or promises of the sellers pertaining to this agreement, or material to inducing this agreement, are listed herein."

Why is this type of clause necessary? To protect you from property buyers who may falsely claim that you made promises—"We'll leave all of the appliances for you" or "The roof's in perfect condition"—that you did not make. In their attempt to void a contract or force you (the seller) to pay for repairs or replacements, buyers (and especially their lawyers) know that cries of "fraud in the inducement" are all that's necessary to threaten or file a lawsuit against a property's sellers.

Will the buyers win? Are you prepared to spend $10,000 or $20,000 in legal fees and court costs to find out? Don't believe for a minute that old saw, "It's just their word against mine." Yes, it is. But that's no guarantee a judge or jury will believe you over them. Don't give your buyers the chance to falsely claim you lured them into a contract through deception.

Default Clause

Your contract default clause should spell out what happens if you or the sellers fail to carry through the terms of your purchase agreement. These clauses address at least four critical areas:

1. Method of resolution
2. Damages
3. Specific performance
4. Who bears the expenses

Method of Resolution. Too many people are quick to file a lawsuit when another party breaches an agreement. Other options for resolution include mediation and arbitration.

If you pursue a lawsuit, you will almost certainly lose even if a court's decision goes in your favor: You will spend tens of thousands of dollars in legal fees; you will see truth and justice perverted beyond recognition; you will encounter lawyers whose dishonesty and incompetence are exceeded only by their arrogance; you will expose yourself and your private life to public view through intrusive discovery procedures that permit lawyers to question you (admissions, interrogatories, depositions) in minute detail about anything that could *in any way* be related to your character or the issues being litigated. The litigation process itself can require you to live through years of anxious uncertainty, and even winning verdicts may be overturned on appeal for purely technical reasons, thus starting the trial process all over again.

Make no mistake about it, lawsuits enrich lawyers, judges, and a myriad of expert witnesses, jury consultants, court reporters, legal secretaries, and photocopying services. They do little to settle disputes in a fair, timely, and cost-effective manner.

Admittedly, mediation and arbitration have their drawbacks. But to their advantage, they are less costly, less adversarial, more timely, and far more likely to emphasize substance over procedure. Go out and talk to people who have sought redress through litigation. Then decide for yourself whether to specify mediation and arbitration as the required method of resolving contract disputes.

Damages. A party who breaches a real estate contract may be held liable for either compensatory damages or liquidated damages. In theory, compensatory damages are supposed to make the innocent party financially whole. Compensatory damages measure the economic loss you've suffered because the other party didn't live up to his or her part of the bargain. Translating the theory of compensatory damages into an actual dollar amount is subject to a great deal of legal argument. Because of this indefinite calculation, no one can predict how much money a jury might award, or whether an appellate court will uphold that amount.

To avoid this legal wrangling over how much you (or the sellers) have lost because of the other party's breach, some contracts specify an amount called *liquidated damages.* For example, in case of buyer default, some real estate contracts permit sellers to keep the earnest money deposit as liquidated damages.

I won't go into all the specific pros and cons of compensatory versus liquidated damages. But as a rule, liquidated damage clauses seem superior because (properly written) they reduce ambiguity and, in the case of buyer default, limit liability to a knowable amount (e.g., the earnest money deposit). Nevertheless, if you can locate an experienced real estate attorney who is both competent and trustworthy, discuss this issue with him or her. At a minimum, make sure you understand the type of damage clause included in your purchase offer. The more you can use this clause to limit your liability, the better off you will be.

Note: In some states, and in some types of contract cases, winning litigants may also recover damages for emotional distress, but this is seldom the general rule. In cases of fraud or other egregious behavior, many states permit awards for punitive damages. In contrast to compensatory damages, punitive damages punish the losing party for reprehensible conduct. Again, these issues involve technical interpretations of statutes and case law in light of the facts of a particular transaction.

Specific Performance.   In addition to a claim for damages, some contracts (or contract laws) give buyers (and, less frequently, sellers) the right to seek specific performance. This right means that through legal proceedings (arbitration or lawsuit), a court could order defaulting property owners to sell their property on the terms specified in your purchase contract. You would pursue this remedy when only a subject property will serve your specific purposes (e.g., to compel the agreed sale of the vacant lot next door to your apartment building so that you can satisfy the city's off-street parking requirements).

Who Bears the Expenses?   Whether you pursue mediation, arbitration, or litigation, the dispute resolution process can easily run up thousands of dollars in costs and expenses. Therefore, look to your purchase contract to see what it says about who pays. Even though today we hear a great deal about "loser pays" types of laws and contract terms, don't accept such a clause without due consideration.

In the first place, realize that lawyers lose many cases where their clients are in the right. Lawyers fail to prepare; they err in tactics or strategy; or perhaps key witnesses may come across poorly on the witness stand. In addition, the other side may lie in a convincing and unshakable manner. Even in the most righteous cases, victory seldom proves easy.

Second, if the other side has far more money than you, they can hire the best and most expensive counsel to overwhelm and intimidate you and your counsel. With such firepower against you, even if you are willing to face the risk of losing your case, you may not be willing or able to face the opponents' legal expenses of, say, $50,000 or $100,000 (yes, even lawyers in small-time litigation can run up fees of this size if someone has the money to pay them). Thus, regardless of the merits of your case, the potential (even if unlikely) burden of having to bear the other side's expenses may force you to accept a quite unfavorable settlement.

◆ ◆ ◆

As in all legal matters, the purpose here is to inform, not advise. Your purchase contract will include many important clauses that govern the relationship between you and the sellers. Mull over these contract provisions before you sign your offer. Only then can you and your counsel rewrite, amend, or strike out unacceptable language. Once you and the sellers commit, you're both bound to the extent of the law. To protect yourself, fashion your offer so that you know and understand the full nature of your agreement—including what recourses and costs apply if the deal falls apart.

SUMMARY

Favorable deals are not just found; they are created. Regardless of the sellers' asking price and terms, investors can frequently use smart negotiating to sort through the sellers' real needs and emotions and fashion an agreement that gives both parties a win-win agreement.

Although all negotiations involve personal and situation-specific issues, you will improve your bargaining skills if you adopt the 15 negotiation principles presented at the beginning of the chapter. One more caveat: Negotiators frequently place too much emphasis on price and terms. Your contract will also include many other critical details. As a minimum, address the following 15 areas of concern:

1. Does the contract include the names and signatures of all buyers and sellers?
2. Are the site boundaries accurately delineated? Have you stepped off the site?
3. Are the building and other site improvements adequately identified and described?
4. Does the contract or contract addendum list all personal property and fixtures included in the sales price? Should you ask the sellers to prepare a separate bill of sale for these items? Does the

seller hold clear title to all the personal property that is to be conveyed?

5. Have the sales price and terms of financing been spelled out so precisely that a disinterested third party could unambiguously interpret the agreement? Should the contract include a financing contingency clause?

6. What is the amount of the earnest money deposit? Under what conditions will it be returned to the buyers?

7. What types of deed must the sellers use to convey title to the property? Is the title free of encumbrances? If not, what liens, easements, encroachments, or other encumbrances cloud the title? Is the title insurable? What exceptions apply?

8. What is the condition of the property? Have you obtained adequate seller disclosures and professional inspections? Have you negotiated an escrow credit for repairs?

9. Who bears liability for preclosing casualty losses? Under what conditions can the buyer (seller) terminate the sales contract as the result of preclosing casualty losses? Who has responsibility for preclosing repair or replacement of systems and appliances?

10. What share of the settlement costs is borne respectively by the buyers and sellers?

11. What are the dates of closing and possession?

12. Have you examined all the leases that apply to the rental units currently occupied by tenants? Has the present owner of the property entered into side agreements with any of the tenants? Have you confirmed with the tenants the rental information provided by the sellers?

13. How many contingency clauses have you included in your offer? Are your contingencies consistent with the negotiation strategy you have adopted?

14. Have you protected yourself against environmental hazards?

15. What methods of dispute resolution are provided by your offer? What types of default remedies are available to you and the sellers? Who pays the costs?

You are negotiating an agreement that includes many issues. Negotiate a full complement of trade-offs and compromises. When you hit a negotiating impasse, shift your focus. Rethink and rework the contract terms. Keep searching cooperatively to satisfy the major issues of concern to all parties.

11

MANAGING YOUR PROPERTIES TO INCREASE THEIR VALUE

Personally owning income property means that you can directly influence the value of your holdings and, consequently, your investment returns. You need not wait and hope for market appreciation. Through effective property management, you can boost the value of your properties within just a few months after acquisition.

THE 10:1 RULE (MORE OR LESS)

Recall from earlier chapters the basic value (V) formula:

$$\text{Value} = \frac{\text{NOI (net operating income)}}{\text{R (capitalization rate)}}$$

When you buy a property that yields an annual net operating income of $15,000 and the applicable R equals .10 (10 percent), its market value equals $150,000. Now, let's say that soon after you acquire ownership, you use the ideas from Chapter 8 to figure out ways to boost rental income and cut expenses. In total, your annual NOI increases by $2,500. Through your management decisions, you've just created an additional $25,000 in market value:

$$\text{Value increase} = \frac{\$2,500}{.10} = \$25,000$$

or, alternatively,

$$V = \frac{15,000 + 2,500 \ (NOI)}{.10 \ (R)} = \$175,000 \text{ (versus the old value of \$150,000)}$$

Are such gains in NOI tough to come by? Not at all. It's a fact of life that most small income properties suffer from subpar management. Ill-informed, poorly motivated, and inattentive property owners seem to dominate the field. (In fact, many smart and successful real estate investors purposely seek out undermanaged properties as a major part of their acquisition strategy.)

Think First

Your opportunity to buy undermanaged properties often arises because too many real estate investors get started in the business without clearly thinking through their total personal and financial objectives. These investors know that they want to "make money in real estate," but they don't critically evaluate the types of tenants, properties, and neighborhoods that best fit their temperament and lifestyle.

Instead they buy their properties according to whether they can get a "bargain price" or "easy financing." Or even worse, they buy a property because some professed guru has urged them to "get started now." (Notice those testimonials on the TV infomercials where people enthusiastically remark, "We were able to buy our first property just three weeks after studying your course. Thank you guru.")

Of course, a few of these investors do get lucky and go on to achieve success. Many more, though, aren't prepared for the potential problems, difficulties, and downside of unwise acquisitions. They find that they hate dealing with their tenants and their properties. Disappointment sets in. Neglect becomes their standard operating procedure. Their properties deteriorate, and their tenant relations sour. Eventually these investors sell out and then lament to anyone who will listen, "Owning rental properties takes too much time and creates too many headaches. It's a never-ending stream of things going wrong."

To avoid this beginner's trap, effective property management requires you to know yourself, your finances, and your capabilities. To succeed in real estate (as well as any other endeavor), honestly inventory yourself. Make sure your properties, tenants, and neighborhoods match up well with who you are and how you want to live your life. Otherwise you'll be swimming upriver.

Know Yourself

Do you want pride of ownership? Would you like to point out the properties you own to friends and relatives? Would you be able to deal effectively with tenants who sit below (or above) your socioeconomic status? (For example, some owners detest their low-income Section 8 tenants, while other blue-collar owners detest their well-to-do, arrogant, college student tenants.) Are there some neighborhoods or types of tenants who might cause you to fear for your safety? Are you the type of person who is a sucker for a hard-luck story? (If so, don't try to personally manage your own properties.)

Before you begin to shop for properties, think through the types of properties that you would enjoy owning. No matter how good the price or how easy the financing, avoid properties that don't fit well with your personality and psychological profile.

I know from experience. When I began buying properties, I looked only at the financials of a deal—not at the personal side. As it turned out, my portfolio came to include an eclectic mix of single-family houses, duplexes, and fourplexes with differing price ranges, types of tenants, and neighborhoods.

Although this odd collection of properties arose more by chance than by design, I learned a great deal from it. As mentioned, I learned that I liked some of the tenants and that some of the properties were great to own. Other types of tenants and properties seemed to evoke a never-ending litany of complaints. Plus, I was one of those suckers who (to my regret) fell for too many hard-luck stories.

However, once I settled on an acquisition and management strategy (including tenant selection) that better fit my personality, I was once again able to enjoy my life and my profits. For me, middle- to upper-middle-income single-family houses proved most desirable. Strictly in terms of cash flow, this strategy did reduce my net income and cash-on-cash return on investment, but I felt the trade-off was worth it.

Nevertheless, some very successful investors do seek out low- to moderate-income tenants (see Roger Neal's *Streetwise Investing in Rental Housing*, Panoply Press, 2000). There's no question that in most cities, low-to moderate-priced properties offer the best cash-on-cash returns. And these types of properties are often loaded with potential for management turnarounds. Regardless of the type of property you choose, you can make good money—as long as the property fits your personal profile. In contrast, properties that evoke personal disappointment, frustration, and neglect seldom yield satisfactory returns.

Know Your Finances

When you begin buying properties (or even as you grow your portfolio), make sure your finances leave you a safe level of cash reserves. For reasons of too little cash or poor budgeting, some property owners fail to invest enough money in upkeep, preventive maintenance, and desirable capital improvements. Your properties will grow in value when you give them the TLC they require. Only when you're holding a specific property for its land value (i.e., a potential teardown or perhaps a major rehab) will shortchanging maintenance pay off.

Effective management means that you just can't pull money out of your property—you must also put money back into it. It's this major point that the "no down payment" gurus fail to emphasize.

Know Your Capabilities

During my early years in property ownership, I tried performing most property repairs, remodeling, and renovations myself. Bad idea! Not only did I lack the required talent and skills, but I also lacked the temperament for this type of work. Rather than save money (my goal), many of these "do-it-myself" projects ended up over budget and low quality.

In addition, projects that I thought I could complete in a week often lasted a month or more. Sometimes I lost more in rent collections than I would have paid a competent contractor. Plus, if I had hired a contractor in the first place, I would have saved myself substantial aggravation.

The moral: Fully and accurately assess your own capabilities *before* you buy a property. Many beginning property owners fudge a property's expense numbers to persuade themselves that a proposed deal looks better than it really is. They tell themselves that there's no need to include an expense for this or that because "I can do it myself." But even if you can do it yourself, at least enter a bookkeeping expense for the value of your own labor.

The most successful property owners do hire out their property upkeep. When you focus on overall management operations and delegate the execution to others, you'll typically find that you will not only make more money but also avoid the burnout that plagues so many owners who try to do everything themselves.

Moreover, delegating the manual labor frees your time for thinking, researching, and planning your investment strategy. In fact, I am convinced that a majority of the people who own small income properties can materially improve their bottom line by simply shifting their efforts from managing details to managing strategy. Think more, work less. That approach is the key to effective, value-creating property management.

SMARTER STRATEGIC DECISIONS

Owners of large-scale apartment complexes routinely invest much time, research, and money into planning their market strategy. These property owners know that carefully thought out marketing efforts pay big returns. Yet the large number of real estate books aimed at small investors don't even mention the terms "strategy" or "market strategy."

Why? For the most part, because the authors of these books believe they have discovered the "one true way" to buy and manage properties. They believe that what has worked for them will work for you. Maybe it will. But more than likely, you can do better if you formulate your own strategy.

In using the term "strategy," I primarily refer to gathering market information and designing a marketing mix (rent level, property benefits, location, promotion) that will permit you to favorably differentiate your properties and management services from those of competing properties. In return for your efforts, you will enjoy higher rent collections, lower turnover, quicker rent-ups, and more satisfied tenants.

Local Markets Require Tailored Strategies

All real estate markets are local. Each one varies by types of properties, price range, rent levels, expense ratios, laws, ordinances, customs, tenant availability, tenant preferences, employment trends, vacancy rates, and dozens of other variables. You can't simply adopt an investment and management style from someone else who gained his or her experience in a different city at a different time. To effectively maximize your rent collections and property values, carefully monitor the ever-changing characteristics of your own potential market(s).

An Example: Craig Wilson's Market Strategy

To see what I mean, consider the successful experience of Craig Wilson. Craig bought an undermanaged eight-unit apartment building located within one mile of a small college. Craig felt that, in general, he wanted to direct his marketing efforts toward college students.

Yet he also knew that "college students" did not define a true market segment. In today's world, college students cannot be stereotyped any more than any other group of people who happen to share one common attribute. Recognizing this fact, Craig set out to learn as much as he could about the various college students who rent off-campus residences, as well as the properties and rent levels from which they could make their choices.

Discovering Student Beliefs and Attitudes

Like all good small business owners, Craig knew that he should begin his market research by learning more about his potential customers. To achieve this end, Craig gathered information by carrying out the following tasks:

- Thumbed through back issues of the campus newspaper to read articles and letters to the editor that addressed student housing issues.
- Met with the director of the off-campus student housing office.
- Talked with a sampling of students who stopped by the off-campus housing office to look at property listings.
- Talked candidly with each of the tenants of his newly acquired building.
- Hired a marketing student to solicit responses to a student housing survey (questionnaire).

Although none of Craig's information-gathering techniques met the sampling and methodological standards of a Gallup Poll, they did provide valuable insights about student attitudes. Overall, Craig found repeated mention of the following complaints:

Too much noise	No laundry facilities
Too little closet space	Rents too high
Inadequate parking	Authoritarian/obnoxious landlords
Unkempt appearance	Inadequate security
Lack of privacy	Plumbing/hot water problems
Too little storage space	Outdated kitchens/baths
Inadequate heating/cooling	No pets
Slow repairs	Cockroaches, ants
Too few electrical outlets	Lack of cleanliness

With this customer information in hand, Craig next turned his attention to a direct study of competitor offerings.

Getting the Details about Competing Properties.   I am forever amazed at the number of property owners who never take the time to personally evaluate their competitors' offerings. This practice is clearly shooting in the dark. How can owners create a competitive edge if they don't collect firsthand information about the features, benefits, and rent levels of competing rental units? Of course, they can't. As a result, they too often set their rents too low or too high. Or they miss easy ways to modify or improve their property's features to gain competitive advantage.

To avoid this common mistake, Craig researched competitors: (1) He telephoned two dozen ads and recorded basic property and rental information; (2) he made appointments and visited a dozen properties; and (3) he performed follow-up research after one-, two-, and four-week intervals.

Calling Advertisers.   From information he culled from newspaper ads, property signs, Internet listings, and the off-campus housing office, Craig telephoned 24 different property owners and managers. From these calls, he tried to discover the following:

- The relative ease or difficulty of reaching these owners and managers
- Their telephone marketing skills (courteous, informative, pleasant, persuasive)
- The addresses of their units and the specific types of property (single family, duplex, fourplex, etc.)
- Property amenities
- House rules
- Important lease terms and rental rates
- Amount of deposit
- Repair, lawn care, and utility expenses (who pays, how much?)

As expected, some owners and managers were more forthcoming than others. But overall, this technique permitted Craig to get a much better feel for the rental housing market. To make sure he didn't forget pertinent facts, Craig faithfully recorded all of these competitive data on a property survey form that he had specifically prepared for this task.

Inspecting Properties.   In follow-up, Craig made appointments or attended open houses for 12 of these units. In making these property visits, Craig was trying to size up both the specific property and its owner/manager. He gathered information about floor plans, bathrooms, kitchens, total square footage, room sizes, decorating patterns, cleanliness, overall appearance, soundproofing, views, ceiling heights, electrical capacity, laundry facilities, appliances, parking, storage, and security.

When possible, he picked up copies of leases and application forms. He also tried to judge the personality and demeanor of the owner/manager. Did this person seem like a plus or a negative for the property? Did he or she seem eager to please and sincerely interested in providing tenants a pleasant place to live? Or did he or she seem more like an army drill sergeant?

The Callbacks. After his inspections of competing properties, Craig ranked each of the properties according to its appeal. Then he buttressed his impressions with market feedback. To learn how quickly (or slowly) each unit rented, he periodically checked back during the following month with each owner/manager to see which units remained on the market. This information added to his store of knowledge about market likes and dislikes, as well as verifying the actual rental amounts that tenants were willing to commit to—not merely the owner's asking price.

◆ ◆ ◆

As you develop a market strategy, search for ways to exploit the weaknesses of competitors and strengthen your own offering in the eyes of the customers (residents) you plan to attract to your property. That's why systematically collecting market information (potential tenants, competitors) stands critical to effective property management.

Without these detailed market data, your strategic decisions (if the term "strategic decisions" even applies) evolve merely from guesstimates or intuition. Or all too often, they arise simply from default—"Well, that's the way we've always done it," or "That's the way everyone else does it." Maybe so. But you can figure out a more profitable approach when you base your decisions on better market information.

How Craig Wilson Used Market Information to Develop His Strategy

Naturally, the methods you use to develop your market strategy will differ from the specific strategy that Craig Wilson (or anyone else) has adopted for his or her properties. Nevertheless, you can profit by following through the several ways Craig chose tenants and designed his property features and operations to gain competitive advantage.

Tenant Segment. In weighing the complaints and comments of various students against the typical rental property and owner/manager, Craig decided to design his property operations to appeal to students who placed high value on quiet, aesthetics, cleanliness, security, and a pleasant, easy-to-get-along-with owner. In addition, he wanted students who had previously exhibited high levels of personal responsibility in their finances, college activities, and employment. Craig wanted to select the cream of the crop from among the many students who were searching for housing. To attract this tenant segment, Craig knew that he had to offer valuable competitive advantages.

Privacy, Quiet, and Storage.   To provide his tenants with privacy, quiet, and storage space, Craig made three changes to his property:

- *Study room.* On a portion of the roof, he built a heavily sound-proofed 20-foot-by-30-foot study room. Many students in his target market had complained that they found it difficult to read or study in their apartments while their roommates watched television, played CDs, or entertained friends. This study room also eliminated another problem: Students who wanted to get in just a couple of hours (or less) of study time no longer had to bear the inconvenience of returning to campus in the evenings.
- *Party room.* As another benefit, residents could reserve the study room on weekend nights for parties or other group gatherings. This use met the needs of not only the building residents who wanted to take advantage of it but also those who did not want to be bothered by the noise of such events.
- *Storage.* To overcome complaints of inadequate storage space, Craig bought eight seven-foot-by-six-foot-high gabled storage sheds and placed them behind a wooden fence on each side of his building. These facilities were more than adequate to hold skis and other infrequently used sports equipment, bicycles, boxes of books, and other assorted items.

Security.   To enhance safety and security in his building, Craig replaced the hollow-core entrance doors to each unit with solid doors equipped with double dead-bolt locks and peep scopes. In addition, he equipped all windows with burglar pins and made certain that all window locks were strong and secure. To add to fire safety, Craig placed a fire extinguisher in each unit and a smoke alarm in every room.

Landscaping, Grounds, and External Appearance.   Although from a street and walk-up view this property looked reasonably good, Craig decided he wanted its attractiveness to stand out. To enhance its appearance, he freshly painted its wood trim; added decorative flowers, shrubs, rocks, mulch, and fencing; and replaced the building entrance doors with heavier carved-wood doors. While from a narrow economic perspective such changes might seem unnecessary, Craig believed they would help achieve four related purposes.

First, these improvements contributed to his pride of ownership and his goal to give students a desirable place to live. Second, since most prospective tenants judge a building from the outside before they even consider looking inside, these improvements would entice students to come in and view the units whenever they became vacant. Third, by keeping the outside especially attractive, Craig felt he could appeal to students who would take better care of the property. (Certainly, tenants cannot be expected to take care of a property if the owner doesn't.) And fourth, by noticeably improving the outside appearance of the property, Craig thought he might encourage other nearby owners to do likewise and thus begin a neighborhood spruce-up campaign from which apartment building owners, single-family residences, and tenants would all benefit.

Laundry Facilities.   Because of its central heating plant, College Oaks had a partial basement. This basement area provided the space necessary to install three sets of washers and dryers, which Craig secured through a lease agreement with a commercial vendor. Under this agreement, the vendor supplied and maintained the machines, and Craig earned a percentage of all revenues. While this operation was not expected to earn much (or any) profit for Craig, it did provide a needed convenience to tenants.

Heating.   The fact that his property did not have individual furnaces in each unit was a constant source of tenant discomfort. In winter months some units always seemed hot, while others were cold. Plus, nearly all units experienced a morning chill from 6:30 A.M. to around 8:00 A.M. To solve this problem, Craig took out each of the wall air-conditioning units and replaced them with units that included both heating and cooling elements. Although these supplemental heating units could not produce heat as efficiently as the central gas boiler, their ability to be controlled as needed made them a cost-effective as well as much-appreciated addition.

Kitchen and Baths.   As Craig knew, both the aesthetics and the functional utility of kitchens and baths contribute heavily to tenant satisfaction or dissatisfaction. To improve appearance, Craig had the kitchens freshly painted and added a splash of color with some use of wallpaper. To enhance function, he added two electrical outlets and six linear feet of counter and cabinet space, and by changing the location of the refrigerator, he improved the efficiency of the kitchen work triangle (see Figures 11.1 and 11.2). Similarly, to improve the baths, Craig enhanced both aesthetics and function by modernizing fixtures and decorating patterns and by installing new storage cabinets and shelving.

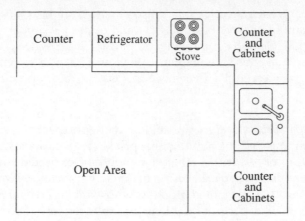

Figure 11.1   Old Kitchen Design

Upkeep and Cleanliness.   Following the lessons of George Kelling and Catherine Coles's book *Fixing Broken Windows,* Craig implemented a cleanliness and upkeep program for his building that never permitted trash, dirt, cobwebs, or deferred maintenance to become an unsightly problem—or even worse, an invitation to residents to drop their standard of care for the property. (As mentioned in Chapter 4, *Fixing Broken Windows* shows that neighborhood and property decline accelerates into a downward spin when "little things" are left unattended.)

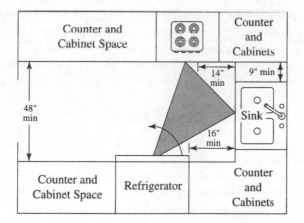

Figure 11.2   New Kitchen Design

234

234   MANAGING YOUR PROPERTIES TO INCREASE THEIR VALUE

Tenant Selection Criteria.   Craig Wilson knew from his market research that a substantial number of students would prefer his property and management style vis-à-vis competing properties and owners. Yet he also knew that to make his strategy work, he would have to screen and select his tenants very carefully. To achieve this goal, Craig took the following four steps:

1. *Appropriate conduct.* In talking with prospective residents, he emphasized the nature of his property operations and the strict types of resident conduct that would be expected and required.
2. *Screening criteria.* In terms of screening criteria, Craig emphasized that he wanted residents who exhibit personal responsibility in all aspects of their lives and thus requested not only credit references but also references from present and past landlords and employers. He also limited his selection to individuals who exhibited these characteristics: nonsmoking, nonuse of drugs, clean and neat appearance, no use of motorcycles or other loud vehicles, and having a B or better grade point average.
3. *Rent level.* Because Craig wanted to offer his residents a strong value proposition, he kept his rent levels in line with other competing (yet inferior) properties. In this way, Craig was not only able to secure many more tenant applications than he could accommodate but also reduced the costly expense of vacancies and tenant turnover.
4. *Deposit.* Although Craig did not exploit the superiority of his property through high rent levels, he did request a security deposit that was double the going rate. In doing so, he explained to tenants that the large deposit discouraged potential residents who were not truly committed to living by house rules. It is a fact that a few inconsiderate people can spoil the peace, quiet, and cleanliness of a property. Steering these people to other buildings would enhance the quality of life for all of Craig's residents.

Overall Results

When combined with a variety of expense reductions, Craig's market strategy paid off big. Virtually every indicator of success (NOI, property value, tenant retention, occupancy rates, word-of-mouth referrals, maintenance costs, pride of ownership, management time and effort) changed for the better.

◆ ◆ ◆

Can you achieve similar positive results with your property or properties? Definitely yes. The opportunities are wide open because so few owner/managers of small rentals think in terms of market strategy. Yet in every housing market, certain types of tenants remain underserved. In every housing market, certain property features, benefits, and management services remain in relatively short supply. When you discover these market gaps and shape your property operations to fill them, you, too, will profit personally and financially.

CUT OPERATING EXPENSES

Every dollar you slice from your property's operating expenses adds $10 (more or less) to your building's value. With figures like that, meticulously keep track of all expenses. Then make continuous efforts to reduce, shift, or eliminate them. The following discussion provide some ideas.

Energy Audits

Nearly all utility companies will help you discover ways to reduce your gas or electric bills. Some will even perform a physical audit and inspection of your property. Others will provide booklets or brochures and perhaps a customer service department to answer specialized questions. You can also find dozens of articles and books at your local library that discuss energy conservation.

Because each type of building construction and area of the country presents different problems and opportunities, you should seek out information that fits your particular situation. In addition, be aware that site placement and window placement can dramatically increase or diminish your energy costs. In fact, you should energy audit a building before you buy it. Then you can judge beforehand the extent to which you can feasibly reduce these costs. Alternatively, you should avoid buying an energy glutton for which no economically practical solution exists.

Property Insurance

There are three requirements for buying the right property insurance that affect your bottom line: (1) Make sure you obtain enough basic coverage to adequately protect your property, your rental income, and your other assets; (2) within your basic protection, look for ways to reduce premiums by increasing deductibles or eliminating some uneconomical coverages; and (3) shop among agents and companies for the best combination of service and low premiums.

Basic Protection.   If you own your home, you've undoubtedly pur-
chased a homeowner's insurance policy—and if you're like many homeowners, you haven't given that policy a whole lot of thought. I know this
from experience. In the early 1990s, I was living in the heart of the
Berkeley-Oakland, California, hills when a wildfire swept through and
completely destroyed 3,300 homes. As many as one-half of the property
owners who suffered losses discovered that they lacked the coverage they
thought they had.

Buying property and liability insurance for income properties
requires even more attention than policies written for owner-occupied
residences. Rental property policies are subject to less standardization of
coverage and greater variance in premiums. Before you simply "buy a fire
insurance policy" and think you're covered, go over the following seven
questions with the insurance agents you're considering:

1. Who is covered? Typically, your insurance coverage protects
    only the named insureds within the policy. Therefore, take care
    to "name" all persons or companies (co-owners, mortgage
    lenders) whose financial interest in the property deserves pro-
    tection.
2. What property is covered? On this point, insurance policies distin-
    guish between the property you own and the property your ten-
    ants own. Policies seldom (if ever) cover tenants' property (advise
    or require them to buy their own tenant policy). Also, policies dis-
    tinguish between personal property (appliances, lawn care equip-
    ment, assorted tools, and other items stored in the garage) and real
    property (the building itself, plants, shrubs, fencing).
        Generally, the real personal-property distinction most
    affects rental property owners who rent their units furnished.
    But if you do keep any personal property around or within a
    rental property, verify coverage.
3. What time period applies? Insurance policies don't just begin and
    end on specified dates. They begin and end at specified *times* on
    specified dates. Assume you close on a property at 9:00 A.M. on 3
    June. A fire breaks out at 10:30 A.M. You've ordered insurance cov-
    erage to begin on 3 June. You're covered, right? Not necessarily.
    That 3 June policy may not begin coverage until 12:00 noon. So
    don't assume; verify your exact dates and timing of protection.
4. What perils are covered? Most people think of fire as the most
    critical type of peril to protect against. But what about flood,
    earthquake, vandalism, tenant abuse, windstorm, hail, mud
    slides, sinkholes, riot, theft, accumulation of snow and ice (on

roofs that collapse), termite infestation, lawsuits, "trip and fall" accidents, and other potential losses too numerous to mention? Your policy will list covered perils. Read them. If not adequate, your insurer may add coverage through a rider or endorsement.

5. What types of losses are covered? Usually insurers classify losses as direct or indirect. A fire that damages your building is a direct loss. The fact that you can no longer collect rents until the damage is repaired is an indirect loss. Your basic policy will not cover many types of indirect losses. For these losses (if coverage is available) you will need to buy a rider or endorsement.

6. What locations are covered? Normally, this question pertains to personal property that you may move from location to location. But also consider the following possibility: You've just loaded your Silverado with $4,000 worth of appliances, plumbing fixtures, and carpeting from Sears. You plan to install these items at a fourplex you own. But while you're in the restroom at a gas station, someone steals your truck and its $4,000 worth of contents. Do you have coverage for these contents? Maybe, maybe not.

7. How much will the insurer pay? Every insurance contract restricts how much it will pay for losses by including some combination of deductibles, policy limits, and coinsurance. In addition, with real and personal property, the policy may pay to replace, repair, or rebuild the damaged items with new items or construction (replacement cost). Or the policy may simply reimburse for actual cash value (replacement cost less depreciation).

Compounding this complexity is the fact that within the same policy, different types and amounts of restrictions may apply to the various types of coverages. For example, fire damage might subject you to a $500 deductible, whereas earthquake damage may subject you to a $10,000 deductible. Don't assume you are buying the right amounts of coverage. Ask your insurance agent to explain *all* of the ways the company may restrict or limit its payment for your covered losses.

Also, even when you buy replacement coverage for your building, your insurer will probably not pay for repair or construction costs mandated by stricter building codes. Without an endorsement, your policy will pay only to replace your current building as it existed before becoming damaged. If to rebuild, current code requires additional fire sprinklers or an upgraded 200-amp electrical system, without specific coverage, you'll end up paying these costs out of pocket.

Look for Ways to Improve Coverage and Reduce Premiums.   After deciding on your basic coverages and endorsements, search through various
policy deductibles, limits, and other fine tuning to find the most cost-
effective combinations. On the one hand, avoid paying a lot for a little:
Often you can save money by increasing your deductibles and eliminating trivial coverages that disproportionately increase your premiums.
Also avoid risking a lot for a little. In other words, don't skimp on coverages that could protect you against large-scale, budget-busting losses
such as huge liability claims.

It's wiser and more economical to avoid coverages for small frequent losses and extend coverage and limits for those rare but cata-
strophic exposures. To further save money wisely, ask your insurance
agent to suggest loss prevention and loss reduction measures that you can
undertake. Some insurers reduce premiums for properties equipped with
hurricane shutters, fire sprinkler systems, burglar bars, and dead-bolt
locks. In earthquake-prone areas, certain types of foundation support systems merit a premium discount. What discounts for loss prevention
(reduction) are available in your area?

Shop Till You Drop.   You may be inclined to place your rental property
insurance with your current homeowner's insurance agent. By all means
do discuss your needs with whomever you're already doing business. But
don't stop there. Secure competitive quotes from at least three or four
other sources. You might also solicit bids through several of the insurance
Web sites that are now operating such as www.insurance.com.

Of course, don't jump for the company with the lowest premium.
Through *Best's Guide* or other consumer rating reports, verify the company's financial strength and its service in paying claims. Also, because
property and liability insurers are licensed by state governments, check
the company's record of performance with your state department of
insurance. (Insurance company financial data and performance records
can be obtained at your local library or through your state department of
insurance Web site.)

Admittedly, few people like dealing with matters of insurance,
but effective property management requires it. Although property insurance premiums may run into the thousands of dollars, failure to obtain
needed coverages can cost you tens, or possibly hundreds, of thousands
of dollars.

Maintenance and Repair Costs

Effective managers also need to reduce and eliminate money-wasting
property maintenance and repair expenses. From experience, I encourage
you to focus on these five measures:

1. *Low-maintenance properties.* When shopping to buy, favor properties that are constructed with materials and fixtures that require less maintenance. Nothing beats a property that's built to last with minimal care. The same advice applies to yards, shrubs, and landscaping.
2. *Tenant selection.* Just as there are both low- and high-maintenance houses and apartment buildings, so too are there low-maintenance and high-maintenance tenants. Avoid the latter and select the former. Watch out for chronic complainers and people who show no "house sense." Overall, I believe that at least one-half of maintenance, repair, cleaning, and wear-and-tear costs can be cut by selecting only tenants who have consistently demonstrated personal responsibility. Contrary to the claims of many tenants, things seldom break by themselves— nor do toilets stop up and overflow as an act of God.
3. *Repair clauses.* To further promote tenant responsibility, a growing number of property owners shift the first $50 or $100 of every repair cost onto their tenants' shoulders. Also, I favor high security deposits.
4. *Handyman on call.* Nothing eases the drain on your time and pocketbook as much as having a trustworthy and competent all-around handyman (or persons) to take care of your property maintenance and repairs. With on-site service calls now costing upward of $100 in many cities, establishing a relationship with a person you can regularly depend on will save you a bundle in cash—and many bottles of Excedrin.
5. *Preventive maintenance.* If you're not penny-wise and pound-foolish, you subject your car to periodic maintenance and inspection. Do the same with your income properties. The operative advice is to anticipate and alleviate when the cost is relatively small. Also, always ask your maintenance experts how you might replace high-maintenance items with low-maintenance items.

Property Taxes and Income Taxes

In addition to cutting all of the expenses just discussed, you can also use a variety of tactics to reduce your property and income taxes. These tips and tactics are covered in Chapter 14.

INCREASING VALUE: FINAL WORDS

For at least the past 10 to 15 years, we've heard about corporate managers who repeatedly downsize, rightsize, restructure, and slash expenses, all the while searching for new customers, new products, and new ways of doing business. Now we know that some of these efforts were nothing more than cheap attempts to excite cheers from Wall Street. But more importantly, such good-faith efforts do illustrate how creative, strategic thinking and the never-ending search to improve can add to the bottom line.

This same principle applies to real estate. When you approach your rental business with the attitude "I can design and develop more profitable (less costly, higher-yielding) ways of operating these properties," you will outperform the results of other owners. The property managers of large shopping malls, office buildings, and apartment complexes have long proved the merits of market research, strategy, property improvement, and cost reduction.

It's now time for owners and managers of smaller properties to adopt a similar entrepreneurial pattern of thinking—and doing. For those who follow this approach, the rewards of increased property values remain readily available.

12

DEVELOP THE BEST LEASE

Within memory, many owners of small income properties (myself included) frequently used oral rental agreements. Today that practice is disappearing. Today lawyers and their legalisms have pervaded (and perverted) ever greater areas of American society—including, of course, the relations of property owners and their tenants. In response, and as a measure of self-protection, property owners now need to write out their rental agreements.

THE MYTHICAL "STANDARD" LEASE

Even though written leases now dominate, don't fall for the myth of the "standard" lease. All written leases are not created equally. Nor will any preprinted "standard" lease necessarily serve your purposes. Before you decide to use any specific lease, consider the following issues.

Your Market Strategy

If you wish to position yourself as a friendly, caring property owner, avoid those multipage fine-print leases written in legal jargon. Yes, these types of lengthy leases do try to nail down what happens under any conceivable contingency. But their long lists of authoritarian dos and don'ts tend to intimidate tenants and tear down trust and a cooperative spirit.

Lawyers, of course, try to justify such leases by claiming that "you want to get everything in writing so that there's no room for dispute or faulty memory." Sounds good, but the reality is something quite different.

Legalisms Bite Both Ways.   If you take an overly legalistic approach with your tenants, don't be surprised when they respond in kind. The more pages your lease entails and the more arcane its language, the more likely your tenants (or *their* lawyers) will find some word or clause to argue about. Lawyers pull in far more money from litigating a lease than they do from drafting a lease. If lawyer and former president Bill Clinton can find a way to legally argue the meaning of "is," you can bet that, if pushed, your tenants and their lawyers can become equally creative is their interpretation of lease clauses.

The Myth of a "Strong" Lease.   Supposedly, a "strong" lease is one where every clause binds the tenants into doing exactly what you want them to do. (Oh, if it were only that easy.) All too often, though, tenants do what they want to do—lease or no lease. Don't believe in the myth of a "strong" or "airtight" lease. In most cases, it's not the strength of the lease that determines whether your tenants conduct themselves in a manner consistent with your wishes. Rather, it's the quality of the tenants themselves.

A strong lease can never substitute for careful tenant selection. When push comes to shove, a strong lease *may* help you mitigate the aggravation and losses caused by troublesome tenants. But regardless of the language in your lease, it is good tenants alone who will make your days as a property owner both profitable and enjoyable.

Joint Responsibilities?   Because most leases are drafted for the primary benefit of property owners, they routinely slight tenant rights and owner responsibilities. In contrast, as part of your market strategy to attract quality tenants, your lease might display a more balanced treatment.

Without a doubt, many tenants do view landlords with suspicion and distrust. If you adopt a more just approach, you will display your good faith. Such an approach will also reveal you to be a cut above other property owners. Plus, since you do intend to fulfill your responsibilities, a listing of these responsibilities will help educate your tenants. More than a few tenants believe that owners of rental properties do little more than collect rents and get rich. You gain when you disabuse them of this notion by listing your responsibilities and expenses within the lease.

Joint Drafting?   People feel more committed to agreements when they help shape them. To put this fact to your advantage, try discussing and drafting your lease agreement with tenant participation. Naturally, you'll have a good idea of which clauses, conditions, and responsibilities you want to address (see "Crafting Your Rental Agreement" later in this chapter). But some give-and-take will make the tenants feel like contributing partners rather than mere vassals or serfs.

Win-Win Negotiating.   Joint drafting can also provide another benefit. Your proposed tenant may suggest trade-offs whereby you both win. Some years back when I first moved to Florida, for example, I tried to rent a place to live for a period of three to six months. Before buying a home, I wanted time to learn the market and explore options. But because I desired a short-term tenancy as well as the fact I owned a pet (a Yorkshire terrier), I faced slim and undesirable pickings. As a result, I stayed at a Holiday Inn for 14 weeks.

However, had I been able to secure a satisfactory rental house or apartment, I would have been a perfect tenant. I would also have been willing to pay a premium rent and large security deposit. Unfortunately, all of the property owners and managers I talked with simply stated their "no pets" rental requirement. None even hinted at the possibility of negotiating win-win.

Think carefully before you adopt such a rigid policy. Even if you don't want to jointly draft a lease agreement, at least keep the negotiating door open. Let the prospective tenants know that you are open to win-win flexibility and mutually advantageous changes.

Searching for Competitive Advantage

By far, most small property owners treat their lease strictly as a document that they can use to compel tenant performance. Although imperfect in that respect, written leases do give you more legal protection than an oral agreement. But your leases also should serve another important purpose: They should help you achieve a competitive advantage over other property owners.

Your Lease Clauses.   Before you decide on the specific clauses within your lease, closely review the leases of other property owners. Look for ways to differentiate your rental agreement that would encourage tenants (your target market) to choose your property over competing properties. For example, you might gain a competitive advantage by lowering your up-front cash requirements, offering a repair guarantee, shortening your lease term, guaranteeing a lease renewal without an increase in rent, or placing tenant security deposits and last month's rent in the investment of the tenant's choice to accrue interest or appreciation for the tenant's benefit.

Or, alternatively, perhaps you could develop very "tight" or "restrictive" lease clauses and position your property as rentals that cater to more discriminating and responsible tenants. You could include severe restrictions on noise and other nuisances common to rentals. In that way you could promote your property as "the quiet place to live."

In other words, you create competitive advantage not only by adapting the features of your property to the wants of your tenant market but also by custom tailoring the clauses, language, and length of your lease to match tenant needs.

Explain Your Advantages.   By adapting leases to better fit the needs of your target market, you can increase your rental revenues, achieve a higher rate of occupancy, and lower your operating expenses. To fully realize these benefits, though, you must make sure that prospective tenants recognize and understand the advantages you're offering. Adopt the strategy of a successful salesman. Rather than show your property perfunctorily, point out and explain (from the tenants' standpoint) the desirable features of both the unit and your lease.

CRAFTING YOUR RENTAL AGREEMENT

In crafting a lease to fit your market strategy, dozens of items, issues, and contingencies present themselves for possible inclusion. Although "typical" practices are featured in the following discussions, stay alert for ways to creatively adapt (or omit) items to better appeal to your tenants. Properly drafted, your lease can materially boost your efforts to attract premium tenants. In contrast, archaic legal jargon and an authoritarian demeanor can drive good tenants into the rentals offered by your competitors.

Names and Signatures

Most property owners require a lease to name all residents who will be permitted to live in the unit—including children, if any. All adult residents should sign the lease. As a general rule, owners do not permit tenants to freely bring in additional tenants or to substitute new cotenants for those moving out. All new tenants are normally required to fully satisfy the application and qualification process.

Joint and Several Liability

When you rent to cotenants (even if husband and wife—divorces do happen), include a "joint and several liability" clause. This clause makes all tenants individually and collectively responsible for all owed rents and tenant damages.

Without this clause, individual cotenants often claim that they're liable only for "their part of the rent." Or alternatively, "I didn't burn that hole in the carpet. Jones did. Collect from him." Most of the time, though, in these cases, Jones has already moved out and disappeared. Joint and several liability at least gives you the legal right to force payment from whichever other tenants have the money.

Guests

As a way around listing roommates, some tenants won't officially bring in new or additional cotenants. When you show up and wonder who these new people are, you'll be told "They're *guests.*" "Joe's just staying here for a couple of weeks until he's called back to work at Ford." Two months later, Joe's still there, and now his girlfriend, Jill, has also taken up "guest" status.

Whether you might get these kinds of tenants depends on the type of people your property attracts as well as your qualification standards. As a precaution, place a "guest clause" in your lease that limits both total permitted occupancy for the residence and the length of time legitimate guests can stay.

Length of Tenancy

Many landlords reflexively set the length of their tenancies at one year. In some markets, though, the preponderance of properties requiring one-year leases creates a shortage (relative to demand) of properties available for shorter terms. Because short-term (especially seasonal) tenancies command higher rents, you might be able to boost your rental revenues by appealing to this potentially underserved market.

As another possibility, to reduce turnover and vacancy expenses, you could give tenants a slight discount on their rents. In exchange, the tenants would sign up for a lease term of, say, two or three years. Either way, leases for terms shorter or longer than one year might prove to be the more profitable strategy.

Holdover Tenants (Mutual Agreement)

A holdover tenant is one who remains in your property after the original lease period expires. In some cases, leases for holdover tenants automatically renew for the same period as the original lease. In other instances, the lease converts to a month-to-month tenancy.

Unless your properties are located in an area with strong peak and valley rental seasons—as are college towns and vacation areas—I would suggest leases that convert to month-to-month tenancies. In my experiences, month-to-month holdover tenants often end up staying for years. But even if they stay for only two to six additional months, you still gain because you've at least postponed your turnover. If, however, you require your tenants to commit for another year, you may precipitate a move that would otherwise have been delayed through procrastination.

Holdover Tenants (without Permission)

Sometimes tenants notify you (or you notify them) that their tenancy is ending. If they move on schedule, all is well. On occasion, though, you may encounter tenants who decide to hold over without your permission. To reduce this possibility and compensate for any problems this delay causes, you could place a penalty clause in your lease for unauthorized holdovers. Penalty fees of $50 or $100 per day are sometimes used.

Property Description

If any possible confusion might arise over the exact physical property your tenants are leasing, supplement the property address with a full description of what they are entitled to. For example, do they obtain the right to use the garage, attic, basement, or outdoor storage shed? Or do you plan reserve areas for your own use or for others?

In addition, your lease (usually through a signed addendum) should fully detail and list any existing damages or imperfections that the property may currently suffer. Your prospective tenants should accompany you while making this inspection. Without this written and signed inventory of prior damages, your tenants may later refuse responsibility for damages they caused with the age-old denial, "Those holes in the wall were already there when we moved in. We didn't do it."

Inventory and Describe Personal Property

If you provide personal property for your tenants (washer, dryer, refrigerator, stove, microwave, blinds, drapes, curtains, furniture), inventory and describe (with photographs or serial numbers where possible) each separate item and include the list as a lease addendum. Unbelievable as it may sound, I know of vacating tenants who have taken their landlord's almost new appliances and left in their place appliances that ranked just above junk.

Absent a specific signed inventory and description of these items, the tenants may get away with this type of theft. If the lease merely says "owner provides washer and dryer," you may find it difficult to prove the exact washer and dryer that you originally placed in the rental unit. (Purchase receipts prove only that you bought the items. They don't prove what you did with them.)

Rental Amounts

Some owners set their rent levels low to reduce turnover, vacancy losses, and tenant complaints. (Complaints fall in number because tenants realize they have a bargain and don't want to give you reason to raise their rent.) In addition, slightly below-market rents will permit you to select the best tenants from a large pool of applicants. Keep in mind, though, it's not just below-market rents that attract a large pool of applicants. In cases where you are offering highly desirable features that are otherwise scarce, you may be able to attract quality tenants even with rents that sit at the top of the market.

Late Fees and Discounts

Ideally, your well-selected tenants will pay their full rent on or before its due date. To encourage early payment, though, some property owners offer their tenants an "early payment discount." Others penalize tenants with late fees if the tenant's check is received, say, three to five days past its due date. In recent years, more owners have adopted the "carrot" approach over the "stick" approach. These owners claim that discounts create better tenant relations, work more effectively, and are easier to enforce.

Regardless of which method you choose, though, do not permit tenants to take the discount, or avoid the late fee, unless they satisfy the respective due date requirements. Plus, never, never, *never* allow tenants to get behind in their rent. Begin your eviction as soon as your lease and local ordinances permit. It is almost a law of nature that tenants who can't pay today, won't pay tomorrow. (Experience has taught me this lesson all too often.)

Nothing stands more important to peace of mind and financial prosperity than renting only to people who pay their rent on time, every time. Accept no substitutes.

Multiple Late Payments

What about the tenant who regularly pays on the eighth or ninth of every month—even though the rent falls due on the first? As long as the late fee is included, some owners do tolerate this behavior. I would not. I want my rents paid on time, every time.

Therefore, to enforce the "on time, every time" requirement, either I work out a new payment date with the tenants that better matches their cash flow needs, or I enforce the "multiple late payment" clause. This clause sets forth a "three strikes and you're out" rule. I realize that anyone can suffer a lapse of memory or cash shortfall once or twice, but chronic lateness warrants termination of the lease, forfeiture of deposit, and any other damages the tenant's breach of contract entails.

Bounced Check Fees and Termination

Likewise for bounced checks. Do not tolerate them. Once or twice, maybe. Three times warrants termination. In my experience, tenants who won't pay their rent on time with good checks don't just create problems in this one area. As often as not, you can expect them to give you other kinds of trouble. In fact, by tolerating this behavior, you actually invite even more troubling conduct. Don't do it. Get rid of these tenants quickly.

Tenant "Improvements"

"If we buy the paint, is it okay for us to paint the living room?" As an owner of rental properties, you may receive requests like this from tenants. Or you may end up with tenants who don't ask. They redecorate first and wait for you to ask questions later—like, "How could you paint the living room deep magenta?" or "What happened to the oak tree that was in the back yard?" (True story: Tenants of a friend of mine cut down a lovely large oak tree simply because they didn't like it.)

To at least try to prohibit tenants from diminishing the value of your property with their "improvements," include a lease clause that requires them to obtain your written permission before they paint, wallpaper, redecorate, renovate, repanel, remove, or in any other way modify your property. If left to their own accord, some tenants will treat your property as if it were their own. (This may sound all right until you see how little care they give their own property.)

Owner Access

Under the laws of most states, you may not enter your tenants' premises without their permission—unless their lease grants you that right. If you do want access to conduct periodic inspections, make repairs, take care of emergencies (e.g., an overflowing toilet), show the unit to prospective tenants (or buyers), or for any other reason, include an "owner access" clause.

Such a clause should not give you unlimited access at any time, night or day. Few tenants would accept such an intrusive demand. But it can give you an automatic right of entry within certain specified hours, say, 8:00 A.M. to 8:00 P.M. daily with 24-hour notice (emergencies excepted). Without an owner access clause, you may find that a difficult tenant may give you the runaround for days, or even weeks. Or worse, they may simply answer your requests for entry with a "No!"

Quiet Enjoyment

Do you want to guarantee your tenants that they will not suffer from noise and disturbances created by other tenants? Then heavily restrict their neighbor-disturbing partying, fighting, arguing, loud lovemaking, and playing of television, radio, stereo, computer, or other electronic devices. Or you could simply place a general clause within your lease such as the following:

> Residents agree not to create, generate, broadcast, or otherwise cause sounds or disturbances to emanate from themselves, their guests, or their residences into the residences of others. All residents agree to supremely respect and promote the quiet enjoyment of the premises by all other residents.

As an additional warning, beware of buying buildings with those notorious "paper-thin" walls. While performing your prepurchase inspection, turn on a portable radio and carry it from room to room and unit to unit. Do sound volumes at reasonable levels penetrate into other rooms or other units? If so, that property presents a large source of potential aggravation to you and your future tenants. Unless you can economically remedy this problem, avoid such a building.

Noxious Odors

As with noise and disturbances, noxious odors wafting throughout a building can stir up tenant dissatisfaction and complaints. Leading sources of noxious odors include smoking, cooking (especially some types of ethnic foods), and heavy use of perfumes. If any of these (or other types of noxious odors) seems as if it could present a problem, then your lease should include a clause that limits or excludes the causes of these odors.

Disturbing External Influences

In some instances, your tenants may be disturbed by noises or odors whose source lies outside your property. If you know of such problems (trains, heavy traffic, school band practice, factory emissions), consider placing a clause in your lease whereby the tenants acknowledge and accept notice. If you know of potential sources of disturbance but don't disclose them, your tenants may be able to lawfully terminate their lease and sue you for any damages they incur because of their "forced" relocation—sometimes called constructive eviction.

In fact, in some instances, even if you've had no prior knowledge of neighborhood noise or odors, such disturbances may give rise to a tenant claim of constructive eviction. If successful in pursuit of this claim, your tenants may also be able to terminate their lease and collect relocation expenses from you. Therefore, with or without actual knowledge of these adverse external influences, you may want to include a lease clause that limits both your responsibility for damages and the tenants' right to terminate their lease.

Tenant Insurance

Because a property owner's insurance does not cover the personal property of tenants, some landlords require their tenants to buy a tenants' insurance policy. These owners have learned through experience that when uninsured tenants suffer damage to their property through fire (or other peril), they invariably sue the owner for negligence. Even if the building burns after being hit by lightning, the tenants (or their lawyers) will claim that you should have installed a better lightning rod.

Sublet and Assignment

When tenants plan to be away from their residence for an extended period (summer in Europe), they may want to *sublet* their unit. When tenants plan to relocate permanently (job change, bought a house), they may want to *assign* their lease to someone else. To deal with this contingency, your lease can adopt one of four different positions:

1. No right to sublet or assign.
2. Right to sublet or assign with owner's written permission. Original tenants and new tenants both assume liability for rent payments and damages.
3. Right to sublet or assign with owner's written permission. Original tenants are released from any liability for future rent payments or damages. Owner must look exclusively to new tenants for financial performance.
4. Unlimited right to sublet or assign. Original tenants remain liable.

Absent a specific lease clause, most courts rule that option 4 is the controlling default option. Because owners dislike this default option, they typically do write in a sublet/assignment clause based on choice 2 or 3.

Obviously, choice 2 is preferred. When original tenants remain liable for rents and damages, they choose their subletees and assignees with far

CRAFTING YOUR RENTAL AGREEMENT

more care. As a negotiating tactic, you could request lease language that reflects the position of number 2. But in response to serious tenant objection, ease up and adopt number 3. Or, as is perhaps most common, stick with the approach of number 2 for subletees and shift to number 3 for assignees.

Pets

Too many property owners reflexively prohibit pets. In my experience, responsible tenants maintain pets in a responsible manner. Irresponsible people maintain pets in an irresponsible manner. If you select out irresponsible people, you usually can eliminate your "pet problems" without excluding all pets.

As a plus, by accepting responsible people who keep well-behaved pets, you can boost profits. Because of widespread "no pet" restrictions, owners who do permit pets can often charge a "pet premium" in both the amount of monthly rents and the amount of the security deposit.

Of course, if you do accept pets, draft a pet rules addendum and attach it to your lease. In drafting your pet rules, though, please consider the needs of the pet. I have seen pet rules that require large dogs to be kept permanently tethered in the backyard on a six- or eight-foot chain. Other rules require that a dog must be kept permanently in a basement or on a back porch.

If you feel so little for the lives of animals, totally exclude them from your rental properties. Moreover, any pet owner who accepts such cruel restrictions does not qualify (in my opinion) as a responsible person or a responsible pet owner.

Security Deposits

Security deposits present at least five issues that you may want to address in your lease:

1. Amount of the deposit
2. When payable
3. Rate of interest, if any
4. Under what conditions tenants will forfeit all or part of their deposit
5. When the deposit will be refunded if tenants satisfy all terms of the lease

To eliminate what often proves to be a source of dispute, your lease (or lease addendum) should clearly spell out answers to each of these issues. (Remember, too, that as you learn the practices of other rental property owners in your area, you can craft a security deposit policy that gives your property a competitive advantage.)

Amount and When Payable. In terms of amount, I favor high security deposits plus first and last month's rent—*always* payable in advance. (This lesson I learned the hard way.) You will undoubtedly get prospects who want to pay their deposit piecemeal over one to three months. Yield to this request, and you invite trouble. (Ditto for postdated checks.)

By urging you to get all of your money up front, I mean only to say that whatever amount you set, collect it before your tenants move into the unit. I favor a large amount because I'm leasing desirable properties to people with financial capacity. However, you may find that your tenant segment doesn't (or can't) meet this requirement.

Interest. Some local and state laws require owners to pay at least some specified rate of interest to their tenants. If this law applies in your area, make sure your tenants know they'll be receiving interest. In fact, I recommend paying interest to tenants even if applicable law doesn't require it. Today many tenants get upset if you insist on a deposit (especially a large one) but refuse to pass along its earnings to its "rightful" owner.

Forfeiture. To minimize controversy, some property owners develop a schedule of costs that they levy against tenants who fail to fully satisfy their lease obligations. For example, this schedule might list broken windows at $25, wall holes at $50, dirty appliances at $35, and general cleaning at $150. Other owners levy actual costs after the remedial work has been performed. And some severe owners simply try to keep the full deposit as liquidated damages—even when the actual damages fall substantially below the amount of the security deposit.

Regardless of which approach you favor, to avoid potential problems, (1) Make sure your tenants understand your deposit forfeiture policy before they take possession of the property, and (2) as soon as they completely vacate the property, perform a thorough property walk-through inspection with your tenants. In this final walk-through, compare the property item by item with the inspection sheet you prepared at the time they moved into the property.

Always perform a final inspection with the tenants present. Never let several days elapse between the tenants' moving out and your final inspection. Either practice can lead to tenant denials and subsequent dispute. Also, at the time tenants first sign their lease, make sure they understand that the security deposit does not limit their liability for rent or damages. Should actual damages exceed this amount, their liability to pay additional sums reaches this higher amount.

Deposit Return.   As a courtesy to your tenants, return their deposits with interest as soon as you know the correct amount. If possible, the best time is at the end of the final walk-through. You pay. The tenants accept. You shake hands with them and wish them well in their new home.

Too many owners needlessly delay returning deposits. That practice not only sours tenant relations but may subject you to legal penalties of treble damages. In some jurisdictions, failure to promptly return a deposit of, say, $1,000 means that tenants can go to court and force the delinquent owner to pay them $3,000. Many states and cities now legislate security deposit procedures. Read these laws closely. As the treble damage penalty shows, violations can cost you plenty.

Yard Care

When you rent out a house or duplex, you will probably want the tenants to care for the yard. But don't just say, "Tenants are responsible for yard care." I once made this mistake with otherwise excellent tenants. To these tenants, "yard care" meant cutting the grass. To me it meant watering the lawn when needed, tending the flowers and shrubs, and trimming the hedges to maintain them at their existing height of four feet.

Because the house was located in Florida and I was living in the San Francisco Bay Area, my visits to the property were not frequent. When after two years I did return, the hedges had grown wildly to a height of seven or eight feet, many flowers and shrubs were dead, and the lawn suffered scattered brown spots.

Learn from my mistake. If you want your tenants to care for the yard, spell out exactly what activities you want them to perform.

Parking, Number, and Type of Vehicles

Some tenants believe that if they can't find parking in a driveway or street, it's okay to park in the front yard. Or they may persist in blocking their neighbors' driveways. Or they leave unsightly junk (inoperable) cars to accumulate around the property. RVs, boats, and trailers also can create aesthetic and parking problems.

To head off these potential trouble spots, place a "parking clause" in your leases. Specify exactly the number and types of permitted vehicles. Then designate the *only* places where they may be parked properly. You may also want to restrict the backyard (or front yard) mechanic who disassembles his car and leaves the parts scattered about for days, weeks, or even months.

Repairs

Increasingly, owners of rental properties are shifting at least some costs of repair onto their tenants. For example, stopped-up toilets or drains and broken garbage disposals seldom occur without tenant abuse. As a minimum, owners may charge their tenants, say, a $50 repair fee for each time a repair becomes necessary. In other instances, owners declare tenants fully responsible for certain types of repairs—unless the service provider establishes that the tenants were not to blame.

Appliances.   With respect to appliances, some owners tell tenants that they may use the appliances currently in the property, but the owner will not pay for repairs or replacement. If the tenants don't agree to accept the appliances on those terms, the owner then removes them, and the tenants provide and maintain their own appliances.

Which Approach Is Best?   As with all lease clauses, no single approach to repairs works best in all situations. It depends on the types of tenants and properties you're dealing with. But undoubtedly, some people will show little care for your property. Yet at the same time, they expect you to jump into action whenever their abuse or neglect creates a problem. These are the people at whom you want to aim your tenant repair clauses. (Of course, ideally you want to avoid these kinds of tenants.)

Roaches, Fleas, Ants

On occasion, roaches, fleas, ants, and other similar pests will invade a house on their own without apparent reason. Usually, though, tenants invite them in through careless handling of food, unwashed dishes, trash, garbage, or pets. Therefore, especially in single-family houses, you may want your lease to assign the cost of extermination to the tenants.

In apartment buildings, the source of such pests may be more difficult to determine. All it takes is one unsanitary tenant, and their roaches or ants can quickly spread to everyone else's units. As a precaution, regular spraying seems to be the preferred method of stemming this potential problem.

Neat and Clean

Regardless of whether you are renting out houses or apartments, your lease should recite acceptable standards of neatness and cleanliness. Proper disposal of trash and garbage are bare minimums. Other dos and don'ts may address unwashed dishes; disposal of used motor oil, broken furniture, and appliances; bicycle storage; materials awaiting pickup for recycling; and vehicles that drip motor oil or transmission fluid.

Rules and Regulations

Especially for apartment buildings—or for rental units in co-ops or condominium projects—prepare a list of rules and regulations that tenants are expected to follow. Make sure your lease incorporates all of these rules (usually by addendum). Also, note within your lease that you (or the homeowners' association) reserves the right to reasonably amend or modify the listed rules.

Wear and Tear

So-called standard leases often state that tenants are responsible for all damages *except* normal wear and tear. I would never use such a clause. It invites tenant neglect and abuse. Many tenants believe that soiled carpets, cracked plaster, broken screens, and numerous other damages reflect nothing more than "normal wear and tear."

I disagree. If a tenant properly cares for a property, that property will not suffer any noticeable wear and tear during a tenancy of one year or less. For such short-term periods of residence, tenants should leave the property in essentially the same condition in which they accepted it. Eliminating the "wear and tear" clause will save you money and argument.

Lawful Use of Premises

As a matter of good business practice, and as a good-neighbor policy, your lease should require tenants to abide by all applicable laws, ordinances, and regulations. However, today's world of asset forfeiture gives you far more reason to strictly prohibit illegal conduct—especially as it pertains to drugs or gambling.

Today, many critics claim that in the zealous pursuit of revenues, law enforcement agencies are increasingly seizing the assets of innocent Americans (for example, see James Bovard's *Lost Rights*, St. Martin's Press, 1994). Many federal, state, and local laws require property owners to forfeit their property (cars, boats, houses, apartment buildings) to the government if drugs (and sometimes gambling) are found in the property—even when the rightful property owners are not accused of any crime. When I was teaching at UVA, the feds seized two or three fraternity houses for drug violations.

Play it safe. Enforce a zero-tolerance rule against illegal drugs or other offenses that can result in asset forfeiture. (As an incentive to law enforcement, the seizing government agency or department shares in the proceeds when the forfeited asset is sold at public auction.)

Notice

To help you reduce rent loss during periods of turnover, your leases should require tenants to give advance notice of the exact date they plan to end their tenancy and completely vacate the property. In that way, you can begin to publicize the unit's upcoming availability. Ideally, you'll find a new tenant who will move in within a day or two after the previous tenants have moved out.

Most owners require 30 days' *written* notice. However, if you're operating in a weak or seasonal rental market, you might ask for 45 or 60 days' notice. On the other hand, if you expect strong and immediate demand for your rental property, you could reduce your advance notice to, say, 15 days. In other words, tie your written notice requirement to the length of time you believe it will take to locate a new, highly desirable tenant.

Failure to Deliver

Sometimes tenants will tell you that they're vacating on the 28th. Yet as of the 31st, they're still packing boxes. This discrepancy could create a serious problem if you've already signed a lease with new tenants and promised them possession on the 30th. Although your "holdover penalty" clause should help you avoid this kind of situation, sometimes it happens nevertheless.

So what do you do? In anticipation of this possibility, some property owners include a "failure to deliver" lease clause. This clause typically accomplishes two objectives: (1) It voids the liability of the property owner to the new tenants for any expenses they might suffer (motel room, furniture storage, double moving costs) as a result of the owner's failure to deliver, and (2) it does not permit the new tenants to immediately cancel their lease. Rather, it simply pushes back their move-in date (and accrued rentals) until the previous tenants do vacate and the owner's "make ready" efforts are complete.

Obviously, if your previous tenants continue to hold over, you can't hang your new tenants up indefinitely. In that case, your lease might release the new tenants after your failure to deliver extends beyond, say, 10 days. Fortunately, you won't often experience the holdover problem. But it's still a good idea to anticipate the possibility and draft a lease clause to deal with it.

Utilities, Property Taxes, Association Fees

Often tenants pay all of their own utilities and waste disposal charges. Owners pay all property taxes and homeowners' association fees. However, this "typical" practice is not written in stone. Sometimes in longer-term residential leases, tenants assume all of these financial responsibilities. And frequently in short-term rentals, owners pay all expenses. Also, some multiunit properties don't separately meter individual tenants. This situation also can shift utility costs to owners.

Regardless of which practice you adopt, your lease should spell out exactly who pays what with respect to these or other similar types of expenses (e.g., heating oil, pest spraying, window washing). Clarity in this regard especially helps two types of tenants: (1) young and old people who are new to renting and may not fully understand their responsibilities, and (2) people who are relocating and would otherwise base their expectations on the different practices they experienced elsewhere.

Liquid-Filled Furniture

Although waterbeds and other types of liquid-filled furniture aren't as popular as they once were, a few old hippies and New Agers still use them. Unfortunately, the water damage created when one of these beds bursts is typically excluded from coverage under most rental-property insurance policies.

Consequently, you may want your lease to forbid this kind of risk. Or, alternatively, require that your tenants' liquid furniture meets rigid industry safety standards *and* require your tenants to pay a "waterbed premium" for the insurance endorsement you'll have to buy to secure coverage.

Abandonment of Property

Sometimes tenants move out and leave various items of their personal property. They promise you, "We'll come back next Tuesday and pick up those boxes in the garage." Of course, next Tuesday comes and goes, and the boxes remain.

What can you do? That depends on your lease. If it's silent on the issue, the law may require you to safeguard the items for some specified period. Then you will have to dispose of the items according to the applicable legal procedure. With a lease clause, though, you can contractually agree with the tenants that any items not removed by the end of the lease will go straight to the dump or (if of any value) to the Salvation Army.

Nonwaivers

For reasons of courtesy or practicality, you may, on occasion, permit tenants to temporarily breach a lease clause or house rule. However, to prevent tenants from stretching this courtesy beyond your intent, your lease can include a "nonwaiver clause." In this clause, you make clear that your obliging actions today in no way waive your right to enforce the letter of the lease tomorrow.

Likewise, this clause can deal with rent collections in a similar way. For example, say you accept a rent check even though you know your tenant is sharing his apartment with an unauthorized cotenant. The nonwaiver clause prevents your tenant from later claiming, "Well, you took our rent check. So you can't tell me now that Joe has to move out." Yes, you can. Your nonwaiver clause voids that tenant defense.

Breach of Lease (or House Rules)

In a breach-of-lease clause, you reinforce your right to terminate the lease of tenants who breach *any* lease requirement or house rule. Absent this clause, tenants sometimes believe that if you accept the rent, you waive your enforcement of other tenant violations. Together, the nonwaiver and breach-of-agreement clauses impress on tenants their obligation to comply 100 percent—or suffer the consequences of eviction.

No Representations (Full Agreement)

On occasion tenants may try to extricate themselves from their lease obligations by claiming that you misled them with false promises. For example, they could claim that you induced them to sign their lease by promising to completely paint and recarpet their unit. You know that the tenants are lying, but a judge may not. To the judge, it's your word against the tenants'.

To prevent this type of charade, include a lease clause that states that the lease and its addenda constitute the full extent of the rental agreement. Further, it could state that the tenants have not relied on any oral or written representations or promises not explicitly included within the lease.

Arbitration

In many cities, the legal process is too slow, expensive, complex, and cumbersome to effect timely and affordable justice. As a result, some property owners include an arbitration clause in their leases. This clause steers unresolved owner-tenant disputes away from the courthouse and into a more informal arbitration hearing.

An arbitration hearing differs from trial litigation in that it typically (1) requires much less time; (2) costs less; (3) avoids formal rules of legal procedure; (4) reduces or eliminates pretrial discovery such as depositions, interrogatories, and request for production of documents; and (5) severely limits the right to appeal. All of these features may sound like a pretty good trade-off against litigation.

But, as they say, "the proof of the pudding is in the taste." Before you adopt this clause for your leases, investigate how well arbitration works in your area. Learn whether your local courts show any noticeable bias for or against property owners. Arbitration tends to work best for landlords faced with courts that generally side with tenants. (Unfortunately, though, some pro-tenant judges—at the urging of lawyers who fear a loss of business—may refuse to enforce contract arbitration clauses.)

Attorney Fees (Who Pays?)

Standard preprinted leases often include an "attorney fees" clause that strongly favors property owners. Typically, in cases where you prevail in court, this clause requires losing tenants to pay your "reasonable" attorney and court costs. In contrast, though, when your tenants prevail, the clause (through its silence) leaves attorney fees and costs on the shoulders of each party who incurred them.

Will the Court Enforce It?   On the one hand, courts that still honor the principle "judges shall not rewrite lawful contracts" will generally enforce this one-sided attorney fees clause. Such courts reason that any tenant who wanted to modify or eliminate this clause was free to negotiate the point before signing the lease.

On the other hand, so-called activist judges may use this clause to declare you liable for a winning tenant's attorney fees and costs. These judges hold that "what's good for the goose is good for the gander." These judges often lean toward the liberal mind-set of "powerful greedy landlords" versus "powerless victimized tenants." They see it as their duty to upset this supposed imbalance of power by placing their thumb on the scales of justice in favor of tenants.

Include or Not?   Whether you should include such a clause remains an open question. As a starting point, note whether courts in your area will enforce it as written. Also, consider how your prospective tenants might view this clause. Will it cause them to mark you down as just another "landlord" rather than see you as "a caring provider of housing services"?

What about the solvency of your tenants? Even if you prevail in court, is it likely you could collect a judgment? Does your state permit wage garnishments? Beware of "activist" tenants. These types of tenants love going to court and often get their legal fees paid by some government agency or "nonprofit" tenants' rights group. Should you eventually fail to win your claim (or defense), these activists know how to work the system to stick you with their substantial legal bills.

Explore Your Best Options.   Don't insert (or omit) any type of attorney fees clause until you explore its practical and legal implications. Try to learn from the experiences of other property owners. Investigate the legal procedure that's typically used for settling owner-tenant disputes in your area. Also, some courts follow a "loser pays" rule regardless of what your lease says—even when it's silent on the issue of attorney fees.

Offer of Settlement Rule.   In other areas, courts may follow some type of "offer of settlement" rule. In these cases, a party who turns down a settlement offer may end up having to pay the other party's fees and costs—regardless of who wins. Say your tenants offer to settle your $8,000 claim for $5,000. You reject the offer and go to trial. The court awards you $6,000.

Guess what? In some areas, you would pay the tenants' legal costs and fees because your court victory didn't win you at least 25 percent more than the tenants offered to settle. (So much for justice!) Of course, this rule does cut both ways. In some cases it can benefit you. Overall, realize that in many jurisdictions, the question of who pays costs and fees is far more complex than a simple clause in a lease may seem to indicate.

Written Notice to Remedy

A "written notice to remedy" requires an owner (or tenant) to give written notice before taking action to legally enforce a lease provision that the tenant (or owner) is currently breaching. From your perspective, written notice can help you in two ways: (1) When you wish to evict a tenant for cause, previous written notices give you a paper trail to bolster your case, and (2) if in defense of an eviction (or suit for rent) a tenant falsely claims, "We didn't have any heat for most of January," you can force the tenants to prove that they sent you written notice of this problem. Because their claim lacks veracity, no such proof will be forthcoming. Their defense fails.

TENANTS RIGHTS LAWS

Because U.S. laws governing landlord-tenant relationships derive from feudal England, our state and local lawmakers, courts, and government agencies have frequently stepped in to "update" this legal relationship. In many cases, these statutes, ordinances, court decisions, and regulations may supersede written clauses in your lease. These laws tend to expand tenant rights and landlord responsibilities in the following areas: (1) tenant selection, (2) property operations, and (3) evictions.

Tenant Selection

Marketing strategy tells you to target your rental units to defined market segments. However, federal law prohibits you from explicitly excluding applicants because of their race, religion, sex, ethnicity, national origin, disability, or family status (households with children). In addition, *some* state and local laws have expanded this list to include various other categories such as homosexuals, welfare recipients, and lawyers. (Yes, many property owners do avoid renting to lawyers because as a class, they rank among the most troublesome tenants. Note, too, that federal civil rights law and nearly all state and local fair-housing ordinances exempt owner-occupied properties of one to four units. If they choose, exempt property owners may discriminate without legal penalty.)

Conduct and Creditworthiness. Laws against stereotyping people because of their race, religion, or occupation do not mean that you must accept individuals who do not meet your legitimate standards of conduct and creditworthiness. You may lawfully turn down any person—regardless of protected status—whose credit, employment, income, or rental record falls below your minimums. Also, you need not accept any individual who does fulfill your minimum standards but nevertheless falls below the superior qualifications of other applicants.

Unlike employers, who are sometimes coerced into quota hiring, landlords are not subject to such laws or regulations. You are free to select those tenants (among all applicants) who *best* match or exceed your standards.

Beware of Inconsistency. However, you are not free to arbitrarily change your standards, or to arbitrarily apply them. In other words, to a large degree, discrimination laws do restrict a property owner's ability to remain flexible. Assume you meet with a nice young couple from your church who have bad credit. You believe they're good people and make an exception to your credit standards.

Subsequently, a nice young couple of a different religion apply to rent a unit in the same building. You turn them down because of their prior credit problems. You've just opened yourself up to a lawsuit. Under the law, you must apply your standards consistently. Exceptions and flexibility can land you in court.

Beware of Testers.   To trap property owners who set and apply their tenant selection standards in an arbitrary or illegal discriminatory manner, various government agencies and activist "nonprofits" employ testers. Generally, these testers differ from each other in terms of race, religion, or family status, but they remain similar in terms of income, credit, and other lawful tenant selection criteria.

In applying to rent from you, various testers will precisely note your words and actions. If you treat any tester differently from the others ("I don't think this would be a good building for your children; mostly singles live here"), you are inviting a charge of discrimination. To avoid trouble with testers and their vigilant search for racist, sexist, and homophobic landlords, apply your tenant-selection standards consistently. Do not encourage or discourage rental applicants because of their protected status.

"I think you'd be happy here, we have many Jewish tenants," and "I don't think you'd be happy here, we have very few Jewish tenants," are equally discriminatory under the law. For your own peace of mind and financial well-being, never say or do anything that takes notice of a person's difference if that difference is covered under some type of discrimination law or regulation. (Of course, this advice applies equally to any leasing agents or property managers that you employ. As a principal, you may be legally responsible for the discriminatory acts of your agents and employees.)

Property Operations

Various laws will govern the operation of your properties. You must abide by zoning, environmental, occupancy, health, and safety codes and ordinances. In addition, rules may apply to matters such as snow removal, approved trash receptacles and disposal, tenant parking, minimum level of heat, security locks, and burglar bars. Some cities and states, too, have enacted "repair and deduct" statutes. These laws give tenants the right to pay for necessary property repairs and then deduct the amounts from their rent check.

As a rule, these laws are just a normal part of doing business. They don't impose any significant costs or problems on landlords. However, compliance can occasionally cost big money (lead paint or asbestos abatement, underground oil tank cleanup, earthquake retrofit). So before buying a property, investigate whether these types of laws could increase the costs of operating your property.

Evictions

States and cities set the legal steps property owners must follow to terminate a lease and evict a tenant. This procedure typically pertains to

(1) lawful grounds, (2) written notice, (3) time to cure or remedy breach, (4) time elapsing before a hearing, (5) allowable tenant defenses, and (6) time to vacate after adverse ruling.

Learn this legal procedure as it applies in your area. Then follow it precisely. Failure to dot your i's and cross your t's can get your case thrown out. You must then go back and start again. Also, never resort to "self-help" by threatening or assaulting a tenant; changing door locks; turning off the tenant's water, heat, or electricity; or confiscating tenant property. Follow lawful procedure. "Self-help" can expose you to personal injury lawsuits and criminal charges.

LANDLORDING: PROS AND CONS

From the preceding collection of possible lease clauses and tenant rights laws, you might say, "Forget it! Landlording involves too many potential hazards, headaches, and risks." But imagine for a moment reading a list of laws, regulations, accidents, breakdowns, repairs, lawsuits, hassles, and expenses that can apply to driving a car. By focusing only on the negatives, you might put your car in a garage and leave it there permanently.

Possibilities, Not Probabilities

In listing various issues, I don't mean to scare you away from landlording; I want to present possibilities for your concern. It is the naive and unknowing property owners who most often experience landlording difficulties.

In more than 20 years of dealing with rentals, I have never suffered through the eviction process. Nor have I ever used a lease that included even one-third of the previously mentioned clauses. Nor have I been sued by a tenant, experienced a charge of discrimination, or run into any serious environmental or building safety and health code problems.

The chances are that you won't, either—if you develop systems of tenant selection and property operation that anticipate, alleviate, and mitigate potential problems. Think of the concerns listed in this chapter as possibilities to prepare for and guard against, not as probabilities certain to make your life a constant source of aggravation. They won't—unless you let them.

Professional Property Managers

You can employ a property manager (not a property management firm) or handyman caretaker to deal with routine tenant relations and property maintenance. For a relatively low cost, you can delegate everyday concerns. As long as you design or retain approval of leasing standards and property operations, delegating tasks to others will save you time, money, and effort. I discourage you from employing a management firm because such firms manage hundreds or even thousands of units for dozens of property owners. How can such a firm closely watch your best interests and develop a marketing strategy to beat your competition? It can't and won't. With a management company, expect mediocre performance (at best), because that's what you will get.

To operate profitably and proactively, set high standards. Show your help how to achieve the performance results you want. Pay them well and frequently tell them how much you value their work and appreciate the job they're doing. Through this approach, your properties will bring you peace of mind and financial security.

13

SELL FOR TOP DOLLAR

At some point, regardless of your specific investment strategy, you will sell (or exchange) one or more of your properties. When that time comes, you must decide whether to sell the property yourself or employ a real estate agent. In making this decision, think not only about the amount of sales commission that you will pay an agent but also about the services that an agent can provide.

AGENT SERVICES

Selling a property involves time, money, effort, and expertise. Investors who are unwilling to take on these obligations will seldom sell their own property successfully.

Because most investors would rather delegate these activities, the real estate brokerage business exists to provide service to sellers. The full range of services that a top agent can provide to a seller are too numerous to mention here, but the more important ones include the following:

- ◆ Works full-time for the seller to find buyers for his or her property. Agents are not just available after work, on certain evenings, or on Sunday afternoons.
- ◆ Relies on sources other than newspaper advertisements to supply a majority of prospects. Agents get prospects from referrals by past customers, Internet and e-mail inquiries, financial institutions, hotels and motels, educational institutions, other professionals such as lawyers and insurance agents, company

personnel departments, builders, other types of advertising, canvassing, and For Sale signs.

◆ Provides sellers with comp sales that indicate the values of their properties. This market analysis is based on what similar houses have *sold* for, not what their *asking prices* may have been.

◆ Gives helpful pointers on how sellers should prepare their properties to improve their value and achieve a quick sale.

◆ Calculates how much sellers will net from a sale after all expenses have been paid, including any balance on a mortgage, taxes, or other liens.

◆ Shows the property to its best advantage and brings out the features that appeal to each prospective buyer. Remember that agents get to know their customers' needs so that they can show only those properties in which a specific buyer is likely to show an interest.

◆ Performs the services that will facilitate the sale, thus freeing the sellers' time for other activities.

◆ Aids sellers in finding their next property and setting up a Section 1031 exchange to save on taxes (see Chapter 14).

◆ Helps negotiate the sale and gives advice concerning the pros and cons of each offer.

◆ Helps buyers overcome obstacles to buying the sellers' property, such as obtaining financing, selling an existing property, working an exchange, or getting finances in order.

◆ Follows up on prospects who have shown an interest in a property.

◆ Exacts from buyers their true objections to a property, so that sellers can attempt to overcome them. Usually buyers will be more direct with an agent than a property owner.

◆ Prequalifies the prospect and helps sellers avoid wasting time in accepting an offer from buyers who cannot put together the financial resources to close the sale.

◆ Handles any details and questions about selling a property that a seller may have from the time of listing to after the closing.

A majority of buyers rely on agents to help them find properties. Therefore, by-owner sellers may miss that large number of buyers who want the services that top agents typically provide.

Obstacles to By-Owner Sales

Although many factors may account for an investor's difficulty in selling a property, the following items are most common:

- An emotional involvement with the property such that buyer criticism results in disputes between the buyer and the owner
- An unwillingness to price the property in line with its market value
- A failure to remain available during the evening hours and on weekends waiting for buyers to call or come by
- An inability to help potential buyers to understand or secure financing of the property
- An overdependence on newspaper advertising to bring buyers to the property
- A personality or emotional makeup that does not lend itself well to direct negotiations with buyers
- An inability to attend to the technical and practical problems associated with selling and buying a property

Cost of Brokerage Services

Instead of focusing on the agent's commission, property owners should focus on the amount they will net from a sale after paying off all necessary mortgages, liens, closing expenses, and selling fees. In effect, the real cost of the brokerage service is the difference between what sellers would net if they employed an agent and the net amount they would receive if they chose to sell the property themselves.

On the surface, it might appear that the difference in net between using an agent and selling by owner would be the amount of the real estate sales commission. However, this situation would result only if all other things were equal. In practice, though, they seldom are.

To obtain a better picture of what this net difference might be, consider four separate items: (1) the selling price of the property, (2) selling expenses incurred by the owner, (3) federal income tax law, and (4) opportunity costs.

Selling Price. The selling price of a property by owner is usually less than that of a similar property sold through an agent. This fact, then, reduces the difference in nets by the amount that the price by owner is less than the agent's price.

Selling Expenses. The selling expenses when using an agent are fixed fairly closely by the amount of the sales commission, which may range between 3 percent and 10 percent depending on the type of property and the type of listing. (Types of listings are discussed later in this chapter.) When an owner sells a property, the amount spent out of pocket on selling expenses varies directly with the length of time the property is on the market.

In some cases, a for-sale-by-owner (FSBO) seller may get lucky and spend only $500 to $1,000 out of pocket. In other instances that expense may go much higher, and the owner may still not succeed. The difference in net is reduced by the amounts a by-owner seller must spend for expenses such as advertising, signs, additional legal costs, appraisal fees, and other miscellaneous items.

Federal Income Tax.   As discussed in Chapter 14, out-of-pocket selling expenses may be deducted in calculating the capital gain resulting from the sale of a property. Therefore, even if out-of-pocket expenses of a by-owner seller are less than those incurred by a seller who uses an agent, the sum is less than the absolute dollar difference between these amounts because of the tax deduction. Again, this factor will reduce the difference in nets between the by-owner seller and agent seller.

Opportunity Costs.   Opportunity costs are costs incurred by a by-owner seller for the time, effort, and aggravation that selling a property entails, such as the cost of time wasted waiting for appointments that may or may not show, or sitting by a telephone that may or may not ring.

The method of calculating the true cost of the brokerage service is illustrated in the following example: Assume that a property can be sold by an agent for $100,000 with a 6 percent sales commission. A by-owner seller can get a price of $97,500 with selling expenses of $1,000. Moreover, assume the seller is in a 35 percent (federal and state) marginal tax bracket. In addition, the closing costs and mortgage balance that will be paid by the seller (regardless of who sells the house) equal $65,000. The nets of each case are computed as follows:

	By-Owner Seller	*Agent Seller*
Sales price	$97,500	$100,000
Mortgage and closing	–65,000	–65,000
Selling expenses after tax break	–650	–3,900
	$(1,000 \times .65)$	$(.65 \times .06 \times 100,000)$
Opportunities costs imputed	–750	0
Net under each method	31,100	31,100
Difference in nets	0	

As you can see, based on the figures in this example, even though the seller who employed a real estate agent to sell her property paid an after-tax sales commission of $3,900, her net of $31,100 equaled the net realized by the by-owner seller.

Although no one can predict what the different net amounts might be to any specific seller, this example seems representative. Only in unusual instances would the net received in a by-owner sale exceed the net received in an agent sale by a substantial amount after all applicable expenses are considered. The actual cost of the brokerage services to a seller can be a positive (benefit) amount, and even in a worst-case scenario, it will seldom come close to approaching the nominal dollar amount of the sales commission. Naturally, this type of analysis shows why 80 percent of owners avoid the FSBO route and sell their properties through a realty firm.

In her book *Housewise* (HarperCollins, 1987, p. 196), rehab investor Suzanne Brangham points out, "Frequently—about once a day—someone asks me why I don't get a real estate license and avoid paying someone else the commission on each property I handle. My answer to this is that I don't want to *sell* real estate—I want to invest in it and renovate it . . . more importantly, if I did try to sell my own properties, I'd lose some of the most valuable assets in this business—the agents I work with. Good agents know what properties are selling for, which areas are strong, and which neighborhoods are getting hot. They know what's gone up in value and which areas may be coming down."

In other words, Suzanne is saying that the agents she works with don't cost her money. Instead, the information, knowledge, and services they provide help her make money. Of course, only you can figure out the sales strategy that's best for you to pursue. But whatever you decide, consider all of the potential costs and benefits of going it alone. Don't naively believe that you can simply sell the property yourself and save the commission.

LISTING AGREEMENTS

A listing contract is the employment agreement between a seller of a property and the real estate brokerage firm. The three most common types of listing contract are (1) open listing, (2) exclusive agency, and (3) exclusive right to sell. Under the first two types of listing agreements, owners retain the right to sell their property themselves without paying a brokerage commission. Under the exclusive-right-to-sell listing agreement, the owners agree to pay as long as a sale takes place within the listing period.

There is no one best listing contract for all sellers. It depends on whether you want to reserve the right to sell your property yourself or hire one or a number of brokers. Each type of contract presents advantages and disadvantages.

Many good agents, though, will hesitate to accept an open or exclusive listing. These agents prefer an exclusive-right-to-sell listing. They want to protect the time and money that they will invest in their efforts to sell your property. Unless you have a good reason to retain the right to sell your own property, give the agent an exclusive-right-to-sell agreement.

If you sign an exclusive-right-to-sell contract, however, make sure that the brokerage firm will allow you to terminate the agreement in good faith at any time with *no further obligation* to that firm. Otherwise you could be prohibited from listing your property with another broker or selling it yourself until after the date that the original listing agreement would have expired.

Note that the preceding advice stresses "termination in good faith." You should have a justifiable cause for canceling. For example, a case where a sales agent of the broker made unauthorized disclosures to buyers would be good cause to terminate. Most reputable brokers will permit cancellations of this nature.

In addition to the termination clause, examine a listing contract for the following points:

- *A written contract.* That the contract should be in writing cannot be stressed too highly. Common sense dictates that any agreement where one party pays a commission to another party should define the responsibilities and obligations of each party.
- *Identification.* The property must be identified. This item does not necessarily mean a full legal description but rather a description sufficiently clear to avoid misunderstanding. "Acreage in Aiken County" is not an adequate description. Court records contain a number of cases where an insufficient property identification caused a misunderstanding between a buyer and seller as to what property was actually sold (or bought).
- *Sales price.* Both the price and terms of the sale should be stated. A broker should not accept a listing at an inflated selling price merely to obtain the listing in hopes of renegotiating the price before the listing runs out. This procedure is unfair and misleading to the seller.
- *Commission.* A negotiable fee, the commission may be any amount both parties agree to. It may be a fixed dollar amount or a percentage of the sales price or a combination of both. "Net listings" in which the commission is all money above a given net amount are prohibited by law in most states. If an offer is submitted substantially below the listing price, some brokers will accept a lower commission than stated in the listing contract to help the sale go

through. It is illegal for real estate boards or associations to set commission rates that member firms must charge.

◆ *Signatures.* All owners of the property should sign the listing contract. It is a good policy for both a husband and wife to sign even though the property is in one name only. The broker should sign also, as he or she is a party to the contract and must be obligated to perform specific duties to the seller.

◆ *Expiration date.* A definite expiration date should be stated in the listing agreement. A typical listing period for a house or small income property is 90 days, although 120 days may not be unreasonable. A listing contract for more than 120 days should not be signed except in unusual circumstances. Listing contracts for larger income properties may reasonably run longer, say 120 days to 180 days, with renewal if the agent seems to be doing a competent job of promoting the property.

◆ *Type of listing.* The listing contract must clearly state and define the type of listing. An exclusive-right-to-sell listing must clearly state that it is such a listing and must contain a statement of the seller's obligation to pay a commission no matter who sells the property.

◆ *Delivery of copy.* Most state laws require an agent to *immediately* give a copy of any listing contract to the parties who have signed it.

◆ *Automatic renewal.* The listing contract should not include an automatic renewal clause. These clauses frequently stipulate that if an owner does not notify the listing broker in writing at least ten days before expiration of his or her intention to cancel the listing, it is automatically renewed for 60 to 90 days. Most courts will not enforce automatic renewals.

◆ *Cancellation of contract.* Either the owner or the real estate broker may cancel a listing contract at any time prior to the execution of a contract of sale with a buyer who is ready, willing, and able to purchase at the listed price. If an owner cancels the listing contract *without clause* before the agent has found a purchaser and before expiration of the listing contract, the broker can sue the owner for any loss or damage that he or she may have sustained because of the cancellation. As a practical matter, most brokers allow cancellation by a client at any time without obligation as long as no buyer has been located. Sometimes, even though you are allowed to terminate the listing, you will be prohibited from listing with another brokerage firm until the time the listing would otherwise have expired.

If a real estate broker fails to perform as agreed in the listing contract, or cancels the contract before its expiration, the owner may recover from the broker the loss (if any) sustained by reason of the agent's default or cancellation. Again, as a practical matter, no compensable damage would have occurred.

◆ *Personal property.* The listing contract should clearly identify personal property that will be included in the sale. Drapes, carpets, window air conditioning units, appliances, and even shrubs are examples of items that often cause disputes between buyer, seller, and broker, when it is unclear whether they are to remain the property of the seller or the tenants.

◆ *Offers.* Real estate brokers may not refuse to forward a bona fide offer because they are not satisfied with it or believe that the seller will reject it. They must present all written offers to the seller. They cannot hold one offer back in favor of another. Brokers cannot assign priorities to offers received. All offers to purchase must be presented promptly to the seller. Once an offer is accepted by the seller, the signed acceptance must be delivered promptly to the purchaser. Delay in delivery could allow the purchaser time to withdraw the offer.

◆ *Earnest money deposit.* A bona fide offer should be accompanied by an earnest money deposit. Many listing contracts stipulate that on default of the buyer, the earnest money is divided equally between the broker and seller. You, however, can change this agreement so that you are entitled to all of the deposit. If the listing contract is silent on this point, the forfeited deposit in most states belongs to the seller.

◆ *Obligations of broker.* Basically, the listing contract obligates the real estate broker to do everything possible to find a buyer for the listed property who is ready, willing, and able to purchase. A broker who advertises and shows a property regularly is thought to be fulfilling that obligation.

◆ *Earning the commission.* Unless otherwise stated in the listing contract, the real estate agent earns a commission by finding a willing and able buyer for your property. If the buyer can't locate financing, if the property does not pass inspection, or if some other buyer contingency clause isn't met, you want your listing agreement to exempt you from paying a commission. Similarly, you also want a provision that releases you from the obligation to pay a commission if for some reason beyond your control you can't close (e.g., a title problem of which you were unaware).

Obligations of the Sales Agent

Although the listing agreement sets forth the basic legal relationship between you and your brokerage firm, you should expect your sales agent to go substantially beyond the bare-bones duties spelled out in the listing agreement. More specifically, the listing firm and your agent should do the following:

- Work actively to *find* buyers for your property, not simply show properties to prospects who come to them.
- Notify you at least weekly what specific actions they are taking to find a buyer for your property.
- Place your property on the market at its market value or only slightly above it.
- When your property has been priced in the right range, agents should not try to talk you into accepting offers substantially lower than its listing price.
- Any undesirable features of your property should have been considered when its market value was estimated; therefore, no need exists for you to reduce your price materially to compensate for any of its disadvantages.
- All offers, with no exceptions, should be presented to you as soon as they have been received by the listing firm. The firm should help you prepare your property for sale by suggesting the types of changes that would increase its market value and marketability.
- A sold sign should not be placed on your property until after the sale has closed. Although a Sale Pending sign may be used, the firm should still work to obtain backup offers on your property.
- You should be given time to consult an attorney prior to signing anything or be free to insert a clause that the sales contract is subject to your rescission if your attorney later finds it unacceptable. In these cases, use your attorney to check the terms of the contract, not to rewrite it or to change for sake of change and inflating his fees.
- The sales agent should help the buyer work out the necessary financing for the purchasing of your property and should not receive a kickback from the lender (this is done in some areas when certain lenders want to encourage sales agents to bring them mortgage business).
- Sales agents should not make contract concessions without your express permission (e.g., telling the buyer without your knowledge that you will include the refrigerator and stove in the sale).

- The sales agent should serve as a good-faith negotiator between you and the buyer without coercing you into accepting an unreasonable offer. He or she should also be able to tell you when the sales contract is signed approximately how much you will net from the sale.
- Your agent should keep you informed about what is happening from the time the sales contract is signed up to the date of closing.
- The sales agent should have an accurate closing statement prepared for you accounting for all receipts and expenditures relevant to you.
- The sales agent should make no unauthorized disclosures to prospects about your personal situation that might harm your strength in negotiating.
- The sales agent should learn all of the information necessary to value and price your property according to the appraisal methods discussed in Chapter 3.
- The sales agent should inform you before you sign a sales contract as to whether the buyer appears financially able to close the purchase.
- The sales agent should try to get at least a $1,000 or more earnest money deposit. The greater the value of your property, the more the agent should obtain. Sometimes buyers tender a relatively small earnest money deposit with their offer but then agree to increase it to 5 percent or 10 percent of the purchase price as soon as you accept the offer.
- Your agent should make all disclosures to you that are required by your state's agency disclosure laws. In addition, the agent should explain the duties and obligations required of agents by your state's agency statutes, case law, and licensing rules and regulations.

Your Obligations to Your Agent

When you employ an agent to sell your property, the selling process becomes a joint effort. First, get your property in tip-top shape. Second, allow the agent to show the property without your interruption and distraction. Would you like your boss looking over your shoulder when you are doing your job? Third, if you have signed an exclusive-right-to-sell listing contract, refer all prospective buyers you meet to the sales agent. Let the agent do what you are paying him or her to do.

And fourth, be fair. If the agent has done the job, pay the commission. Don't try to negotiate or make side deals with buyers around an agent you have hired on an exclusive-right-to-sell basis. Owners have the right to sell their own property, but when they use an agent, that relationship should be on a good-faith basis, or it should not be entered into.

PREPARE THE PROPERTY FOR TOP DOLLAR

To receive top dollar for your property in the shortest time, you may need to spend time and money getting it ready for sale. Your property should immediately impress your prospective buyers. Few things turn buyers off as fast as a property that lacks curb appeal and interior decor. Yet many sellers surprisingly ignore even a basic sprucing up of their property before placing it on the market.

This tendency of sellers to let their properties run down works to your advantage as a buyer; but as a seller, you don't want your property's poor condition to detract from your selling price. Furthermore, a subpar property draws inferior tenants at lower rent levels. And because buyers of income properties (should) pay close attention to tenant quality and operating income, these deficiencies, too, will contribute to a lower selling price. In other words, put your property in tip-top condition. To do so, you follow not only a sound philosophy of property management but also an important part of your sales strategy.

To illustrate the importance of preparing a property for sale, consider the following example. Although the property in question is a single-family home, the same principles apply to all types of properties.

Some years back, a friend asked me to see if I could determine why his house would not sell. He had had it on and off the market for over a year with no success. Yet the house was priced reasonably for its location and physical condition.

When I inspected it, several problems were apparent. The wallpaper in the bedrooms, kitchen, and living room was faded and drab in color. The kitchen floor tile was permanently stained and discolored, and two of the bedrooms had asbestos tile floors rather than more desirable hardwood or carpeting. The upstairs attic had been converted into a children's bedroom and recreation area; however, because no ductwork was available to the upstairs, a gas space heater had been installed.

Overall, prospective buyers would feel that the interior of the house lacked warmth and color and were leery of having children playing unattended near a gas space heater. I recommended that the owner install light-colored, inexpensive carpeting in the bedrooms and repaper the rooms with an attractive, inexpensive prepasted wallpaper. I also suggested that he put a new bright flooring in the kitchen and take the space heater out of the attic and replace it with baseboard electric heat. Furthermore, I advised the owner to remove about 60 percent of the overgrown shrubs and plants from the yard because it looked like a jungle.

After four days of work and $1,837 in expenses for the carpeting and electric heat (including hired installation), paint, wallpaper, tile (which he installed himself), and rental of a chain saw for removal of the bushes and shrubs, the owner again placed the house on the market. It sold 45 days later for $8,000 more than he had previously been asking. At that time, this was not a bad return for $1,837 and four days of work.

The people who owned the house were so accustomed to its short-comings that they just didn't see them. When you try to sell (or rent out) a property, evaluate it as buyers (or tenants) in the market will view it, not according to your own tastes and what you have grown accustomed to.

Usually, it's best when redecorating to use colors that will blend with about any color of furnishings. A fresh coat or two of off-white paint will refresh most rooms. And buyers won't have to worry about refurbishing right after they take possession.

Compliance Issues

Real estate law has shifted from *caveat emptor* (let the buyer beware) to *caveat vendor* (let the seller beware). Consequently, as part of your property preparation, discuss the issue of seller disclosures with your attorney and your real estate agent. A variety of disclosure laws (which differ by state and city) now apply to property condition (roof, foundation, heating and air conditioning, plumbing and electrical systems, etc.), environmental hazards (lead paint, asbestos, underground storage tanks, water quality, electromagnetic fields, radon, etc.), code compliance (zoning, building permits, safety regulations, etc.), location (floodplain, mud slide area, earthquake fault line, excessive crime, nearby landfills, other off-site hazards, etc.), and virtually anything else that might tend to upset someone, at some time, for some reason.

In other words, sellers must ward off buyer claims of nondisclosure, misrepresentation, or fraud. Although investors who sue are typically accorded less status under the disclosure laws than homebuyers, you can never be certain how a court will rule. Therefore, when you prepare your property for sale, do it honestly. Don't try to hide, cover up, or disguise any property defects or problems. Either comply with acceptable standards of physical condition and applicable laws or truthfully disclose deficiencies.

"As-Is" Sales Still Require Disclosures

Some property owners know that their buildings suffer from an unsound foundation, a leaky roof, or an unused underground heating oil tank. To get around disclosure, however, these owners (or their agents) will advertise such properties "as is." By putting prospective buyers on notice that they must inspect the property for themselves, some sellers think they have fulfilled their legal obligation. But these sellers are mistaken. If you know of a "material defect" in your property, you must disclose it. Otherwise you run the risk of being sued for fraudulent nondisclosure.

Describing a property "as is" does not relieve you of the legal responsibility to tell buyers about significant problems that lie within your knowledge. In selling property, full disclosure is always best. If for some reason you can't repair, alleviate, or eliminate a property defect, then explicitly inform the buyer (preferably in writing so that, if necessary, you can later prove your truthfulness).

ATTRACTING BUYERS

If you have listed your property with a real estate firm, the firm will get the word out about your property. However, you still need to learn how the firm intends to promote a sale. Today most top agents prepare marketing plans for their listed properties. Meet with your agent and decide the best ways to reach prospective buyers. These methods should include:

 ◆ Newspaper advertising
 ◆ Word-of-mouth referrals
 ◆ Networking through apartment owners' association groups
 ◆ Electronic information highway (Internet—commercial on-line services, Realtor.com, FSBO sites, Multiple Listing Service, etc.)
 ◆ Advertising in specialized investor publications
 ◆ Cold calling current or prospective real estate investors

Advertising and Promotion

In advertising circles, the elements of a good advertisement form the acronym "AIDA": (1) attention, (2) interest, (3) desire, and (4) action.

Attention.   Advertisements for your property need to grab the attention of prospects. You (or your agent) must select the media that best reaches your targeted prospects. In the sale of real estate, this step is relatively easy because many publications, on-line bulletin boards, and other promotional outlets offer specialized listing sections for income properties. Buyers who are in the market know where to look for properties.

Nevertheless, your ad will compete with dozens (sometimes hundreds or even thousands) of other ads. You must figure out some way to set your ad apart by size, typography, color, illustration, headline, word choice, or other creative techniques. To achieve this goal, look closely at other ads for similar properties. Then do something different. Design, write, and position your ad so that it catches the prospect's eye.

Interest.   Once your ad has grabbed the prospect's attention, next interest him or her in your property. Give the prospect concrete information about your property. Avoid clichés like "real moneymaker," "fantastic opportunity," or other grandiose, abstract claims that have been touted by others since newspapers first published classified ads. Stick to the facts and criteria that serious investors will use to judge properties such as gross rent multiplier (GRM), net operating income (NOI), cap rate (R), and property location and description (e.g., Westside brick fourplex: three 2BR, 2BTH units plus oversized owners' suite).

Desire.   Your ad should stimulate desire. Make the property sound good relative to other advertised properties. Cite specific facts (not vague claims) that give your rentals a competitive advantage over others. Have you rented your units to good, long-term tenants who take excellent care of the property? Does the building require low maintenance expense? Are you offering a bargain price, owner-will-carry (OWC) financing, a low-rate assumable mortgage, lease option, master lease, or other "easy-to-buy" technique? Does the property offer strong fix-up possibilities and above-average rate of appreciation, or perhaps condo conversion potential?

Few buyers call every ad, so give them reasons to call about your property. Study other ads. Then use your ad to highlight your property's competitive advantages.

Action.   As a final step, tell your prospects what to do. Don't leave the action stage to their imagination. Don't simply list a telephone number. Tell the prospects to call for an appointment, attend an open house, drive by the property, or make an offer. Also, give them a reason to take action now. Although saying "won't last" approaches the cliché, it still conveys a sense that prospects should not put off until tomorrow what needs to be done today. Convey the message "those who snooze, lose."

Honesty.   Although not typically considered a part of the AIDA framework, a fifth and crucial element of your advertising is honesty. Many real estate ads grab attention, create desire, and generate action, but the property fails to deliver as promised. Some real estate agents explicitly use this tactic to obtain leads. In running ads, their goal is not to sell properties per se. Rather, they use their ads to get the names of potential buyers and then try to talk them into using the services of that agent to help locate the type of property that the buyers are looking for.

In theory, this approach may seem like a good idea. But in practice, if the lead-generating ad deceives, misleads, or overpromises, the prospect not only won't buy the advertised property; he or she will doubt the agent's competence and integrity. Regardless of whether you are trying to sell a specific property or generate a lead, your advertising should not disappoint prospects when they inspect and evaluate the actual property. Do accent your property's advantageous features or terms of financing. Don't presell a product you can't deliver.

NEGOTIATING THE SALES CONTRACT

Chapter 10 discusses this topic from your position as a buyer. Because the same negotiating strategies and tactics can be employed by sellers, we won't again go over that ground. Just recall that in talks with buyers, you are not negotiating price; you are negotiating an *agreement*. Never let your negotiations center exclusively on price. This mistake puts the buyer and the seller into polar opposites, where each one is trying to pull the other toward his or her position.

Your sales agreement will incorporate many issues such as earnest money deposit, closing date, possession date, personal property, lease guarantees, closing costs, prorations, repair escrow, contingencies, terms of financing, type of financing, amount of financing, type of deed, quality of title, casualty risks, and default remedies. Price need not represent the only, or even the most critical, issue.

Most importantly, negotiate an agreement that closes. No lawyer has ever drafted a contract that was immune to challenge in the courts (either on bona fides or pretense). Sales contracts seldom close because of legal threats. They close because both parties believe they are gaining more than they are giving up. By keeping the other party's full complement of needs in view along with the multiple possibilities for give-and-take, you create a win-win agreement that both you and the other party will want to honor.

14

PAY LESS TAX

For many real estate investors and owners of property, taxes represent their largest single expense. Income taxes, property taxes, estate taxes, unemployment taxes, social security taxes, special assessments, sales taxes, and disguised taxes such as rent controls, property regulations, and the costs of liability litigation can deeply cut into your cash returns. Although the United States was founded on the idea that people are entitled to their property and the fruits of their labor, governments (federal, state, and local) have pushed that founding idea into the dustbin of history.

As a result, to build wealth and a secure future, you must protect what you earn. Otherwise you will find yourself working and investing so that others may spend the wealth that you have produced through your sustained efforts. That task is becoming more difficult. Not only do present-day governments generally suppress our rights of property and industry, but they also ignore the fundamental principle of justice that law should remain simple and stable.

THE RISKS OF CHANGE AND COMPLEXITY

At the Constitutional founding of the United States of America, Publius (John Jay, Alexander Hamilton, and James Madison) wrote in *The Federalist*:

> It will be of little avail to the people that the laws are made by men of their own choice if the laws be so voluminous that they

cannot be read, or so incoherent that they cannot be understood; if they be repeated or revised before they are promulgated, or undergo such incessant changes that no man who knows what the law is today can guess what it will be tomorrow.

Can anything contradict these founding principles more than the current federal income tax laws? At present, the Internal Revenue Code (IRC) court cases, regulations, interpretive rulings, and journal commentary take up more than one million pages of text. Moreover, the Internal Revenue Service (IRS), the U.S. Department of the Treasury, and Congress change or threaten to change the tax laws on an almost daily basis.

Given this high degree of complexity and instability, you may decide to shun the field of taxation and turn all of your financials over to a tax professional. Unfortunately, such planned ignorance can cost you thousands (or even hundreds of thousands) of dollars. Instead, as a smart, tax-savvy investor, you must at least learn the basics of tax law. In doing so, you will discover what tax questions to ask your adviser, and perhaps, even more importantly, you will learn how to plan your tax strategy to legally reduce or avoid the amounts governments will try to extract from you.

All too often, naive investors act, then ask their tax pro to calculate their taxes. In contrast, the tax savvy investor first anticipates the tax effects of various alternatives and then chooses with full knowledge.

Now, with those words of advice in mind, let's begin our review of federal income tax law by looking at some ways owning a home can save you taxes.

HOMEOWNER TAX SAVINGS

Because government policy favors home ownership over renting, Congress has provided homeowners with several great tax-reducing advantages.

Capital Gains without Taxes

Under current tax law, homeowners receive a big tax break. You can now sell your principal residence and pocket up to a $500,000 gain tax free (married filing jointly). If you're single, your maximum untaxed profit is capped at $250,000.

Although the law generally requires you to have lived in the home for two of the past five years, it does not limit the total number of times that you may use this exclusion. It merely limits you to one capital gains exclusion every two years. In other words, over the next 24 years, you could buy and sell a personal residence up to 12 times—and escape capital gains taxes every time (subject, of course, to the $250,000/$500,000 limits).

Flipper's Paradise.   For investors who would like to buy properties, improve them, sell, and move up to bigger and better, this law offers a "flipper's paradise." Granted, most people do not want to change residences every several years. But for those willing to tolerate this inconvenience, even an 8- or 10-year plan could easily help you gain $500,000 to $1,000,000 in tax-free profits.

As noted before, this is exactly how Suzanne Brangham, author of *Housewise* (HarperCollins, 1987), earned a fortune. Starting with a $40,000 condominium, over a period of 16 years, she rehabbed herself up to a $1.8 million mansion. However, in contrast to Brangham's day, the beauty of the law now is that when you sell that last "flipper," you can avoid paying taxes on the gain. (Under previous tax law, homeowner capital gains were primarily deferred, not excluded.)

Tax-Free Capital.   In addition to flipping homes, you might benefit from this law in another way. Say you own a home with a substantial equity. The kids are gone, and you want to downsize. You can now (without the previous once-in-a-lifetime age-55 restriction) sell that large, expensive house and unlock your equity tax free (up to $500,000). Then split your cash proceeds into several piles. Use this money as down payments on a lower-priced replacement home as well as several income properties. Finance all of the newly acquired properties with 15-year mortgages. With property appreciation and mortgage payoff quickly building your net worth, you'll be set for life within a relatively short time frame.

RULES FOR VACATION HOMES

Increasingly, Americans are buying vacation homes for both personal and investment purposes. As covered by income tax laws, vacation homes are defined quite broadly and can include a condominium, apartment, single-family house, house trailer, motor home, or houseboat. Unfortunately, unlike personal residences, your profits from the sale of a vacation home will be taxed as a capital gain. No exclusion applies. However, if you earn rental income from this vacation property, you may deduct some of your expenses according to the following three rules:

1. If the vacation home is rented for less than 15 days, you cannot deduct expenses allocated to the rental (except for interest and

real estate taxes), but the rental income doesn't have to be reported to the IRS.

2. If the vacation home is rented for 15 days or more, then you need to determine if your personal use of the home exceeds a 14-day or 10 percent time test (10 percent of the number of days the home is rented). If it does, then you are considered to have used the home as a residence during the year, and you may deduct rental expenses only to the extent of gross rental income. The amount of rent collected in excess of expenses becomes taxable.

3. If you rent the vacation home for 15 days or more, but your personal usage is less than the 14-day/10 percent test, then tax law ignores this minor usage of the property during the year. In this case, the amount of expenses that exceed your gross rental income may be deductible against your other salary or business income. Court cases have allowed deductions for losses when the owner made little personal use of the vacation home and primarily bought the property to earn a profit on resale.

This brief description shows that the income tax laws that apply to vacation properties relate directly to how many days you use the property relative to how many days it is available for rental. Plus, your principal reason for buying the property can affect your tax liabilities. Advance planning with your tax pro in each of these areas can help you avoid or reduce your vacation home tax bill.

MORTGAGE INTEREST DEDUCTIONS

In most instances, you will finance at least part of your property acquisition costs (purchase price, settlement fees, loan points) and property improvement expenses with mortgage money. Accordingly, you may deduct the interest you pay on these borrowed funds. However, if you later do a cash-out refinance on your home (refinance and pay off your old mortgage, plus borrow more to put in your pocket), you may not deduct interest on the cash-out portion of that loan unless you use the money for property improvements or for certain other costs such as medical or education expenses.

CREDIT CARD INTEREST

As a rule, tax law treats credit card interest as a personal expense, and as such you may not deduct it from your wage or business income to reduce your tax liability (as you can with mortgage interest). But here's an important exception: If you use credit card borrowings or cash advances to help fund your rental property acquisitions, improvements, or operations, then you may deduct the interest you pay on those funds.

However, if you comingle personal and business credit card charges, make sure your records fully document the business portion. For ease of record keeping and documentation, reserve one of your credit cards exclusively for business charges. Of course, in times of cash flow short-falls, you may have to violate this practice and dip into the credit available on your personal cards. If (or when) you do resort to your personal cards, though, don't get sloppy. Accurately segregate business from personal. Otherwise the IRS may try to invoke the general rule against deducting credit card interest.

RULES FOR YOUR HOME OFFICE

As an owner of rental properties (and possibly other investment and business interests), you may be able to set up a tax-deductible home office. To legally claim a deduction for a home office, the area must be used *exclusively* and on a regular basis for work (a room where your spouse watches television or sews while you use the telephone does not qualify).

When you do qualify for a home office, you're entitled to deduct pro rata amounts for property depreciation, insurance, telephone, computer, office furniture, and any other items that relate to your work. However, if your rental properties don't show a taxable income (because of other allowable deductions), you can't deduct office expenses for that year. You can, however, carry these expenses forward and use them as deductions as needed in later tax years.

DEPRECIATION EXPENSE

Real estate investors deduct a noncash expense called depreciation. Income tax law assumes that your buildings, their contents (appliances, carpeting, HVAC), and various on-site improvements (parking lot, fencing, sidewalks) wear out over time. Accordingly, various IRS depreciation schedules permit you to reduce your taxable income to allow for this supposed deterioration that is occurring.

Note that this deduction stands on top of already deductible expenses for repairs, upkeep, maintenance, and property improvements. That's why investors call depreciation a tax benefit. You don't have to write a check to pay for it, but it knocks down your tax liability as if you did.

Land Value Is Not Depreciable

Tax law does not permit you to depreciate the land on which your rental buildings sit. Thus whenever you buy a property, to calculate your depreciable basis, you must first subtract the value of the land from your purchase price. If you buy a property for $200,000 and its lot value equals $50,000, your original depreciable basis equals $150,000. Tax law permits an assumed life for the house itself of 27.5 years. Divide $150,000 by 27.5 and you get $5,455. That's the amount of noncash depreciation that you can deduct each year to reduce your otherwise taxable rental income. (If you held this or any other residential property for 28 years, your annual depreciation deduction would then cease.)

Land Values Vary Widely

To maximize your depreciation expense, look for properties in neighborhoods with relatively low land values. On holding land value constant, look for lots with the largest quantity (or quality) of improvements. On the other hand, I recently looked at a small (900 square feet) 100-year-old rental house in Berkeley, California, that was priced at $525,000. In that case, the land value alone probably totaled $500,000. The actual building was a teardown. As a result, even though the property was worth in excess of a half million, the buyer would be entitled to less than $1,000 in annual depreciation deductions.

Simple rules that pertain to land/building value ratios don't exist. You must scout neighborhoods and geographic areas. Talk with appraisers and sales agents. Other things being equal, the larger your deduction for depreciation, the larger your annual after-tax cash flow. Unfortunately, the "other things being equal" caveat seldom applies. So when you compare properties and estimate returns, the potential depreciation deduction becomes just one more factor among others that you should weigh, consider, and possibly trade off.

After-Tax Cash Flows

To illustrate how depreciation can serve to reduce your taxable income, let's go through a simple example. Say that a property you own produces a net operating income (rent minus operating expenses) of $10,000 per year. Your mortgage payments total $9,500 a year, of which $9,000 represents deductible mortgage interest (hence $500 went to reduce the balance on your mortgage). With building and improvement value of $135,000, you're entitled to a depreciation deduction of $4,909. Furthermore, let's say you're in a 35 percent income tax bracket, and without your rental property, your taxable wages (and other income) equal $75,000. Here's how these numbers work out to save you taxes:

NOI	$10,000
Less	
Mortgage interest	9,000
Depreciation	4,909
Tax loss	(3,909)

You use this tax loss from your rental property to offset your taxable income from a job (or other sources).

Taxable income	$75,000
Tax rate	.30
Taxes owed (excluding property tax)	$22,500

Now with the tax loss from the property:

Taxable income	$75,000
Property tax loss	(3,909)
New taxable income	71,100
Tax rate	.30
	$21,330

Taxes saved because of rental property:

Taxes owed without property	$22,500
Taxes owed with property	21,330
Tax savings	$ 1,170

Total yearly benefit (without appreciation):

NOI	$10,000
Mortgage payment	9,500
Before tax cash flow	$ 500
Before tax cash flow	$ 500
Principal reduction	500
Tax savings	2,170
Total benefit	$2,170

Naturally, the numbers for a specific property and investor could yield higher or lower annual operating benefits than shown here. However, the basic purpose of this example is to show how and why investors can gain from a property—even when, for tax purposes, that property shows a tax loss. As a noncash expense, tax-deductible depreciation (even though in reality the property is appreciating) helps investors reduce their tax payments and increase their after-tax cash flows.

Passive Loss Rules

The tax law described in the previous section applies to most real estate investors, but not all. If you fall into a technical tax swamp called the "passive loss rules," a different set of laws apply to you. Although too complex to detail here, the passive loss rules generally ensnare investors who report taxable incomes in excess of $100,000 a year. Additionally, investors who take no role in the operational or managerial decisions that affect their properties may also be subject to passive loss rules.

Overall, the passive loss rules were primarily enacted to keep high-wage earners from sheltering their earnings through deductions for depreciation—a widely adopted practice (including by yours truly) before the 1986 Tax Reform Act (TRA). (Unfortunately, the amounts that investors, as well as other taxpayers, must now pay to CPAs and tax attorneys to figure their taxes far exceeds any revenue gains to the U.S. Treasury.)

Taxpayers in the Real Property Business
(No Passive Loss Rules)

More complexity: Congress has created another investor tax category called "taxpayers in the real property business." This category includes (but is not limited to) real estate agents, contractors, property managers, leasing agents, converters, and owners of rental properties. The great advantage of fitting yourself into this category is that you are exempt from the passive loss rules and may use your rental property tax losses to offset the taxable income you receive from any other source including wages, commissions, dividends, interest, and royalties.

However, here's the catch: You must work in a real estate–related trade or business at least 750 hours per year, or an average of slightly over 14 hours per week. In addition, more than one-half the personal services you perform each year must fall within the definition of a real property trade or business. In other words, you can't simply go out and get a license to sell real estate and automatically qualify for this preferred tax treatment. Nevertheless, for people who actually do (or can) work in real estate, the "hours worked" test won't prove difficult to meet.

Even if you work as, say, a schoolteacher or an auto mechanic, once you begin to build a portfolio of properties, you may be able to meet the "hours worked" test if you can somehow spend at least one-half the hours you work each year on your real estate activities. Obviously, to do so, you would either cut back on the hours you work in your regular job, or almost work a second job with your properties. However, if you are putting a lot of time and effort into fixing up and renovating your properties, you might be able to pull it off. Time spent working evenings and weekends can add up.

ALTERNATIVE MINIMUM TAX

Because of the complexities of the alternative minimum tax (AMT), only a brief overview deserves mention here. The subject of the AMT requires a tax pro's attention to enable you to get an understanding of the subject and to learn whether you may be exposed to the AMT. Both passive losses and capital gains may throw you into the AMT. Originally, only the wealthiest and most heavily tax-sheltered taxpayers would run into serious AMT tax liabilities. Today the reach of the AMT has pulled in millions of other unsuspecting taxpayers. (For more information on the AMT for individuals, including the new rules, see IRS Publication 909, Alternative Minimum Tax.)

CAPITAL GAINS

Lower tax rates for capital gains have traditionally benefited real estate investors. Under current rules, gains realized in the sale of a property will be taxed at a maximum rate of 20 percent (18 percent maximum if the property has been held for at least five years)—and possibly lower.

A Simplified Example

As stated often throughout this chapter, the tax law incorporates far more complexity and technical nuances than discussions here can adequately explain. Still, the following example does illustrate the basics of the capital gain tax:

Sales Price		$600,000
Tax Calculation		
Original cost		$300,000
Less: Accrued depreciation		100,000
Adjusted basis		200,000
Total gain		400,000
Less: Depreciation recapture	100,000 at 25% =	$ 25,000
Capital gain	300,000 at 20% =	60,000
Total taxes		$ 85,000

Under current law, accrued depreciation is recaptured at a tax rate of 25 percent, and the remaining part of the capital gain is taxed at a rate of 20 percent (or less). If you fit into the 15 percent ordinary income tax bracket (as opposed to the higher brackets), your capital gains are taxed at 10 percent rather than 20 percent. The depreciation recapture rate remains at the 25 percent rate.

To qualify for lower capital gains taxes, you must own a property for at least one year. In addition, your property "buying and selling" activities must not occur so frequently that they throw you into the IRS "dealer" category.

How often and how many deals? No one knows for sure. Occasional sales by rental property investors clearly don't cross into dealer tax territory. However, investors who fix and flip numerous properties (other than their successive personal residences) may get tagged as dealers. Don't unknowingly get caught in the "dealer" trap. Anticipate this potential problem. Seek the advice of a tax pro.

The Installment Sale

If you elect to carry back financing (owner will carry, or OWC) when you sell an investment property, you need not pay all of your capital gains taxes at that time. Instead, you spread them out on a pro rata basis as you actually receive your money.

Assume that at closing you accept 20 percent down and finance the balance of the buyer's purchase price over 15 years. Say also that your total taxable capital gain equals $300,000, which accounts for 50 percent of your selling price. You would immediately incur a tax liability on $30,000 (20% x 50% x $300,000). Thereafter you would owe taxes on the pro rata amount of gain you would receive in each of the following years. The exact formula for calculations is shown on IRS Form 6252.

Pros and Cons. In his excellent book *Aggressive Tax Avoidance for Real Estate Investors* (Reed Publishing, 2001), John Reed argues that investors should not sell their properties on the installment plan. Reed maintains that with the now lower tax rates on capital gains, postponing the day of reckoning doesn't really save a great deal of money. Moreover, because of technical complexities, use of installment sales may expose you to the black hole of the AMT.

Overall, Reed's points are sound. He deserves credit for forcing investors to look more carefully at whether an installment sale will produce the tax savings that are popularly believed. In another sense, though, Reed, doesn't go far enough in his analysis. Certainly, you want to carefully examine the tax effects of all your decisions before you make them; the installment sale may not yield the tax savings that some believe it will.

Nevertheless, you can't let your investment decisions be driven by tax strategy alone. (That's why so many pre-1986 TRA investors ended up with real cash losses. Their deals were driven exclusively by tax-shelter benefits. After the tax shelters were reduced or eliminated by the passive loss rules, the tax value of those investments collapsed.) Reed alludes to this point in bringing up the issue of opportunity costs. He says, "Why leave your money tied up in OWC financing just to save taxes when you could instead use those sales proceeds to buy more properties and earn much higher returns?"

Here's the Answer. As Robert Bruss frequently points out in his columns, owners should consider OWC financing because it can help them get their properties sold faster and at a higher price. This is especially the case when mortgage lenders are going through one of their tight money phases and are refusing to make investor loans except on onerous terms with rigorous qualifying standards. Therefore, don't measure your profit from the installment sale by just the tax savings and interest earnings on the buyer's mortgage. Also determine whether OWC financing will get you a quicker sale and a higher price. It probably will.

In addition, your interest earnings can prove quite lucrative, especially if you're able to use wraparound financing. Moreover, interest earnings on a buyer mortgage (depending on creditworthiness, amount of down payment, and the quality of the collateral) deserve a lower risk category than does property ownership. And it requires less effort to pull a mortgage check out of the mailbox each month than it does to manage apartments and collect rents.

What's the Bottom Line for Sellers?

That old equivocating answer "It all depends" applies to installment sales. As John Reed ably points out, the potential tax savings of the installment sale may not loom as large as many sellers anticipate. However, the benefits of an installment sale extend beyond tax savings. If you have reached the stage in life where you want to enjoy a stable monthly income without the efforts of property ownership, then when compared with long-term bonds at 4.5 percent to 7 percent interest, a seller mortgage that earns, say, 8.5 to 12 percent interest might look pretty good. And if OWC financing helps you get a better price for your property, all the better.

As with other business decisions, to decide the merits of an installment sale, consider not only the tax effects but also your personal situation, your tolerance for risk (not all buyers make their payments), and any other direct or indirect costs and benefits. You should neither accept nor reject it out of hand. Instead give it considered thought and work through the numbers with a tax pro and a Realtor experienced in investment properties.

Implications for Buyers

Nothing in this preceding discussion of installment sales is intended to discourage buyers from seeking OWC financing. As a buyer, whether you borrow from a bank or a seller will not change your federal income tax liabilities. However, once again take note. If you do agree to pay the seller a higher price in exchange for favorable terms, make sure you include a prepayment discount. If you refinance or sell the property early, you won't want to pay the seller for terms that you end up not using. In addition, when you arrange seller terms, try to negotiate assumable financing that you can pass along to your buyers when you sell (or exchange) the property.

TAX-FREE EXCHANGES

When you own a corporate stock that has had a big run-up in price, you may think that now is the time to sell before the market stalls or turns down. But selling creates a serious problem. Thanks to federal income tax law, you will lose a big part of your gain to the U.S. Treasury. As a result, many stock market investors hold their stocks long after they should have sold them because they can't bear the thought of immediately throwing away part of their profits in taxes.

In contrast, real estate investors need not face this dilemma. As explained earlier, for many investors, the installment sale can help them defer, and perhaps reduce, the amount of their profits they lose to taxes. Just as important, but not nearly as well known, real estate investors can also eliminate or defer their federal income tax liabilities by trading up. These two techniques—installment sales and exchanging—give owners of income properties a substantial tax advantage over investors who choose stocks, bonds, and most other types of real or financial assets.

Exchanges Don't Necessarily Involve Two-Way Trades

Owing to lack of knowledge, most real estate investors who have some awareness of tax-free exchanges believe that to use this tax benefit, they must find a seller who will accept one or more of their currently owned properties in trade. While this does represent one way to enter into a tax-free exchange, it does not represent the most commonly used exchange technique. Most exchanges, in fact, actually involve at least three investors.

The Three-Party Exchange

Three-party exchanges outnumber two-party "trade-in" exchanges because it's usually difficult to find an owner of a property you want who will accept the property you plan to trade up. True, it's sometimes possible to negotiate a two-way trade by convincing an unwilling seller to accept your property in trade and then turn around and sell it. But to do so may cause you to spend too much negotiating capital that you could otherwise devote to issues such as a lower price or OWC financing.

Instead, most serious real estate investors arrange a three-party exchange through the following steps: (1) Locate a buyer for the property you want to trade; (2) locate a property you want to buy; and (3) set up an escrow whereby you deed your property to your buyer, the buyer pays cash to your seller, and your seller conveys his or her property to you. In effect, no property has really been "exchanged" for another property. Because of this anomaly, John Reed (a leading expert on exchanges) suggests renaming this technique the "interdependent sale and reinvestment" strategy.

Exchanges Are Complex but Easy

As you might suspect, anything that involves federal tax laws will be entangled in a spider web of rules and regulations, and Section 1031 exchanges (as they are called in the Internal Revenue Code) prove no exception. However, even though exchange rules are complex, exchange transactions are relatively easy to administer when you work with a pro who is experienced in successfully setting up and carrying out tax-free exchanges.

John Reed says the total extra costs (including attorney fees and escrow charges) of conducting an exchange should run less than $2,000. Professional Publishing Company (now taken over by Dearborn Financial in Chicago) even publishes standard forms that may be used to complete the required paperwork according to law. Even if you rely on standard forms, use a tax or realty exchange pro. Be aware, too, that the great majority of CPAs and real estate attorneys know little about Section 1031 exchanges. Unless your accountant or lawyer has definitively mastered this area of the law, find someone else who has this expertise. (If you live in at least a midsize city, there's probably an exchange club whose members include investors and commercial realty brokers who will be able to recommend competent and experienced exchange professionals.)

Note: Some accountants and lawyers have frequently told me things like "Oh, you don't want to get involved in something like that," or "That's more trouble than it's worth," or "Sure, I can handle it, no problem." In my inexperienced days, I simply accepted such comments without question.

"Surely, I can count on the wisdom and good faith of my accountant or lawyer," I told myself. (Okay, those of you who have worked with lawyers and accountants can now stop laughing. I have already confessed to my early naïveté.) The point here is twofold: (1) To hide their own ignorance, lawyers and accountants who do not understand an issue will often advise against "getting involved with that," whatever "that" may be, so as not to disclose that they really don't know what they are talking about; or (2) depending on how much they need the business (or perhaps they don't want to lose you as a client), accountants and lawyers frequently claim competency in areas where they lack expertise.

Either or both of these tendencies can cost you. (Yes, you can sue for malpractice, and I have. But it's not a recommended course of action.) To reduce the chance of professional error, misinformation, or just plain bad advice, don't let your accountant or attorney bluff you. Pepper them with detailed and specific questions about the issue at hand and their actual experience in successfully dealing with these issues. Whatever you do, don't naively accept the counsel of any professional (lawyer, accountant, real estate agent, medical doctor, etc.). These are not demigods but people with serious limitations. Require them to *earn* your trust and respect through knowledge and performance, not expect it simply because they list a string of initials after their name.

Are Tax-Free Exchanges Really Tax Free?

Some people quibble with the term "tax-free exchange." They say that an exchange doesn't eliminate taxes but only defers payment to a later date. This view is wrong on four counts:

1.   The exchange itself is tax free if you follow the rules (see following section).
2.   Whether you must pay taxes at a later date depends on how you divest yourself of the property. If you hold it until death, the property passes into your estate free of any capital gains taxes.
3.   As another alternative, you could arrange a sale in a later year in which you have tax losses that you can use to offset the amount of your capital gain.
4.   If Americans are sensible enough to elect legislators who understand the importance of productive investment, we may see the income tax, or at least the capital gains tax, abolished.

The most important point is that exchanges eliminate capital gains in the year you dispose of a property by trading up. Whether you pay in future years will depend on how savvy you are in developing your tax-avoidance strategies, and on the tax law that exists in some future year. By exchanging, you eliminate a definite tax liability in the year of disposition and accept an uncertain and contingent future tax liability. That's a tax trade-off you should always try to make.

Section 1031 Exchange Rules

Stated as simply and briefly as possible, Section 1031 tax-free exchanges must comply with five principal rules:

1. *Like-kind exchange.* Here's another source of confusion: The tax law states that only exchanges of "like-kind" properties qualify for the preferred tax treatment. However, "like-kind" doesn't mean fourplex to fourplex, or even apartment building to apartment building, as some people believe. The concept is actually much broader and includes "all property [types] held for productive use in a trade or business or for investment." As a matter of law, you are permitted to exchange nearly any type of real estate for any other type of real estate and still arrange your transaction to fall within Section 1031 guidelines.

2. *45-day rule.* If all parties to an exchange are known and in agreement, you can close all properties simultaneously. Otherwise you can use a delayed exchange procedure that specifies two separate time deadlines. One of these is the 45-day rule, which says you must identify the property you want to acquire within 45 days after the date of closing with the buyer of your present property (i.e., before midnight of the 44th day).

3. *180-day closing.* The second time requirement states that you must close on your acquisition property within 180 days of closing the disposition of the property that you are "trading up."

4. *Escrow restrictions.* Tax-free exchanges generally require exchange proceeds to be paid into and distributed out of an escrow arrangement. The escrow agent must be completely independent of you (e.g., not your attorney, real estate agent, bank officer, spouse, company's employees, or anyone else who is subject to your exclusive control or direction). Most important, you must not be able to withdraw any money from this escrow or otherwise pull out of the exchange agreement before the date the escrow agent has scheduled disbursements and property conveyances.

5. *Trading up.* To gain the benefit of a tax-free exchange, you must trade for a property of equal or greater market value. Trading down or accepting a cash "boot" exposes you to a liability for capital gains taxes. If because of this tax liability your "seller"

doesn't want to trade down or accept a cash sale, then you (or your realty agent) can create a daisy chain of exchange participants until a property owner is found who wants to cash out or trade down real estate holdings and is willing to pay his or her capital gains tax. (A seller who has planned a total tax strategy may not have to pay any taxes despite realizing taxable income from a specific transaction. Also, because heirs receive properties on a stepped-up basis, they will incur little or no capital gains tax liability unless they sell their inherited property for substantially more than its estimated market value at the time it entered the deceased's estate.)

To keep lawyers and accountants fully employed, the tax law embellishes the preceding rules with various details, definitions, regulations, and requirements. So, as noted earlier, the trick is not only to use an experienced exchange professional to guide you *before* you enter into any purchase or sale agreement but also to keep the exchange process in compliance throughout each step until all closings are completed.

REPORTING RENTAL INCOME AND DEDUCTIONS

Rental income and expenses are reported on Schedule E of your federal tax return. You report the gross rents received, then deduct expenses such as mortgage interest, property taxes, maintenance costs, and depreciation. The net income is added to your other taxable income. If you realize a loss, you can reduce the amount of your other taxable income within certain limitations (see passive loss limitation rules, discussed earlier).

To pay less tax, keep detailed records for all allowable deductions. Don't shortchange yourself with sloppy bookkeeping. Deduct every expense that you believe reasonable and necessary to operate and maintain your properties. Among the most common deductions are the following:

- ◆ *Real estate taxes.* Property taxes are deductible, but special assessments for paving roads, sewers, or other public improvements may have to be depreciated or added to the cost of the land.
- ◆ *Depreciation.* Be sure to deduct depreciation; it is the tax-shelter benefit of real estate ownership.
- ◆ *Maintenance expenses.* These expenses include repairs, pool service, heating, lighting, water, gas, electricity, telephone, and other service costs.

- *Management expenses.* You may deduct all fees paid to a professional management firm. However, you can't pay yourself a deductible fee unless the property is owned by a separate corporation or partnership. You could, though, pay your wife or kids for helping out and then deduct these amounts.
- *Traveling expenses.* These include travel back and forth from properties for repairs or showing vacancies.
- *Legal and accounting expenses.* These could include the costs of evicting a tenant, negotiating leases, or keeping financial records and filing tax returns.
- *Interest expense.* This category includes interest on mortgages and other indebtedness related to the property or property operations.
- *Advertising expense.* This includes the cost of signs, newspaper advertising, Web sites, and referral (bird dog) fees.
- *Insurance expense.* This includes the cost of premiums for property and liability coverages.
- *Educational investment.* To consistently improve your motivation and performance, read books, attend seminars and conferences, join investor organizations, and subscribe to magazines and newsletters. These educational costs are legitimate tax deductions.
- *Capital improvements.* Income tax law does not permit you to write off a new roof, a new heating, ventilating, and air-conditioning (HVAC) system, a major kitchen remodeling, or other long-life expenditures in the year you incur such an expense. Instead, the law requires you to depreciate the cost over, say, 5 to 10 years, depending on the precise nature and expected longevity of the improvement. (For specifics, talk with a tax pro.)

TAX CREDITS

In addition to deductible property expenses and capital improvements, you may also be entitled to reduce your income liability through the use of tax credits. Whereas a tax deduction serves to offset income, tax credits offset your actual tax liability dollar for dollar. They're much more valuable than tax deductions.

Say you subtract all tax-deductible expenses from your gross income and calculate your taxable income at $40,000. If you are in the 28 percent tax bracket, you would owe $11,200 (.28 x 40,000) in income taxes. But instead, let's assume that you are entitled to a tax credit of $4,000. After accounting for this credit, your tax liability falls from $11,200 to $7,200 (11,200 − 4,000).

How do you get these tax credits? As tax law stands today, tax credits aren't as easy to come by as they once were. However, to win support of special interests, Congress continually adds (or deletes) tax credits. So stay alert for updates. Currently, the law offers five possibilities:

1. *Mortgage credit certificates (MCCs).* These tax credits are available only to first-time homebuyers whose state or local governments participate in a program Congress created in 1984 and has continued to reauthorize since then. To calculate the amount of tax credit permitted, you multiply 0.2 times the amount of your annual mortgage interest. If you paid $9,000 in mortgage interest this year, in addition you would receive a $1,800 tax credit (0.2 x 9,000). If your area offers an MCC and you haven't yet invested in your first home, get the details on this program as they apply to homebuyers where you live (or plan to live). This is truly free money.
2. *Low-income housing tax credits.* These tax credits are available to real estate investors who build new or substantially rehabilitate rental housing that is rented to households with low incomes.
3. *Nonresidential rehabs.* Nonresidential rehabilitation tax credits are available to investors who substantially renovate commercial buildings that were originally constructed before 1936.
4. *Certified historic rehabs.* Historical societies in various states have the authority to certify residential and nonresidential buildings as "historically significant." Investors who rehabilitate and restore these structures to meet historical preservation standards are entitled to tax credits.
5. *ADA building modifications.* The Americans with Disabilities Act (ADA) requires owners (or lessees) of some existing public or commercial buildings (not including rental housing) to adapt their properties to meet the accessibility and use needs of people who are physically disabled. Meeting the financial burden of these ADA requirements may entitle the owner (lessee) to tax credits to partially offset these expenses.

Although calculating the amount of tax credits available through the MCC program is quite straightforward, the other tax credits cited require the application of complex formulas involving tax credit percentages and the amounts of qualified rehab, renovation, or restoration expenses. For further information, the IRS publishes updates from time to time on each of these tax credits.

Complexity, Tax Returns, and Audits

All investors face the risks of tax complexity. Without a doubt, income tax laws are "so voluminous that they can't be read, and so incoherent that they can't be understood."

Several years ago, *Money Magazine* created an income and expense profile for a hypothetical investor and sent the figures to 50 certified public accountants (CPAs), tax lawyers, and the IRS. *Money* asked these tax experts to calculate this hypothetical household's federal income tax liability. Guess what? Among these 50 separately prepared tax returns, no two produced the same answer. In fact, the difference between the high and low tax bill was a whopping $66,000.

What does this mean to you? The complexity of tax law makes it uncertain and incomprehensible not just to average citizens but also to tax preparers. This doesn't mean that some parts of the law aren't relatively certain (e.g., the deductibility of mortgage interest paid to finance rental properties). It does mean that in many instances, figuring your tax liability will require judgment calls (e.g., the allocation of property value between land and improvements for purposes of calculating depreciation).

Therefore you will need to choose whether to take an aggressive stance on matters of judgment to reduce your taxes to the lowest possible level. Or should you play it safe? Pay more, take less than the law *might* allow, and reduce your chance of an audit?

You and your tax adviser can answer this question only after considering your total personal situation in light of current IRS audit standards and the "hot issues" that may flag your return for audit. Nevertheless, before you choose to play it safe and pay more than you owe, consider the following points.

Audits Are a Tactic of Intimidation.   Playing it safe is exactly what the IRS wants you to do. The IRS operates primarily through intimidation. It wants taxpayers to fear an audit. The fewer the number of people who push the envelope, the more money the IRS collects for the government. However, the lawful role of the IRS is not to raise the maximum amount of revenue. Rather, statutorily, the IRS is charged with enforcing the tax laws. Therefore, as long as you can support an aggressive position that reduces your taxes, you have little to fear from the audit itself. (Of course, the time, effort, and expense an audit requires remain a valid concern.)

Renegotiate Your Assessment.   Even if an audit goes against your position, that doesn't mean you have lost completely. When the IRS assesses you more in taxes, you can renegotiate the amount (based on the facts of your case and applicable tax law, not simply, "I'll give you 50 cents on the dollar") with the examiner, another examiner, or the manager of the IRS office responsible for your audit. In many cases, you (or your tax pro) can persuade the IRS to reduce its additional assessments.

Appeal Your Assessment. Absent a satisfactory resolution at the local level, you can ask the district appeals office to reduce or eliminate the additional assessment. Although theoretically the appeals office could reopen your file and bring new challenges and even higher assessments, it rarely does so. The prime task of the appeals office is to get cases settled as quickly as possible. As a result, appeals officers acquiesce (on the merits) to lower assessments in more than 50 percent of the cases that come before them.

Litigate Your Assessment. Some cases aren't settled on appeal. But again, you aren't compelled to accept the decision of an appeals officer. You have further appeal possibilities through several different court procedures. Furthermore, because of the large cost of litigating tax cases and the limited number of government lawyers to handle them, few cases actually go to trial.

Represent Yourself without Worry or Large Costs. You may think that audits, appeals, and court litigation will cost you far more than you could possibly save in taxes. While that may be true, it's not *necessarily* true. Up through the appeals office, you can represent yourself as long as you are willing to prepare your case (facts, records, laws) in a way that meets IRS standards. This task is not difficult (see the excellent book by tax attorney Fred Daly, *Stand Up to the IRS*, Nolo Press, 2001).

Furthermore, if you move your case from the appeals office to the small-claims tax court (tax assessments of less than $10,000 for each year in question), you still can represent yourself. If you choose to litigate in regular tax court or a U.S. district court, however, retain a tax pro to carry on your battle. At that point, your legal expenses will shoot up. But keep in mind that the time, effort, and expenses you incur to win your position shouldn't be measured against the tax savings of just one year. If the issue affects your future tax returns (or past returns that are still open to audit), then you've got more at stake than just the initial assessment. Failing to argue for the position you believe is correct could cost you additional taxes over a larger number of years.

Relatively Few Returns Are Audited. Your aggressive position to minimize income taxes won't be challenged automatically. Even if IRS computers flag your return, that doesn't mean you will be called in for an audit. In recent years, the IRS has scheduled office or field exams for fewer than 1 percent of all tax returns filed. Even then, most returns are not examined in total. Typically, only certain items are questioned as a matter of law or documentation.

This brings us back to where we started this IRS discussion. Because it has the personnel to investigate (not to mention litigate) fewer than 1 percent of all tax returns filed, the IRS realizes that it must appear more formidable than it actually is. Don't let the intimidating image of the IRS deter you from lawfully minimizing your tax payments. Even in the event that the IRS does choose your return, as long as you (or your tax pro) can plausibly support your positions by citing case law, statutes, or revenue rulings and provide some reasonable (not perfect) records, you need not fear the audit.

At the worst, you will have played the game with odds in your favor. And even though at times the dice may roll against you, over the long run, an aggressive (but lawful) tax position will yield more wins than losses.[1]

"Plausible" Position.   In taking an aggressive tax position, you should *avoid* paying taxes that you do not owe—not *evade* paying the taxes that you do owe. Do not spend $20,000 to renovate your personal residence and then claim this expense was invested to upgrade your rental properties. Do not collect rents in cash so that they will leave no paper trail for the IRS to follow. Do not sell your properties privately on contract so that you can try to hide your capital gains and interest income from the IRS.

Before you take action to reduce your taxable income (or, correspondingly, increase your deductible expenses), verify your position with a tax pro. A "plausible" position is one that is supported by one or more recognized tax authorities (cases, statutes, regulations, or revenue rulings) and some personal records (contemporaneous or ex post). Failing to report rental income or running personal expenses through your rental property accounts does not meet this test. Interpret facts and law to favor your position, and at most you'll end up owing more in taxes (plus interest and maybe some penalties). Purposely misrepresent the facts, and you subject yourself to the possibility of steep penalties, fines, and criminal prosecution.

---

1. John Reed, author of *Aggressive Tax Avoidance for Real Estate Investors* (self-published, 2002), was subjected to the excruciatingly detailed Taxpayer Compliance Management Program (TCMP) audit, but he emerged from this torture with zero additional tax liability.

Use a Tax Pro

Although you can represent yourself at an audit or appeal, consult a tax pro to help you plan your tax strategy, prepare your returns, and, if necessary, prepare for an audit. Tax law complexity makes it nearly impossible for the great majority of Americans to fully understand the tax laws.

This chapter goes through some basics of income tax law as they apply to property owners. But this discussion remains a starting point—not the last word. I again emphasize the need to consult a tax pro *before* you buy or sell a property, and *before* you develop your operating budget or plans for capital improvement or exchange. How you structure your transactions and how you structure and document your spending can dramatically increase or decrease your federal income tax liabilities.[2]

PROPERTY TAXES

"If you think that your property taxes are too high," writes tax consultant Harry Koenig, "you're probably right! Research shows that nearly half of all properties may be assessed illegally or excessively" (*How to Lower Your Property Taxes*, Simon & Schuster Fireside Books, 1991). While Koenig may overstate his point, no doubt, millions of property owners do pay more in property taxes than they need to. With just a little attention and planning, you can avoid falling into this trap by taking several precautions:

 ♦ *Check the accuracy of your assessed valuation.* Tax assessors usually base their tax calculations on a property's market value. Look closely at the assessor's value estimate on your tax bill. Can you find comp sales of similar properties that would support a *lower* value for your property? If so, you may have grounds to request a tax reduction. (See Chapter 3 for more details on appraisal techniques.)
 ♦ *Compare your purchase price to the assessor's estimate of market value.* Apart from providing comp sales, if you can show the assessor that you recently paid $190,000 for a property that he or she has appraised at $240,000, you have a prima facie case for lower taxes.

---

2. A former secretary of mine was billed $12,500 by the IRS to recover tax benefits she had previously claimed from the sale of a property. She had timed a second sale two months too soon. Although she had been represented in these transactions by a lawyer, he claimed that tax issues were not his specialty. If taxes were her concern, she should have asked specifically about them. Lesson: Don't assume! Inform yourself. Then ask.

♦ *Look for unequal treatment.* Under the law, assessors must tax properties in a neighborhood in an equal (fair) and uniform manner.
This means that you might be able to argue successfully for lower
taxes even though the assessor has accurately estimated the market
value of your property. How? By showing that the assessor has
assigned lower values to similar nearby properties. (All property
tax data are publicly available.) If faced with this issue, the assessor
will have to cut your taxes because after everyone's tax notices
have been sent out, it's not politically feasible (even if lawful) for
the assessor to start telling people he or she has made a mistake
and they actually owe more than is stated on their tax bill.

♦ *Recognize the difference between assessed value and market value.* Typically, property taxes are based on assessed value, which is calculated as a percentage of market value. If your tax notice shows an
assessed value of $80,000 and you know your property's worth
$120,000, don't conclude that you've been underassessed. If tax
law states that assessed values should equal 50 percent of market
value, then your assessed value should come in at $60,000
(.50 × 120,000), not $80,000.

♦ *Does your property suffer any negative features that the assessor has not
considered?* Even though comp properties may appear similar, are
there really significant differences? Does your property abut rail-
road tracks or a busy, noisy highway? Does it lack a basement,
built-in appliances, a desirable floor plan, or off-street parking?
Does it have a flat roof? (In some areas, flat roofs reduce value
because they tend to leak and are quite costly to replace.)

♦ *Do you or your property qualify for any property tax exemptions?* Most
property tax laws grant preferential treatment to various persons
or properties. For example, veterans, seniors, blind persons, and
hardship cases may be entitled to reduced assessments based on
their special status. Similarly, historic properties, properties in
areas designated for revitalization, energy-efficient properties, or
properties rented to low-income households may qualify for
reduced assessments. Check with your assessor's office to see
what exemptions might apply in your city or county.

♦ *Verify that your property assessment meets all technical requirements
specified in the law.* Tax assessors and the legislative bodies that
levy property taxes must operate within a set of rules, regulations, laws, and even constitutional requirements. For instance,
some technical or procedural requirements may pertain to
assessed value ratios, property classification, land-improvements
ratio, conducting public hearings, notice of public hearings, per-

missible valuation techniques, and allocation of assessed value between real and personal property.

◆ *Learn tax assessment laws before you improve or rehabilitate a property.* The property tax laws of every state list the types of property improvements that are taxed and the applicable rates. Once you discover the detailed nature of these laws, you can develop an improvement strategy that adds value without adding taxes. For an excellent discussion of this topic and numerous case examples, see the book by Steve Carlson, *The Best Home for Less: How to Drastically Reduce Your Taxes, Utility Bills, and Constructions Costs When You Build, Remodel, or Redecorate* (Avon Books, 1992).

A related issue is building permits. Some investors remodel or renovate without bothering with the appropriate permits. They think that the government can't tax what it doesn't know. As pointed out, this approach presents the danger that at some future date the building inspector may discover the unpermitted work. In some cities, that means the inspector can require an owner to tear out the work and do it over. This risk arises especially when unpermitted work doesn't meet code requirements. In the past, governments often overlooked unpermitted work and failed to keep their property tax records up to date. But now, with computer data banks, buyer prepurchase inspections, and mandated seller disclosure statements, such work is more likely to be discovered.

Furthermore, in their unrelenting quest for greater tax revenues, local governments recognize that unreported remodeling and renovations are costing them billions of dollars each year in lost tax revenues. The trend throughout the country is pushing toward more thorough property investigations and harsher penalties. While many city and county governments still lack the personnel, resources, or political will to change their careless practices, don't bet that these assessment inefficiencies will continue forever.

SUMMARY

Income taxes and property taxes take large chunks out of your earnings. To reduce this drain on your livelihood, you can either practice tax evasion or tax avoidance. Tax evasion refers to illegal schemes such as maintaining two sets of books, not reporting rents, overstating expenses, or running personal expenses through your tax-deductible property accounts. In contrast, tax avoidance refers to perfectly legal strategies and tactics you can use such as depreciation deductions, tax credits, installment sales, tax-free exchange, and income shifting (e.g., timing of receipts and converting ordinary income into capital gains).

The key to a successful tax evasion plan is to line up trusted and competent property managers who will look after your properties while you are in jail. The key to successful tax avoidance strategies is knowledge and planning. By knowing the law, you can structure your income, expenses, and transactions to minimize, if not eliminate, your income tax liabilities. Before you act, ask your accountant three questions: (1) How can I arrange and document this spending to make sure it's tax deductible? (2) How can I structure my receipt of income and capital gains to keep from losing it to the IRS? (3) Can I arrange this spending or investment to qualify for any allowable tax credits?

Although the income tax law stands as a fact of life (at least for the present), the amount of income tax you pay does not. Through careful planning at the *start* of each year, you will find that you can slice your income tax bill at the end of the year by thousands of dollars.

Similarly, all property owners must pay property taxes. But the amount of taxes you pay need not be the amount indicated on your tax bill. Through negotiations with the tax assessor's office or through formal appeal procedures, you may be able to pay less than the sum the assessor originally said you owed. By learning the details of property tax laws and assessment practices *before* you remodel or renovate a property, you can make your improvements with an eye toward keeping your assessments down while enhancing the desirability of the property for your tenants.

Although you never want to let tax avoidance drive your investment strategy, neither should you develop an investment strategy that fails to explore all available opportunities for tax avoidance. The stakes have climbed too high. With governments' insatiable appetite for more of your money, your best defense is a strong offense. And a strong offense necessitates wisely informed tax planning.

15

AN INCOME FOR LIFE

No one knows the future for social security, stock prices, bond returns, or inflation. Consequently, as long as the population and economy continue to increase, rental housing will provide the safest and surest path to both long-term real wealth and high spendable cash returns. A $10,000 to $20,000 down payment today will multiply itself into an equity of $50,000 to $100,000 over a period of 5, 10, or at most 20 years. During this same period, your rent collections will increase by at least 50 percent, and they could even double if you choose a soon-to-be hot area (see Figure 15.1).

LESS RISK

You will also enjoy great safety of capital with rental housing. Even in recessions, property values and rent collections for owners of small properties generally remain stable. In such down periods, home building and apartment construction fall, thus slashing new supply. Hard times also tend to draw more households toward renting and away from homebuying. Then, when we return to a normal economy, rising employment, incomes, and general prosperity push rents up. Plus, households "unbundle." Many of those live-together multigenerational households and boomerang kids become able to afford a place of their own.

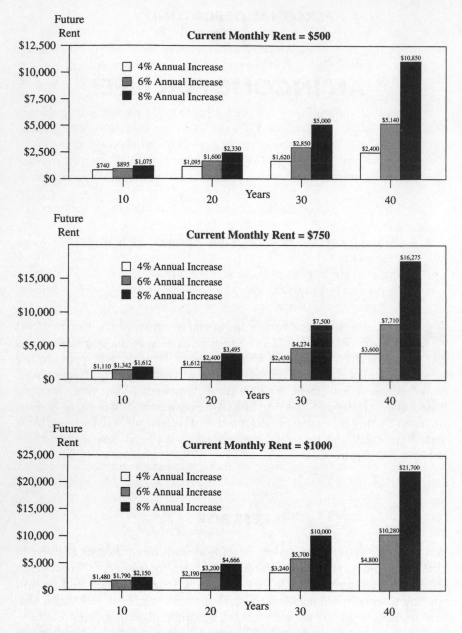

Figure 15.1   Future Rent Levels at Various Rates of Increase

PERSONAL OPPORTUNITY

When you rely on stocks, bonds, and even social security, your fate spins out of your control. Other than buying, selling, or perhaps voting, you can do nothing to influence the returns you would like to receive. Not so with income properties.

When you depend on your properties to build wealth and a lifetime of income, you can achieve good returns, even in a recession. (Or, as some might say, especially in a recession, because that's when you can best pick up bargain-priced properties.) Best of all, investing in property provides you with profit opportunities that stock investors can only dream about:

- Buy properties at prices substantially less than their current market value.
- Through creative finance, acquire properties with little of your own cash.
- Improve properties to enhance their current market value.
- Improve your market strategy to boost rents and lower vacancies.
- Cut operating costs to increase net operating income.
- Sell your existing properties and trade up without paying tax on your capital gains.
- Change the use of a property from one that's less profitable to one more profitable (apartments to condo, residential to office).
- Refinance your properties and pull out tax-free cash. (You can borrow against a stock portfolio. But margin requirements, price volatility, and little or no cash flow load that choice with costs and risks.)

To profit from some or all of these real estate opportunities does require knowledge, effort, and market savvy. Unlike those who buy stocks, property investors don't whimsically follow hot tips from their barber, auto mechanic, or the noise-making talking heads on FNN. You can't buy, own, or sell real estate with the click of a mouse.

But that so-called disadvantage explains why, over time, real estate provides a safer, surer path to wealth and income. Today a great majority of stock market investors still foolishly believe that they and tens of millions of other Americans can achieve wealth without work. Just buy stocks, and voilà—your portfolio will grow. Supposedly, easy street awaits all investors who faithfully contribute money to their 403(b)s, 401(k)s, Keoghs, 529s, and IRAs. But it won't happen. It can't happen.

At some time in the future, Americans will realize that income from corporate stock portfolios can never exceed the yearly amount of corporate dividends. And these dividends will never grow large enough to support the more than 50 million individuals and households who continue to send their monthly retirement contributions to Wall Street.

At present, income property provides true *investment* opportunities. You can *speculate* in stocks. You can even *speculate* in real estate. You can buy lottery tickets. You can shoot craps in Las Vegas. Maybe any or all of these will pay off for you. But the odds are stacked against you. In contrast, selectively acquire just four or five rental properties, and you will build an income for life—a monthly cash flow that will generously finance the life you would like to enjoy.

I wish you success. And if you get the chance, let me know how you're progressing. I like to hear from my readers.

INTERNET APPENDIX

Throughout this book, you have been referred to a variety of Web sites that complement or expand on the topics covered. For your added convenience, I have assembled these Web sites by category and have listed them here. In addition, for readers who want to learn more about Web-based homebuying and mortgage lending, I highly recommend *How to Find a Home and Get a Mortgage on the Internet,* by Randy Johnson (Wiley, 2001). You can also profit by roaming through Randy Johnson's Web site at www.loan-wolf.com.

CITY AND NEIGHBORHOOD DATA

www.census.gov
http://stats.bls.gov
http://usacitylink.com
www.virtualrelocation.com
http://verticals.yahoo.com/cities
http://venus.census.gov
www.ojp.usdoj.gov.bjs
www.crime.org

COMP SALES

www.dataquick.com
www.propertyview.com

www.latimes.com
www.domania.com
www.iown.com
www.ocpa.gov

CREDIT INFORMATION

www.econsumer.equifax.com
www.experian.com
www.transunion.com
www.creditscoring.com
www.creditaccuracy.com
www.myfico.com
www.qspace.com
www.credit411.com
www.ftc.gov
www.creditinfocenter.com
www.fairisaac.com

FINANCIAL CALCULATORS AND SPREADSHEETS

www.loan-wolf.com
www.moneyweb.com
www.mortgagewizard.com
www.mortgage-minder.com
www.hsh.com

FORECLOSURES AND REPOS

www.brucebates.com
www.bankhomes.net
www.4close.com
www.all-foreclosure.com
www.homesteps.com
www.hud.gov
www.va.gov
www.bankreo.com
www.treas.gov

www.premierereo.com
www.fanniemae.com
www.bankofamerica.com

HOME IMPROVEMENT

www.hometime.com
www.michaelholigan.com
www.askbuild.com
www.hardware.com
www.bhglive.com
www.housenet.com

HOME INSPECTION

www.ashi.com
www.creia.com

HOMES FOR SALE

www.realtor.com
www.homeseekers.com
www.homeadvisor.com
www.cyberhomes.com
www.homes.com
www.bamboo.com
www.ipix.com
www.owners.com
www.efsbo.com
www.buyowner.com
www.fsbo.com
www.realfind.com

INSURANCE INFORMATION

www.cpcu.com
www.statefarm.com

LAW INFORMATION

www.lectlaw.com
www.lexis.com
www.lawstar.net
www.nolo.com

MORTGAGE APPLICATIONS

www.interest.com
www.mortgage101.com
www.mortgagequotes.com
http://mortgage.quicken.com
www.lendingtree.com
www.fhatoday.com
www.loanweb.com
www.mortgageauction.com
www.clnet.com
www.eloan.com
www.iown.com

MORTGAGE INFORMATION

www.loan-wolf.com
www.mortgageprofessor.com
www.hsh.com

MORTGAGE PROVIDERS (UNDERWRITERS)

www.fanniemae.com
www.homesteps.com
www.va.gov
www.hud.gov

REAL ESTATE INFORMATION

www.inman.com/bruss
www.ired.com

www.stoprentingnow.com
www.ourfamilyplace.com
www.realtor.com
www.johntreed.com
www.arello.org

SCHOOL DATA

www.2001beyond.com
www.schoolmatch.com
www.schoolreport.com

With thousands of Web sites dealing with real estate and mortgage lending, this list samples only some of the most popular sites. Nevertheless, if you have the time and the will to sort through the data overload that the Web offers, you can make a more informed homebuying and borrowing decision.

But beware. Many sites do not provide accurate data, nor do the data necessarily relate to your specific need. For example, neighborhood data and school data are plagued with inconsistencies, omissions, errors, and ill-defined measures. Don't accept Web-based data as the last word. Verify all information. The Web does not reduce your need to "walk and talk" the neighborhood; visit schools, shops, parks, and other facilities; physically view comp sales; and drive through areas to look for Home for Sale signs.

On a final note, I will admit that buying investment properties can seem challenging at times. But persevere. You'll never regret investing in real estate. In the meantime, should you have questions, give me a call at (800) 942–9304 ext 20691 or e-mail me at garye@stoprentingnow.com. If you e-mail me, please include your address and phone number. I will respond one way or another.

I hope you profit from the successes (and mistakes) of the thousands of people who have in one way or another contributed to the content of this book. Good luck and good fortune.

INDEX

Cost approach, 58, 66–69
Cost estimates, 184
Creating value, 168–169, 239–240
Creative finance, 21, 41–47
Creativity, 186
Credibility, 24
Credit counselors, 128
Credit history, 52
Credit score, 54

Dealer status, 290
Debt coverage ratio, 50, 91–92
Default clause, 217–218
Demographics, 2, 96–97
Depreciation, 67
Depreciation deduction, 285–286
Disclosures, 119–121, 150–151
Distressed owners, 125–128
Down payment, 22–23, 33–39,
    49–50

Earnest money, 210
Echo boom, 9
Employment, 97–98
Energy audit, 235
Environmental hazards, 176,
    216–217
Estate sales, 161–162
Evictions, 262–263

Fannie Mae homes, 158–159
Federal Reserve, 15
FHA loans, 34–35
First–time buyer, 36
Fiscal solvency, 98–99
Fix and flip, 165–166
Flipper's paradise, 283
Forecasts, 2, 19
Foreclosure auction, 139–141
Foreclosure financing, 141–142
Foreclosure follow–up, 145

Foreclosure process, 123
Foreclosure specialist, 146–147
Foreclosure speculators, 160–161
Freddie Mac homes, 158–159

Grass–is–greener sellers, 104–105
Gross rent multiplier, 72–73

Holdover tenants, 246
Home office deduction, 285
HUD bid package, 153–154
HUD homes, 35, 147–156

Improvements, 168–169
Income approach, 59, 72–73
Income statement, 74
Inflation, 16–17
Information highway, 117–119
Installment sale, 290–292
Insurance, 235–238
Interest rates, 14–16
Investment analysis, 81

Joint and several liability, 244–245

Land contracts, 45–46
Landlording, 263–264
Land–use laws, 100–101
Late fees, 247
Lead paint disclosure, 150
Lease option, 187–191
Lease option sandwich, 191–192
Lease provisions, 244–259
Lease purchase, 193–194
Leverage, 25–29
Limiting conditions, 80–81
Listing agreements, 269–272
Loan–to–value (LTV), 32–33
Loan workout, 124, 136–138
Location, 177
Low–income tax credits, 298